Economic, Social and Demographic Thought in the XIXth Century

Yves Charbit

Economic, Social and Demographic Thought in the XIXth Century

The Population Debate from Malthus to Marx

Springer

Prof. Yves Charbit
Université Paris Descartes
UMR CEPED (Université Paris Descartes-INED-IRD)
75006 Paris
France

ISBN 978-1-4020-9959-5 e-ISBN 978-1-4020-9960-1

DOI 10.1007/978-1-4020-9960-1

Library of Congress Control Number: 2009920976

Printed on acid-free paper

9 8 7 6 5 4 3 2 1

springer.com

For Véronique

Contents

Chapter 1
The Population Controversy and Beyond

The two intellectual figures who dominated the whole of the nineteenth century, Malthus and Marx, were and still are systematically opposed. A "clash of prophets" claimed in 1970 the title of an American textbook, which usefully provided large excerpts of what Marx and Engels wrote against Malthus. According to current understanding, Malthus is hostile to an excess of population because it causes social sufferings, while Marx is favourable to demographic growth in so far as a large proletariat is a factor aggravating the contradictions of capitalism. This is unfortunately an oversimplification and a few scholars have long established that in his later works Malthus seriously retrenched from his earlier opinion: population, far from being redundant, might well be insufficient to ensure sustained economic growth. As for Marx, he proves extremely ambivalent towards Malthus, simultaneously denouncing the sycophant of the Tories while claiming him to be an economist far superior to Ricardo. To be more precise, Malthus and Marx can be reasonably be opposed only in so far as their *demographic* theories are concerned, and again only if one refers to the first edition (1798) of the*Essay on the Principle of Population.* As soon the analysis is broadened to the later editions of the *Essay* and to the economic writings of Malthus, it is clear that he constantly raised the same question: when considered as an economic variable, how does population fit into the analysis of economic growth? Marx also addressed the problem, assuredly less obsessively and both Marx and Malthus were concerned with growth and not *equilibrium*, a major difference from the orthodoxy of the classical school. From the same starting analytical standpoint, Marx established a very different diagnosis from that of Malthus and built a social doctrine no less divergent: there was no way out of increased poverty and class conflicts were unavoidable.

What was left to lesser thinkers to say about one of the major social issues raised by industrialisation? Whereas important scholars concentrated on the English scene, relatively little is known about nineteenth controversies over population debates in France. They are dealt with here and again sweeping generalisations prevail. The French liberal economists, who prolifically wrote on population at the onset of the industrial revolution in France (1840–1870) are commonly assumed to be the uncompromising keepers of the Malthusian faith. Pierre-Joseph Proudhon's views are usually considered as those of a socialist, who shared with Marx a vehement denunciation of the very same capitalist society which the French economists

Y. Charbit, *Economic, Social and Demographic Thought in the XIXth Century*,
DOI 10.1007/978-1-4020-9960-1_1, © Springer Science+Business Media B.V. 2009

praised during exactly the same decades. Again it would be too simple if that sketchy opposition were true. As for the so-called neo-Malthusians, a closer study reveals them to be *anti*-Malthusian, not only, as it is often believed, at the doctrinal level of the plea for contraception, but by questioning the very principle of population which constitutes the core of the Malthusian theory. A careful examination of Proudhon's conceptual framework shows that his ideas differ from Marx on two fundamental points. Far from being a materialist in the Marxian sense, his thought has a strong metaphysical dimension, in which the idea of God is central. He also pays a great deal of attention to what should be a *moral* demographic behaviour, a doctrinal preoccupation totally absent from Marx's writings. Such is the rather puzzling scene of the nineteenth century, as far as ideas on population are concerned in France, not to mention the fact that the stage was also quite encumbered: radicalism (although it was declining along with Godwin's fading star), Christian political economy, the social catholics in France and later the hygienist movement. Much the same can be said about other European countries.

Theoretical Progress and Affiliations

Is it possible to escape these moving sands by safely confining oneself to the more tranquil path of the history of ideas, and to the analysis of the progressive construction of demography as a science? After all since Malthus, the French liberal economists, Proudhon and Marx claimed in turn to have produced a *theory* of population, we would therefore expect some sort of a continuously enriched scientific corpus, like a majestic river growing thanks to successive confluent streams. Indeed there was a vast circulation of ideas in an intellectual space transcending the borders of nation-states. The English political economist Malthus was inspired by his compatriots Wallace and Petty, but the idea of an imbalance between *vis nutritiva* and *vis generativa* had been clearly formulated by Botero in Italy in 1635. Inspired by the French physiocrats as well as by Ricardo, Marx tried to revolutionise an economic system that was firmly entrenched in English capitalist society.

But what is under question is precisely the very idea of progress. Indeed the French economists (as well as Marx) are *post*-Malthusians, and not only chronologically. But did their population laws progress from the base line drawn by Malthus. Were they so to speak more proven? Letting aside Proudhon's disconcerting computations, the French economists made a major contribution to what was to become the modern economic theory of fertility. According to the *standard of living argument* (which they actually borrowed from English writers) the increase in welfare automatically induces the desire to reduce fertility, whereas Malthus had stated the opposite causal relationship. Progress can also be assessed by looking at the problem from the angle of the progressive construction of the theory of population. Actually, demography stands out among the social sciences because of the paucity of theory, there being only one model, namely the demographic transition, formulated in 1934 by Landry.[1] The theory of the demographic transition is the overwhelming dominant explanation of the past of European populations. As is known, the demographic transition is no more than a generalisation based on available long term statistical series of deaths and births in several European countries. For centuries the mortality rate compensated for the birth rate, with no overall demographic growth. Then the transition began with a first stage of a declining mortality rate (except in France), while fertility remained high, hence an accelerating pace. Then again a decline followed in the birth rate, now resulting in a more and more slow growth. At the end of the process (towards the end of the nineteenth century and until the end of the Second World War) both rates were low and since they compensated each other, once again population grew slowly. Now, if it is recalled that Malthus and Marx were acute and widely-read observers of nineteenth century England, it is tempting to relate their theory to the stages of the transition. We would then have the possibility to reveal a continuum between past and present theories. Let us examine this possibility and assume that the Malthusian system of 1798 expresses the demographic logic and equilibrium prevalent before the advent of demographic transition (high fertility and high mortality), while Marx writing in the 1860s would somehow echo the demographic regime characterising the second phase of transition (drop in the death rate followed by lower fertility). Transition would then be a powerful synthesis of Malthusian and Marxist laws on population. The idea is attractive, but the first claim, as will be demonstrated in the chapter on Malthus, does not hold. It applies at the most to the first Malthusian model of regulation through mortality, but it does not take into account later models where Malthus observes that the middle-classes, by and large, practised prudential restraint in England during the years 1820–1830. It is equally questionable to link the second phase of transition to Marx. He was certainly interested in capitalism in its most ruthless form, but if the fertility decline can be explained as part of capitalism's evolution, it is more with regard to the half-century that followed (1870–1914) the publication of *Das Kapital* in 1867. There was a general rise in the standard of living and an improvement in the status of women as well as a rise in the cost of child-rearing due to the increase in the number of years spent in school, a rise in the expenditure on housing and health-care, a demand for skilled workers for industrial production, etc. Looking at the demographic transition as a synthesis of a large set of demographic facts, one must therefore give up this

---

[1] But the illustrative data gathered subsequently (in Europe and the industrialised countries, and later in the developing countries) led to the conclusion that there are so many different paths leading to the end of transition that ultimately it is the parameters of the model that are really important (Coale, 1973). Finally, later efforts at abstraction and modelling, particularly the theory of socio-cultural modernisation formulated by Thompson (1929) and Notestein (1953), were marked by a strong ideology which further weakened the model's theoretical validity and therefore its universality. The article by Szreter (1993) on the historical and political reasons for the success of Notestein's modernisation theory as compared to the poor reception of Thomson's theory is worth reading.

alluring idea that it "inspired" these great intellectuals during each of its phases. Nor, if the transition is considered as a theory, can it be regarded as a logical continuation from Malthus' and Marx's theories. There is a good reason for pleading this case.

Demographic Theory and Economic Theory

One also tends to forget that from the eighteenth century onward population became an *organic* part of economic thought as seen in the inevitable chapters on population in treatises on economics. So it is not possible to analyse Malthus' theory independently of his economic theory and population as a concept finds its logic in the field of economics where it was initially theorised, much before it became a demographic concept. What is true of Malthus as a mainstream thinker applies even more to his strongest opponent, Marx, whose economic theories formed the basis of his population law which he opposed to that framed by Malthus. Consequently, the problem is that of the epistemological status of demography in relation to economics, which has direct implications with regard to the mere possibility of writing a history of the theory of population. One is reminded of Canguilhem's position vis-à-vis the life sciences. He rejects the very idea of looking for precursors to reconstruct the history of a science and calls it "the most evident symptom of the incapability of epistemological criticism." As a matter of fact, if a concept is meaningful only within a given system and historical context, a precursor cannot simultaneously belong to his time and to a later period. What is being questioned is the historical contextualisation itself. "So the precursor is a thinker who the historian believes he can remove from his cultural background and insert into another. This amounts to considering concepts, discourses and speculative or experimental actions as capable of being moved and replaced in an intellectual context where the reversibility of relations has been obtained by forgetting the historical aspect of the object he is dealing with."[2] So what about demography?

As a first step in our analysis, if we consider the population theory as a subset of the economic theory, it will be observed that its concepts, and particularly the most central of them all, the demand for labour, are not really "exported". This lessens, at least in the case of demography, the impact of Canguilhem's criticism. As for Malthus and Marx, who illustrate the two theoretical streams that succeeded one another between the eighteenth and nineteenth centuries, it is evident that the latter borrowed from the former, but this does not justify the powerful accusation that "the same word does not mean the same concept."[3] But by the same token, this organic relationship between demography and economics is structured so differently that it

[2] Canguilhem, 2002: 20–22.

[3] 2002: 177.Contrary to Canguilhem's radical position, one can quote the idea that was developed from the physiocrats to Malthus and Marx, that all revenue is not automatically reinjected into the economic circuit, giving rise thereby to under-consumption due to a real lack of demand (see Blaug, 1986: 35).

is not possible to find an intellectual affiliation between a thinker and his followers that could be deemed complete and perfect. As for Marx, his "population law" is inseparable from the theory of capital accumulation and there is no epistemological discrepancy except, as we shall see, in his writings prior to 1859. Malthus poses a more formidable problem. His demographic theory is as coherent as his economic theory and he made remarkable sociological observations. He was after all an Anglican pastor who never stopped affirming that his work was a contribution to the implementation of the Creator's designs. But if we take into account his entire work, we are struck by serious theoretical contradictions. Far from adhering to his initial denunciation of the risk of overpopulation, Malthus seriously foresees the risk of an insufficient growth. It will be shown that only an interdisciplinary approach can avoid such contradictions, reconcile the demographic viewpoints of the economist, the empirical sociologist, the man of the cloth and, finally, establish epistemological coherence. We thus find ourselves far from the simplistic neo-Malthusian interpretation that Malthus' thinking can be reduced to the idea of regulating population growth by a decrease in fertility. And to conclude our discussion on the problem of theorisation in the field of demography, we will agree with Canguilhem who says, "Paying attention to epistemological obstacles will allow the history of science to be a true history of thought."[4] The line of research followed in this book enables us to easily incorporate the classical typology of population theories without confining ourselves to it alone, to explain their origin and the internal logic of their evolution or, on the contrary, their absence in a given society and in a particular period. What can be done when dealing with demographic doctrines?

Demographic Doctrines and Ideology

It should first be noted that as is the case for theories, doctrinal affiliations should not be taken for granted. The best example is Malthus, who must not be considered as a precursor of the so-called "neo-Malthusians". As mentioned above, the divergence has a bearing on a crucial issue, that of contraception. For the wretched proletarians, whose fertility was unlikely to diminish with economic progress, birth-control methods seemed a most practical means of escaping poverty, and was overtly advocated, while Malthus always refused to recommend it. As Keyfitz put it, "It is a strange injury that posterity has inflicted on Malthus when its calls contraception 'malthusian' or 'neo-malthusian'".[5]

All the writers dealt with here were keen observers of the European societies in which they lived. They were eager to describe, measure and analyse, not for the sake of a positivist attitude but because they wanted to influence the course of events, at a time when industrialisation had deeply shaken the social, economic, moral and political patterns inherited from the past. Viewed from that angle, their demographic

[4] Cangilhem, 2002: 177.

[5] Keyfitz, 1983: 5.

doctrines must be examined within the historical context. A doctrine being a body of normative arguments, based on value systems, which define the goals to be attained, either general (the growth or control of population) or specific to major demographic variables (in the past, it was more often than not fertility, marriage and migration rather than mortality), by nature the goals of a demographic doctrine cannot be purely demographic. The above example shows clearly enough that the doctrinal goal was the welfare of the poor, as a response given by the French bourgeoisie to the sufferings created by industrialisation. Reducing fertility is evidently not a desirable objective per se, it is so only in view of social, economic, political or ideological goals. Let us turn to the other branch of the alternative: *increasing* fertility can be desirable from the point of view of the country's military, economic, fiscal, social or political requirements. It is therefore important to understand, keeping in mind the economic, social and political context prevailing at the time of formulating any given demographic doctrine, to what stakes these doctrinal positions responded. One may discuss the legitimacy of increasing or restricting fertility, recommend marriage at an earlier or later age, but to a large extent the examination of the demographic doctrines in the following chapter will be inspired by the central ideological conflict of the nineteenth century, the defence of the triumphant bourgeois values and their contest by the heralds of the poor.[6] In brief, demographic doctrines can be considered as the subsets of these ideologies. Now the prime role of all ideologies being to provide solutions to the problems of their times, they are likely to change in order to find satisfactory solutions for new or unforeseen problems. Like any other ideology, doctrines on population are thus domed to be abandoned when they become obsolete and are no longer capable of providing ideologically satisfactory interpretations of historical change. The decline of the Malthusian doctrine (as commonly understood, i.e. the condemnation of excess demographic growth) during the second half of the nineteenth century is a magnificent *cas d'école.*

Interpreting Theories and Doctrines

Demography stems from a double line of historical descent. On one hand, political arithmetic, whose main contribution was the construction of an original tool, the mortality table, and was nothing but applied statistics focused on very concrete actuarial problems, without any theoretical ambition. Political arithmetic gave birth to what is now regarded as the heart of the discipline, namely *population dynamics* (referred to in France as demographic analysis). On the other hand, from the sixteenth and seventeenth century political and moral philosophy, relayed from the eighteenth century by political economy, provided the concepts and intellectual frameworks to understand and analyse demographic behaviours. They are the classical foundations

[6] In a democracy nobody would contest the validity of protecting life and contrary to other variables, there is total consensus on mortality. Only under totalitarian regimes, particularly Nazism, there was no hesitation in recommending euthanasia for the mentally and physically handicapped under the pretext of protecting the country's higher interests.

of today's *population studies*. Among these concepts, the principle of rationality, inherited from both the English Utilitarism and the French Enlightenment, underlies modern demographic theories, particularly those pertaining to mobility (the so-called neo-classic theory of international migrations) or to human reproduction (the economic theory of fertility).[7]

To analyse theories as well as doctrines, this book borrows from both conceptions of demography. Demographic facts are taken into account, in as much as the authors were concerned with the heritage of political arithmetic and more generally with population dynamics. By "facts", we do not mean of course what we now know of the demographic dynamics of the nineteenth century, but those data they had access to and which they used to support their theoretical or doctrinal statements. Malthus' travels in Europe and his wide readings served him to confirm his central argument that if population had not grown in a geometrical ratio, it was because it was universally checked, except in the United States of America. More interestingly, some facts were ignored although they were largely publicised. If major intellectual figures such as Malthus, Marx or Proudhon, and if excellent experts like the French economists (who lengthily commented the 1846, 1856, 1861 and 1866 censuses, and the cholera epidemics of 1832 and 1854), ignored some facts, there must be good reasons for that, and they are worth elucidating. We shall pay particular attention to the internal coherence of what they wrote not for the sake of our own intellectual satisfaction, but because it raises the question of the causes and significance of evident inconsistencies. Even if Skinner is right to denounce "the myth of coherence"[8], we shall try to reconcile conflicting or inconsistent *demographic* views, by focusing on other dimensions of the author's thought such as political philosophy or economic theory. An author can be inconsistent in his analysis of a given demographic fact because of ideological biases which force him to do so. Only when no coherence is found at any analytical level of analysis, may we conclude that serious intellectual pitfalls exist. The French economists and Proudhon are not free from such an interdisciplinary screening, but more surprisingly it is also true of Malthus and Marx. Social, economic and political facts are no less important than the demographic ones. Malthus, the French economists and Marx commented upon short-term economic crises. Marx made massive use of social surveys and Engels' survey on Manchester is well known, but at least three major figures among the French economists (Villermé, Reybaud, Blanqui) undertook field surveys which are

[7] This hybridisation has produced a permanent tension between theory and empiricism which could have been fruitful, but which often produced two types of results: either descriptive statistical works without a theoretical base or research work having ambitions of producing theories which have not been empirically confirmed due to lack of data (e.g. mortality models). In such a situation, it is difficult to trace the origin of the transition theory because the advance of political arithmetic in the seventeenth century was not incorporated in the transition structure and also because the inventors of transition did not take into account Adam Smith's economic theory on the demand for work formulated in 1776. Transition confines itself to the gross mortality rate that is compared with the birth rate while ignoring the mortality tables because different analytical processes are involved. Coontz's book (1961) is one on the most interesting attempts to theorize demography on the basis of the concept of the demand for labour.

[8] Skinner, 1969: 16–22.

valuable testimonies of the social condition of the industrial workers throughout France, not to mention many books and articles devoted to *La question sociale*.

Before the age of Malthus and the birth of demography, attention was paid to population, indeed not in modern terms, notably by Plato, the mercantilists and the physiocrats. In order to interpret what they wrote, we have no other choice, as was noted above, than to refer to the most legitimate intellectual field into which we can enter them. Philosophy, and its two major branches, moral and political philosophy, is an evident choice when reading Plato, the mercantilists and the physiocrats. For the mercantilists and the physiocrats, political economy must enter the lice.[9] What economic or philosophical stakes are to be considered in the nineteenth century? Let us briefly quote social inequality and access to welfare, social and economic justice, the control of political power by the few versus democratic legitimacy, the potential ethical conflict between the liberty of the individual and his responsibility, and last but not least in such an unstable century, the dialectics between revolutionary movements and the defence and enforcement of social order.

If these questions are of primary concern when dealing with demographic doctrines, they are also important for theories. A careful study of their writings reveals that the accepted distinction between theories and doctrines must be questioned. Their theories were grounded on their doctrines, in the sense that central theoretical concepts were in fact constructed on premises which were directly borrowed from doctrines. The most striking example is the central argument Malthus uses to demonstrate that a sustained economic growth is possible, a purely psychological conception of human indolence, and he goes as far as asserting that God wisely gave the human species a high reproductive power: it would compel man to work harder produce more to feed his offspring, hence consume more, which in turn guaranteed at the macroeconomic level the maximisation of economic growth. Such an argument, clearly derived from the utilitarian philosophy, is no more than a purely moral value judgement on mankind.

To sum up, the following chapters deal simultaneously with doctrines and theories, paying special attention to the coherence of the overall intellectual argument. This coherence has two dimensions, external, meaning it is consistent with facts as they were known by the author; internal, by which we imply that there are no contradictions in the conceptual construction. Both types of coherence are assessed from an interdisciplinary point of view, in order to avoid a careless dismissal of what is written because, so to speak, of the somewhat short-sighted vision induced by a monodisciplinary analysis. Such is the methodology used to achieve the purpose of the book, which is to provide an evaluation of the exact place of the Malthusian theories and doctrines in the nineteenth century, beyond the shortcomings of the classification between pro- and anti-populationists. Why France? The debate is of particular historical relevance in a country well-known to be obsessed with demography as a condition to its grandeur...

---

[9] On Plato and on the physiocrats, see Charbit, 2002a; 2002b.

Chapter 2
Population, Economic Growth and Religion: Malthus as a Populationist

A conversation between a young man named Thomas Robert Malthus and his father Daniel, an admirer of the French Enlightenment and a friend of Rousseau,[1] led to the writing of *An Essay on the principle of population as it affects the future improvement of society with remarks on the speculations of Mr. Godwin, M. Condorcet, and other writers*, the author having felt the need for "merely stating his thoughts to his friend, upon paper, in a clearer manner than he thought he could do in conversation."[2] When the *Essay* was published anonymously in 1798, no one could have imagined that it would deal a fatal blow to the radical theories of William Godwin, then at the height of his glory, that it would be used against the French Revolution and, finally, that it would serve as a formidable weapon against egalitarian ideologies all through the nineteenth century. But although the *Essay* written in 1798 was aimed at English radicalism and, more generally, at the Jacobinism of the French revolution, it also had a more fundamental objective which would be confirmed by the rest of Malthus's writings, namely enlarging upon Adam Smith's *Wealth of Nations* by suggesting both theoretical and empirical solutions to the problem of structural poverty related to industrialisation. At the same time, major political factors, particularly the Napoleonic wars, provided food for his ideas on the relationship between population and the short-term economic crises that England was going through at the time.

But this is where the ambiguity begins for we have not one but two fundamentally different works, both having almost the same title. In the second edition, however, the *Essay*, originally a short philosophical pamphlet published in 1798, was transformed into a treatise on population laden with sociological observations gleaned by Malthus during his numerous travels. For example, John Harrisson points out that in the first *Essay*, an octavo volume consisting of 396 pages, Malthus claims to have reasoned out the principle of population after having read Hume, Wallace, Smith and Price, while the quarto edition published in 1803 has 610 pages with quotations from 112 works. In the sixth edition, which came out in 1826 and was

---

[1] Regarding the relations between Daniel Malthus and Rousseau, see Keynes (1972: 74–77). For a psychological portrait of Daniel Malthus see Grampp (1974).

[2] *Essay*, 1798: 61.

Y. Charbit, *Economic, Social and Demographic Thought in the XIXth Century*,
DOI 10.1007/978-1-4020-9960-1_2, © Springer Science+Business Media B.V. 2009

the last one to be published during Malthus's lifetime, he has counted quotations from 133 works and 1054 references.[3] The first problem is one of coherence between what is commonly accepted as the "first" *Essay* of 1798 and the subsequent editions. Contrary to a generally accepted opinion, there is a strong theoretical and doctrinal continuity between the successive versions and it is thanks to a new line of research that this coherence has been brought to light.[4] This brings us to another prevalent but erroneous belief that the Malthusian *theory* of population underwent a basic change. It is true that while according to the first edition of the *Essay* all population growth is necessarily checked by mortality, the second and following editions give an important place to two other possibilities, "prudential restraint" (essentially controlling fertility not only before but also during marriage through the use of contraception or other methods such as abortion) and "moral restraint" or raising the age of marriage until a man is capable of providing for his family, it being understood that he abstains from all sexual activity during his bachelorhood, but that after marriage the couple does not practice contraception and willingly accepts all the children that God bestows on them. However, it is usually forgotten that most of these *theoretical* concepts are present in the first *Essay*, but that a profound *doctrinal* change occurred later. By admitting that man is capable of controlling his destiny through the exercise of his willpower and thus escaping from vice and poverty, Malthus considerably diluted the uncompromising tone and the metaphysical pessimism of the first edition; but at the same time, he laid himself open to controversies of a doctrinal nature. In other words, could moral restraint be an effective remedy or would it lead to overpopulation in England and in the rest of Europe? Was not contraception, later recommended by neo-Malthusians but strongly condemned by Malthus for reasons that we shall mention later, a better "solution" to the problem of poverty among the working classes?

But there is also another problem. Since the time of Adam Smith, population is an indispensable chapter in all treatises on economics; it is an integral part of the theoretical construct of which it is a variable just like land and capital. This is also the case with Malthus's *Principles of Political Economy, with a view to their practical application,* published in 1820 and his *Summary View on the Principle of Population*, which appeared in 1830. These works suggest that far from forecasting the risk of overpopulation, as he claimed in his *Essay on the Principle of Population*, he was in fact worried about insufficient demographic growth. Moreover, since he based this opinion on theoretical and empirical, as well as on demographic and economic arguments, the epistemological problem, to say the least, is stimulating: either there is incoherence at the theoretical level or it is necessary to look for internal coherence in the thinking behind the apparent interdisciplinary contradictions. In short, how to account for the complexity of Malthus's thought?

---

[3] Harrisson, 1983: XV.

[4] We refer to the works of British and North American scholars on *Christian Political Economy*. For the principal bibliographic references, see Waterman (1991: 58–59).

Last but not least, analysing Malthus's thoughts is not easy as his style is frequently obscure and ideas are lost in digressions and the reader cannot expect well-structured thoughts as in Ricardo's or Marx's writings. In an article published in January 1825 in the *Westminster Review*, John Stuart Mill, whose comments on his contemporaries were usually quite moderate, wrote that Malthus made what was obvious seem astonishing, what was simple complicated, what was clear obscure and what was easy difficult. It may be added that Malthus, undoubtedly toughened by the discussions with his father and his mentors in Cambridge, possessed a strong questioning and provocative disposition and this Whig, who was sincerely concerned about both individual rights and social progress, but never to the point of adopting a democratic position like Samuel Whitbread, had an innate talent for creating confusion.[5] For example, deciding whether Malthus gave up his protectionist ideas has given rise to a debate between two specialists, Pullen and Hollander, both of whom refer to the same texts, the ambiguities of which are such that that their views cannot be reconciled.[6] Further, his attitude being essentially pragmatic, the chapters of his *Principles of Political Economy* read like answers to a series of questions, without any logical sequence. It may be recalled that in a letter to Ricardo dated 21 October 1818, he described his hesitation about the use of the word *Principles* in the title and regretted not having been able to use the term "essays" or "tracts" which were more in tune with the book's format. In 1804, Malthus thought of bringing out a new edition of Adam Smith's *Wealth of Nations*, but finally published in 1815 his *Inquiry into the Nature and Progress of Rent*, which constitutes the core of the long Chapter 3 of *Principles*.[7] But this empiricist, who reproached Ricardo for giving too much importance to the theoretical aspect of things, did not hesitate to write in 1803 in the preface to the second edition of the *Essay*, "Should any of them [facts and calculations] turn out to be false, the reader will see that they will not materially affect the general scope of the reasoning", a statement which, to say the least, is quite nonchalant. Another source of difficulties and ambiguities is the opinions expressed by Malthus as an expert before Parliamentary Commissions on the various reforms proposed in his time. Considering the amendment of the Poor Law in 1834, which offers an excellent case study, one would have expected to find in the *Essay* of 1798 all the arguments in support of conservative reforms. It is a well known fact that posterity considers him to be the father of the law of 1834, thus reinforcing his image as a stone-hearted conservative. But this belief is mistaken because in the first place,

[5] The psychology and intellectual training of Malthus the man have been skilfully described by Grampp (1974) in an article on "Malthus and his Contemporaries". John Stuart Mill quoted by Grampp (1974: 285).

[6] See Hollander (1995) and Pullen (1995).

[7] Letter quoted by Pullen (1989: xxxi). As regards their organisation, all the essays are not treated systematically; see Pullen (1989: xxxvi). It is known that Ricardo and Malthus exchanged a series of letters, which provide ample material for studying the differences between Ricardo and Malthus, notably on the subject of under-consumption and the crisis which followed the Napoleonic wars in 1815 (for example, Bonar, 1924; Hollander, 1969; Churchman, 1999; Rashid, 1981; Cameron Maclachlan, 1999).

Malthus did not take part in the Commission's proceedings and secondly, in the later editions of the *Essay* he expounded a view that was totally against the interests of the landowners who were defended by the Tories.[8] Malthus was certainly not the only thinker to have committed the sin of lack of clarity or coherence. But then there is another difficulty. While analysing the development of ideas, it would have been ideal if each edition of the *Essay* had introduced new and decisive elements; unfortunately, that did not happen and the crucial points required for demonstrating our case, which figure in the later editions of the *Essay*, are already there in the 1798 edition, though they are not fully developed and properly argued. It would however be wrong to deduce from this that his thinking did not progress further. On the contrary, it became richer with successive additions, but at the cost of contradictions and swings of opinion. As a result, there is a greater need to look for the overall coherence in his writings concealed behind these apparent contradictions and this obliges us to move constantly from one edition to another.[9] To resolve the apparent contradiction – whether Malthus was for or against population growth – this chapter, after a brief summary of the main Malthusian concepts, proposes an interpretation of Malthus's thinking that is simultaneously demographic, sociological and economic, and is illustrated by four models, keeping in mind all the time that Malthus was a clergyman who did not take his religious convictions lightly.

Finally, let us point out that unlike the other chapters in this book, more importance is given here to the overlapping of the doctrinal and theoretical dimensions than to the historical context because the detailed contextualisation of the genesis of Malthus's ideas and their extraordinary success is not possible within this limited space.[10] The oft-repeated question about the lack of originality of Malthus's ideas will not be dealt with in these pages. However, when Malthus formulated his theory on population, he based himself on numerous examples, both contemporary and from the past, to illustrate the principle of population and the role of destructive as well as preventive checks. As regards the past and particularly ancient Greece and Rome, an empirical verification has little relevance because the information that was lacking then is still fragmentary and, in any case, unusable for the purposes of verifying Malthus's law. Since figures are not available for the past, especially the growth rates of population and the means of subsistence as well as the rates of mortality and fertility, there is no question of commenting on the role of different controls. This is evident, for example, when reading *Histoire de la population mondiale* by Reinhardt, Armengaud and Dupaquier, where more or less careless assumptions are

---

[8] Grampp (1974 : 283–284), who bases himself on Malthus's testimony before the Commission in charge of drafting the *Combination Act*, certainly goes too far when he suggests that they are not particularly useful.

[9] Besides the *Essay* of 1798, we have used the seventh edition, published in England before his death.

[10] In France, for example, the analysis of the debates on Malthus, although focused only on the group of pro-free trade French economists between 1840 and 1870, (see Chapter 6), involved taking into account the works of some forty writers and going through more than sixty thousand pages of articles published during these decades.

scattered throughout the chapters on the population of Greece and Rome.[11] On the other hand, because Malthus's thinking has a solid empirical dimension, it will be briefly compared in each of our models, with reference to certain theoretical points and to a lesser degree its doctrine, to the demographic and economic data pertaining to his time.

The Central Concepts

Unlike Godwin, who maintained that inequality of property was the reason for mankind's misfortunes, Malthus believes that "human institutions" are much less responsible for poverty than the principle of population.[12] He based his argument on two postulates, namely that food is necessary for human existence and that the sexual instinct (or "the passion between sexes" as Malthus calls it) will always remain powerful. Taking for granted that these two assumptions will be accepted, he claims that if population is not controlled, it will grow in geometrical progression while the means of subsistence will increase in arithmetical progression. He claims that in the North American States where "means of subsistence are abundant, manners are pure and marriages take place early", it is quite evident that the principle of population has been in action and the population has doubled every twenty-five years. Everywhere else, it is neutralised by strong checks which have always brought down demographic growth to the level of the available means of subsistence. The comparison of the two progressions is taken up right from Chapter II of the *Essay* of 1798, with Malthus concluding the first chapter of his book, which would immortalise him, by recognising "this natural inequality" between population and the means of subsistence as an insurmountable obstacle to the attainment of perfection by mankind. This would radically change the way the population problem was perceived all over Europe and give rise to an extensive literature during the following decades. But if the book appeared to be marked by a pessimism which contrasted sharply with the euphoria generated by the egalitarian ideologies blossoming in France and in England at that time, it was also because of the nature of the checks described by Malthus. He first analysed mortality and its main causes and considered it a positive check: "The positive checks are extremely various, and include every cause, whether arising from vice or misery, which in any degree contribute to shorten the natural duration of human life. Under this head, therefore, may be enumerated all unwholesome occupations, severe labour and exposure to the seasons, extreme poverty, bad nursing of children, great towns, excesses of all kind, the whole train of common diseases and epidemics, wars, plague, and famine".[13]

---

[11] It is nonetheless true that in 1968 it appeared to be an innovative book.

[12] As regards the controversy with Godwin, works by Waterman (1991) and Winch (1996) are much more informative than the articles by Spengler (1971) and Petersen (1971). On some points, these two articles are subject to debate.

[13] *Essay,* 7th Edition, I: 13–14.

Preventive checks are of two types: *moral restraint*, and *prudential* or *vicious restraint*. The first, as it has been pointed out, means that a man should not marry until he is in a position to provide for his family and that he should observe complete celibacy before marriage. From the demographic viewpoint, a preventive check means raising the age of marriage and a higher proportion of bachelors. The second preventive check, which is prudential or vicious restraint, covers all other types of behaviour. Malthus first mentioned "vicious celibacy", or the absence of chastity. For example in England, to which he devoted an entire chapter, among the upper classes, especially in urban areas, some persons were "deterred from marrying by the idea of expenses that they must retrench, and the pleasures of which they must deprive themselves, on the supposition of having a family."[14] He also severely condemned "promiscuous intercourse, unnatural passions, violations of the marriage bed, and improper arts to conceal the consequences of irregular connections, [which] are preventive checks that clearly come under the head of vice."[15] As for contraception, Malthus realised what it was only when he brought out the fifth edition in 1817. In 1798, he confessed that he "could not understand" how Condorcet, in *Esquisse d'un tableau historique des progrès de l'esprit humain*, could raise the objection that the increase in the number of men would compromise the progress of activity and happiness: "he alludes either to a promiscuous concubinage, which would prevent breeding, or something else as unnatural. To remove the difficulty in this way will surely (...) be to destroy that virtue and purity of manners which the advocates of equality, and of the perfectibility of man, profess to be the end and object of their views."[16] In 1830, Malthus finally understood what contraception was. In *Summary View*, he includes among vicious preventive restraints, "the sort of intercourse which renders some of the women of large towns unprolific; a general corruption of morals with regard to the sex, which has a similar effect."[17]

These were then the core concepts of Malthus's population *theory*. The following pages attempt to clarify a series of epistemological contradictions: why is it that Malthus, being a *theoretical economist,* never *recommended* prudential restraint, i.e. the refusal to marry or the use of contraception, although he was perfectly aware, *as an empiricist observer* (because strictly speaking, it would be anachronistic to talk of him as a sociologist), that several social strata took recourse to such restraints to avoid lowering their standard of living due to family responsibilities? On the *doctrinal* level, Malthus continued, however, in edition after edition to deplore contraception, continuing to classify it as a prudential or vicious restraint and refusing to look at it as an acceptable method of counterbalancing the principle of population. On the contrary, neo-Malthusians in France, the Netherlands, England and Sweden, recommended contraception and, breaking away from Malthusian orthodoxy in the early years of the nineteenth century, they condemned moral

[14] *Essay*, 7th edition, I: 236. Same observation as in the first edition: *Essay*, 1798: 91.

[15] *Essay,* 7th edition, I: 14.

[16] Mac Cleary, 1953: 85–93. *Essay*, 1798: 124. Same quotation in *Essay*, 7th edition, II : 5.

[17] *Summary View*: 250.

restraint as unrealistic advice to the poor. Actually, Malthus had only suggested postponing marriage until the time a man expected to earn enough to provide for his family. He understood the need to be more "operational" by defining an exact criterion and he indicated that the worker should earn a wage that would be sufficient to "feed, at the average price of wheat, the average number of children produced by a marriage."[18] The objections are quite obvious: was he capable of assessing the cost of providing for a family? Was the average price of wheat the right index given the fluctuations caused by poor harvests? What if the person was a victim of unemployment? Besides, was chastity before marriage possible for persons considered by the middle-class as being demoralised by poverty? On the other hand, contraception within marriage was a remedy more suited to the social reality prevailing in the early years of the industrial revolution. How do the empirical observation of society and the demo-economic theory fit in together and, from a different angle, how to ensure that Malthus's theory is coherent with his doctrine on population? The various models in the following pages will clarify the problem.

The First Model: Regulation by Mortality

The simplest model is defined by the decisive role played by the means of subsistence and by positive checks: "Among plants and animals the view of the subject is simple. They are all impelled by a powerful instinct to the increase of their species, and this instinct is interrupted by reasoning or doubts about providing for their offspring. Wherever, therefore, there is liberty, the power of increase is exerted, and the superabundant effects are repressed afterwards by want of room and nourishment, which is common to animals and plants and among animals by becoming the prey of others."[19] In this model (Fig. 2.1), population is governed by the available

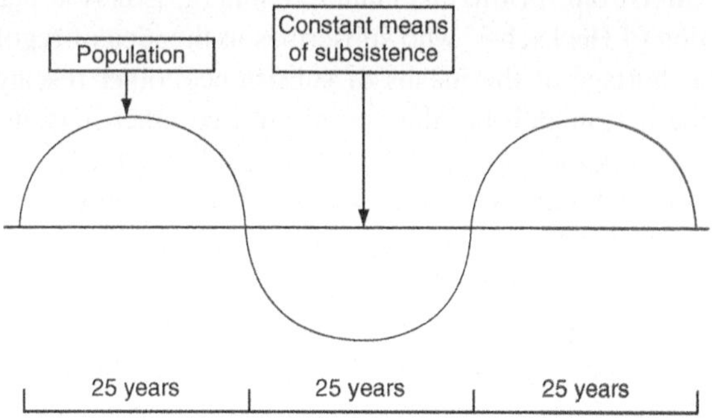

Fig. 2.1 First model: regulation by mortality

[18] The note figures on p. 600 (Book III, Chapter 4) of the Guillaumin Edition of 1852, which gives a translation of the 5th edition published in 1823. See Charbit (1981: 62–64) for the reactions of French Malthusians to moral restraint.

[19] *Essay*, 1798: 76.

means of subsistence. Both a demographic increase and a decrease are possible. The model shows a sinusoidal fluctuation because of a certain inertia related to the combination of causes of mortality. Let us consider a famine or an acute shortage of means of subsistence, very common in France during the *Ancien régime*. Even after the high mortality had brought the population back to the level of the available means of subsistence, the large number of deaths made it impossible to find enough burial places and delayed burial. An uncontrollable typhus, cholera or dysentery epidemic, given the epidemiological conditions at the time, was bound to break out and the mortality curve would continue to go down, below the level of the available means of subsistence. On the other hand, if the means of subsistence are abundant, the increase in the number of men will first lead to growing malnutrition. Population will continue to exceed the maximum level of available resources and death will first strike the weakest persons before the situation becomes a demographic catastrophe.

This mechanism applies to economies based on food-gathering and hunting where men, like all species of animals, are not in a position to increase their means of subsistence. But according to Malthus, this model was also applicable in England "to the lowest orders of society".[20] Was it historically relevant? We will limit ourselves to the Scandinavian countries that Malthus visited in 1799 and to England, a country evidently crucial to understand the genesis of the *Essay*.

The First Model: Scandinavian Countries

Malthus compares the material well-being of the Norwegians, which he attributes to late marriage, to the poverty prevailing in Sweden, where death took a heavy toll of the population dependent for its living on inefficient farming practices.[21] Magnusson has assessed Malthus's analysis on the basis of the work done by Heckscher, Utterström, Fridlizius, Gaunt, Winberg, Eriksson and Rodgers.[22] With the exception of Heckscher, who subscribes to the idea of regulation by mortality because of a shortage of the means of subsistence, other researchers also follow the logic of the first model, but they point out two other reasons for mortality, viz. epidemics and lack of hygiene (Utterström, Fridlizius); some others, on the contrary, totally reject Malthus's argument, arguing that demographic growth stimulated agricultural growth and encouraged proto-industrialisation in the early nineteenth century. Gaunt opposes two demographic structures in Sweden corresponding to two distinct types of agriculture: firstly, nuclear families, late marriage and low fertility in the cereal-growing areas and secondly, large families and high fertility in areas where

---

20 *Essay*, 1798: 93.

21 Norway: *Essay*, 7th edition, I: 154–159. Sweden: ibid., I, 164–173. Also see the pamphlet published in 1800 under the title: *An Investigation of the Cause of the Present High Price of Provisions*.

22 Magnusson, 1986: 60–70.

small landowning farmers could earn an extra income by working in the mines and producing handicrafts. Finally, Winberg draws attention to differences in marrying patterns according to the social status in a parish in western Sweden. Though later research showed that Malthus made a mistake when he attributed the situation in Sweden to high mortality, it concedes nonetheless that the Malthusian theory is relevant as a demo-economic system, particularly because it gives importance to nuptiality, as we shall see later.

The Reform of the Poor Laws in England

Taking England as a case study to assess the relevance of Malthus' ideas is more complex for not only do Malthus's theories and doctrine overlap, but there is a constant fluctuation of his opinions regarding a major social issue of his time, namely widespread poverty. It is well known that the success of Malthus's *Essay* first published in 1798 as well as of its later editions is explained by the socio-economic situation in England. As a result of the exceedingly poor harvest in the years 1795–1796, 1800–1801, 1812–1813, there was a marked inflation during the period 1794–1813 and the price of wheat skyrocketed; a quarter (28 lbs), which was worth 46 shillings on an average between 1777 and 1793, rose to 83 shillings (1793–1813) and the same was true of other cereals. Following the reform of the Poor Laws and the spread of the *Speenhamland System* devised in May 1795 by the Justices of the Peace in Berkshire (according to which the amount of aid was decided by the price of wheat and the number of children), the contribution of the parishes to the upkeep of the poor assumed the proportions of a national tax, data about which speaks for itself: 2 millions in 1784, 4 millions in 1803 and 8 millions in 1818. Thus Sidney and Beatrice Webb wrote in 1929, "To a generation unaccustomed to public expenditures, such a sum seemed stupendous."[23] The idea that the Poor Laws contributed to the continuation of poverty by encouraging the poor to multiply thoughtlessly and that population could be regulated only through mortality, found its theoretician and it is easy to understand why the reasoning in the anonymous pamphlet seemed perfectly convincing to those who discovered it in 1798 in a situation of ideological, political and social unrest, one of whose key elements was the publication by Godwin in 1793 of *Political Justice*, that Malthus sought to refute.[24] However, it is not right to consider Malthus a champion of the established order for reasons that need to be mentioned, even if briefly, because they are a good example of the general problem of the book's ambiguity that we have

---

[23] 1929, II: 2. Statistics for the entire period (1688–1847) figure on pp. 1036–1043. Regarding the rise in prices and wages, see Mingay (1986: 91–100) and Eccleston (1986: 143).

[24] The grave mistake made by Malthus in the 1798 edition is mentioned often and rightly so (for example Wrigley, 1986). He underestimates England's population by 56% and places it at 7 millions while the 1801 census places it at 10.9 millions. See *Essay*, 1798: 74–75. But this is true only of the first *Essay* as Malthus later used figures provided by the census.

raised in the introduction to this chapter. The first paradox is that while the *Essay* of 1798 is generally considered a formidable weapon against the ideology of 1789 strongly supported by Godwin, Malthus calmly stated that the French Revolution was the best proof of the inefficacy of the English Poor Laws because it made each person more independent instead of depending on others. Thus French workers became more industrious, they saved more and married later.[25] The paradox is easy to spot: it was not an argument *in favour* of the French Revolution; the question is just not relevant here as Malthus developed a purely utilitarian argument. Let us remove a gross error that is often made: even though history associates Malthus with the reform of the Poor Laws in 1834, only the 1798 *Essay* contains a total condemnation of the system of aid. The first *Essay* claimed that this aid had encouraged population growth although sufficient means of subsistence were not available, reduced the quantity of food meant for the more active workers by giving it to those employed in *workhouses* and had weakened the English workers' spirit of independence; finally, since the workers were attached to parishes, the system of assistance had introduced an element of rigidity in the labour market by reducing the workers' mobility. Malthus's conclusion is inexorable: had there been no Poor Laws, there would certainly have been "cases of extreme distress, but the sum of happiness among the people would have been greater."[26]

But what was his position later? In the 1826 edition, he defended himself vigorously against the accusation that he had forbidden marriages among the poor and declared, "What I have really proposed is a very different measure. It is the *gradual* and *very gradual* abolition of the poor laws." And as if this repetition was not enough, he added an explanatory note saying, "So gradual as not to affect any individuals at present alive, or who will be born within the next two years." Even better, he explained that the abolition of the Poor Laws would not only add to the distress of the poor but also lead to a stagnation of the demand for labour.[27] This profound doctrinal change is very clear in a letter to Chalmers in which he declared that he was convinced that it was above all necessary to improve the management of aid. Finally, when circumstances made it necessary, assistance was justified for humanitarian reasons as well as political calculations.[28] The conservatives who demanded an urgent reform of the law because of the fiscal pressure exerted by the

---

[25] *Essay*, 7th edition, II: 69.

[26] *Essay*, 1798: 94–101.

[27] *Essay*, 7th edition, II: 61, 63–64. The adjective "gradual" has been put in italics by Malthus himself.

[28] Letter dated 21 July 1822, quoted by Winch (1996: 320–321). But the *Summary View* published in 1830 again warns its readers that everything depends on the manner in which the poor perceive assistance: if receiving aid is not considered demeaning, then there is a great risk that the aid will create a larger number of poor than it provides succour to (*Summary View*: 271–272). Improvement of assistance: *Essay*, 7th edition, II: 53. Humanitarian and political reasons: ibid.: 47.

Poor Tax must have been somewhat perplexed when they found the author of the principal argument in favour of its abolition backing out. Without any ambiguity whatsoever, Malthus wished to postpone by at least two decades the amendment of the Poor Laws which appeared so urgent to them. But things are not so simple: in spite of this doctrinal about-face, he maintained his condemnation of 1798 in the chapter on the Poor Laws and often repeated word for word the arguments advanced in the first *Essay* that although assistance brought succour in individual cases, it was basically pernicious.[29] There is no choice but to accept the confusion in his thinking, either because the subject did not really interest him or because he was looking for a more comprehensive solution to the problem of poverty. We shall see that the latter hypothesis is the right one. As early as 1800, in *An Investigation of the Cause of the Present High Price of Provisions* whose sole object was to explain why the price of wheat was so abnormally high as compared to its availability, he declared that the system of parish assistance had raised the price of wheat above the market price, but that the poor had no reason to complain because the problem for them would be solved by importing more wheat and encouraging farmers to produce more. What is important is that he no longer insisted on the condemnation based on the principle of population but declared that in the years when wheat was in short supply, imports were beneficial for the country.[30] Once again, the utilitarian interpretation is relevant because Malthus took into account the compensations that benefited the poor on another level.

To conclude this discussion, we may ask whether the Poor Laws really encouraged population growth. The answer to this question involves a comparison of the normal demographic rates (birth, marriage and mortality) before and after the reform of 1834. Data was collected by the Cambridge Group for some parishes which had set up a system for providing assistance. An analysis of the data related to 15 of these parishes shows that none of Malthus's mechanisms were confirmed – neither the increase in the birth rate nor the fall in the death rate. In addition, cases where assistance was provided for children independently of the assistance provided for unemployment also show that the law had no effect. These results led Huzel to oppose the reformers of 1834 and conclude that the old law did nothing to encourage growth but was a response to poverty. This can be shown by taking into account the per capita income; immigration was highest in the poorest parishes despite a higher per capita expenditure by way of assistance.[31] If these results can be extrapolated – as they are yet to be proved (Boyer, for example, reaches a conclusion opposite to Huzel's) – the reform of the Poor Laws is not of much interest from the viewpoint of social history; it can only be considered as being of ideological interest, which it certainly was.[32]

---

[29] *Essay,* 7th edition, II: 47, 48–51.

[30] Also see *Essay,* 7th edition, II: 42, note 1.

[31] Data taken from Huzel, 1986.

[32] Boyer, 1989: 111.

The Second Model: The Demo-Economics of Fertility and Nuptiality

The Agricultural Employment Market and Demographic Growth

Even though Malthus believed in the first *Essay* of 1798 that population was regulated by mortality, the demo-economic dimension was very clear. Like all classical economists, his conception of dynamics meant, at least in the first *Essay* though not in his later works, analyzing the fluctuations around a point of equilibrium in distinct markets – in this case the labour market and that for agricultural produce. We may briefly recall the concepts related to the employment market and their demographic implications. Agricultural (or even industrial) workers *supply* their labour: if the population increases, it will be followed by an increase in the supply of labour. Enterprises *demand* labour for production and wages are the point of intersection of the curves representing supply and demand. Hence according to the classical economists, economic factors govern demographic behaviour, as is clear in Malthus's formulation of the demo-economic dynamic: "The constant effort towards population, which is found to act even in the most vicious societies, increases the number of people before the means of subsistence are increased. The food, therefore, which before supported seven millions, must now be divided among seven millions and half or eight millions. The poor consequently must live much worse, and many of them be reduced to severe distress. The number of labourers also being above the proportion of the work in the market, the price of labour must tend toward a rise. The labourer therefore must work harder to earn the same as he did before. During this season of distress, the discouragements to marriage, and the difficulty of rearing a family are so great that population is at a stand. In the meantime the cheapness of labour, the plenty of labourers, and the necessity of an increased industry amongst them, encourage cultivators to employ more labour upon their land, to turn up fresh soil, and to manure and improve more completely what is already in tillage, till ultimately the means of subsistence become in the same proportion to the population as at the period from which we set out. The situation of the labourer being again tolerably comfortable, the restraints to population are in some degree loosened, and the same retrograde and progressive movements, with respect to happiness are repeated."[33]

In this model (Fig. 2.2), unlike the previous one, the fluctuations are part of a long growth movement. It is the principle of population, an independent variable, which induces the growth of agricultural production and, contrary to the first model, the population is regulated not by mortality but by marriage.

---

[33] *Essay*, 1798: 77.

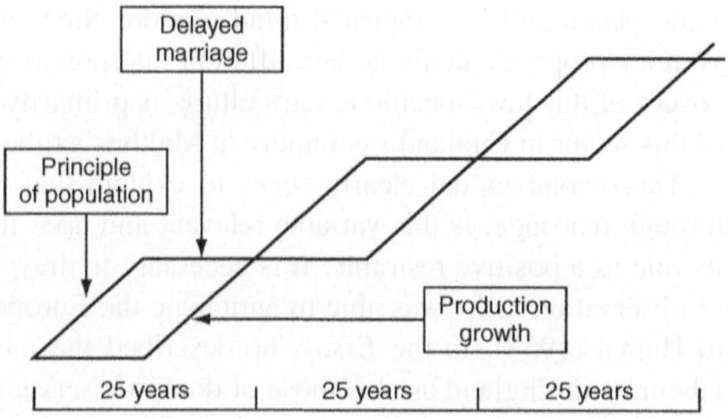

Fig. 2.2 Second model. Regulation by marriage

The Law of Diminishing Returns

It is possible to propose a variant of this model by introducing the law of diminishing returns, which is of major consequence considering that sooner or later population reaches a point of equilibrium. David Ricardo theorised the process as follows: due to the absolute scarcity of land, the law of diminishing returns implies that in the long run the price of the means of subsistence must necessarily increase. As a result, the price of labour must also increase because workers must at least reproduce their labour force by buying necessaries, (i.e. goods essential for their survival such as food). Since profits can increase only at the expense of wages, the rate of profit tends to be zero in the long run. Entrepreneurs are therefore not interested in investing and the demand for labour gets stabilised. At the same time, the supply of labour also gets stabilised and population remains stationary.[34] Figure 2.3 below expresses the tendency towards the stationary state.

Von Tunzelmann rightly notes that Malthus finally gave little importance to the law of diminishing returns even though he was its author. According to him, this is because Malthus proposed a demo-economic system that is above all dynamic and based on the analysis of disequilibria. It is therefore very different from Ricardo's

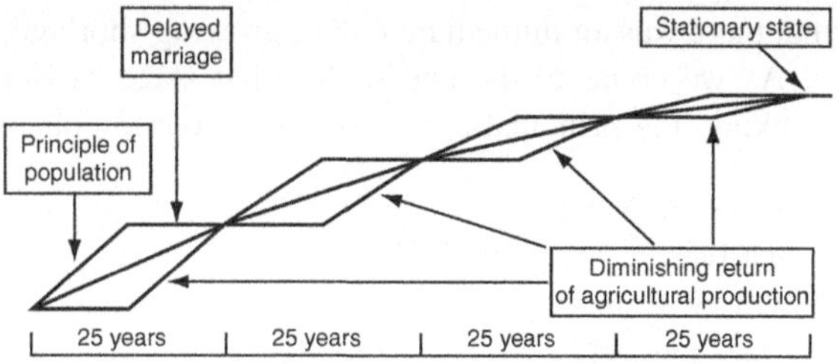

Fig. 2.3 Second model. Regulation by marriage (with diminishing agricultural returns)

[34] Ricardo, *The Principles of Political Economy and Taxation*: 52–53. Regarding Ricardo, see Hollander, 1987: 191–207.

static vision and his empirical mind is more concerned with short term results.[35] Wrigley proposes an altogether different interpretation according to which the discovery of this law, specific to agriculture, is primarily explained by the central role of this sector in England's economy in Malthus's time.[36]

The second model clearly seeks to explain that population can be controlled through marriage. Is this variable relevant and does it mean that mortality has lost its role as a positive restraint? It is necessary to draw attention to Malthus's power of observation as he was able to anticipate the European nuptiality model credited to Hajnal (1953). In the *Essay*, he described the motivations of agricultural day labourers in England as also those of domestic servants living with their employers who also took care of all their needs.[37] But in a more general way he points out, "In no other country to the same extent is there to be found so great a proportion of late marriages, or so great a proportion of persons remaining unmarried, as in Great Britain"[38] and he explains a little later that in Europe these two characteristics were the two main factors through which preventive restraint regulated the growth of population, while the positive check (i.e. mortality) was a thing of the past.[39] Though Malthus did not describe in detail how these checks worked, there is no doubt that he had an intuition about the role of nuptiality, confirmed by the reconstitution of the population of England by the Cambridge Group. Initially, till 1781, population growth was the driving force behind the rise in food prices and as Wrigley puts it, "it was entirely rational for him, on the basis of recent history, to detect a sound link between the population growth rate and food price rises and to fear the effect of rapid population growth." Later, the two variables developed independently. Similarly, the prices of food varied inversely with the real wage. But what was important was that the relation between the real wage and life expectancy at birth disappeared, which means that demographic growth was no longer regulated by mortality but by nuptiality, as claimed by Malthus.[40] On the other hand, we are now aware of the long-term changes and short-term fluctuations in the major aggregates.[41] For example, between 1520 and 1820, agricultural production increased at the same rate as population, while the population working in the agricultural sector decreased. Wrigley, who has drawn attention to some shrewd observations made by Malthus on these issues, concludes on the basis of this data that the latter could not believe that there was an immediate risk of growing shortages in the agricultural sector.[42]

As we come to the end of the first stage of our reconstruction of Malthus's thinking, the principal concepts get organised coherently in two models in which

[35] Von Tunzelmann, 1986: 67–71.

[36] Wrigley, 1986: 50–53.

[37] *Essay*, 1798: 91.

[38] *Summary View*: 237.

[39] Ibid.: 251, 264.

[40] Wrigley, 1984: 214–219.

[41] Wrigley and Schofield, 1981.

[42] Wrigley, 1986: 50–53.

demography and economics seem to more or less agree. The third model will bring us face to face with more profound thinking focused on the crucial concept of effective demand.

The Third Model: Effective Demand

The third Malthusian model has been reconstituted on the basis of three major sources – the two editions of *An Essay on the Principle of Population, Principles of Political Economy, with a view to their practical application* published in 1820 and *A Summary View on the Principle of Population* which came out in 1830 – as well as other texts, notably articles, letters and pamphlets. Joseph J. Spengler's seminal article published in 1945 entitled *Malthus's Total Population Theory*, to which this chapter owes a lot, even though Spengler underestimates the role of agriculture in Malthus's thinking and lays greater stress on industry, has guided us during this reconstruction.

Production and Population

Malthus's statement that "What is mainly necessary to a rapid increase of population is a great and continued demand for labour" is fully representative of the orthodox stream of classical economic theory according to which the demand for labour is determined by its supply. This statement is illustrated at least twice in the *Essay* by comparing two recent periods in England (1735–1755 and 1790–1811), the marked increase of wealth during the second period having been translated into much faster demographic growth.[43] But does it not go against his frequent claim that the population principle is an *independent* variable, a vital and uncontrollable force? There is no doubt whatsoever that there was a change in his thinking on this point and a complete break with the ideas expressed in the first *Essay*. "To suppose an actual and permanent increase of population is to beg the question. We may as well suppose at once an increase of wealth; because an actual and permanent increase of population cannot take place without a proportionate or nearly proportionate increase of wealth. The question really is, whether encouragements to population, or even the natural tendency of population to increase beyond the funds for its maintenance, so as to press hard against the limits of subsistence, will, or will not, alone furnish an adequate stimulus to the increase of wealth. And this question, Spain, Portugal,

[43] *Principles*: 261. Examples mentioned: *Essay*, 7th edition, II: 95, 139. Smith, for example, in the chapter on workers' wages, writes in 1776 in the *Wealth of Nations*: "*If this demand increases continuously, the remuneration for work should necessarily encourage marriage and the multiplication of workers so that it allows them to respond to this demand with a constant increase from a constantly growing population. (...) The demand for men, like the demand for any other good necessarily regulates its production. It increases it when it grows too slowly and it stops it when it increases too fast.*" (*The Wealth of Nations*: 183, in Book 1, Chapter 8).

Poland, Hungary, Turkey, and many others countries in Europe, together with nearly the whole of Asia and Africa, and the greatest part of America, distinctly answer in the negative."[44]

Actually, the demographer ceded his place to the economist or, to be more precise, demographic reasoning became a part of a much larger construct. Although Malthus, in accordance with the classical economic theory, ruled out that population growth (supply of labour) could control production (demand for labour), it could be said that it is so because poverty is not solvent, an idea underlying the following quotation: "There must be something in the previous state of the demand and supply of the commodity in question, or in its price, antecedent to and independently of the demand occasioned by the new labourers, in order to warrant the employment of an additional number of people in its production."[45] A superficial reader of Malthus's writings would assert that the latter constantly feared that the means of subsistence would fall short of the population's needs. And therein lies a second contradiction because contrary to this common perception, Malthus no longer believed in this risk and the *Summary View* is perfectly clear on this point, namely that the means of subsistence only represented a ceiling that is never reached: "While land of good quality is in great abundance, the rate at which food might be made to increase would far exceed what is necessary to keep pace with the most rapid increase of population which the laws of nature in relation to human kind permit."[46]

This would be true even in the old countries and the living conditions would not worsen. More importantly, in the *Summary View* as well as in the *Principles* the question of the relation between the population and the means of subsistence is included in the wider framework of the effective demand: "It appears to me perfectly clear in theory, and universally confirmed by experience, that the employment of a capital, too rapidly increased by parsimonious habits, may find a limit, and does, in fact, often find a limit, long before there is any real difficulty in procuring the means of subsistence; and that both capital and population may be at the same time,

Fig. 2.4 Third model. Demand for labour as a long-term driving force

[44] *Principles*: 350–351.

[45] *Principles*: 349. Regarding demand for labour see Coontz, 1961 On Sismondi, Lauderdale and Playfair as contributors to the theory of effective demand see Spiegel, 1955: 529–530.

[46] *Summary View*: 239.

and for a great length, redundant, compared with the effective demand for labour."[47] Figure 2.4 shows how the demand for labour acts as a driving force in the long run.

Short-Term Demographic Responses

In response to the fluctuations in the demand for labour resulting from phases of recession and recovery, the population, in order to maintain its standard of living, adjusts the age of marriage while the married population uses contraceptive methods whenever necessary (Fig. 2.5).

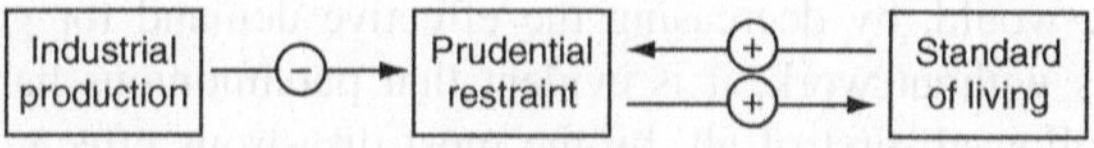

Fig. 2.5 Third model. Short-term demographic responses

But though it is logical that there should be an interaction between prudential restraint and the standard of living (as shown by the double arrow in the figure), prudential restraint cannot have a long-term effect on production because, according to the classical theory, the demand for labour always controls its supply and that is why a single arrow links prudential restraint and industrial production in Fig. 2.5. Malthus is remarkably explicit about the practice of prudential restraint, arguing that if the poor wish to improve their condition, they should marry at a time when their wages together with the savings collected during bachelorhood would permit them to have 5–6 children without having to depend on assistance. Only then will prudential restraint bring about a "striking" improvement in the condition of the poor.[48]

As mentioned above, the idea of a short-term response is at the core of the doctrinal arguments advanced by twentieth century neo-liberal ideology, exactly as it was in the writings of the French economists of the nineteenth century (see Chapter 3). However, in Malthus's case, it was not a doctrinal position but an empirical observation. So far, we have emphasised the key role of the demand for labour as compared to its supply. It is now necessary to explain its nature since Malthus raised the question of effective, and not potential, demand because only the former was likely to result in an increase in production.

Effective Demand

When he analysed the conditions of a strong and sustained demand, Malthus the economist surveyed the social groups and income categories likely to generate it.

[47] *Principles*: 469.

[48] *Essay,* 7th edition, II: 254.

From where could such a demand arise? Certainly not from the lower classes: "An increase of population, when an additional quantity of labour is not wanted, will soon be checked by want of employment and the scanty support of those employed, and will not furnish the required stimulus to an increase of wealth proportioned to power of production.[49] A second argument was developed regarding the psychology of the workers who were supposed to be satisfied with essential goods and, having obtained them, preferred "indolence" to "activity".[50]

Which were the groups having sufficient savings to make investments? Malthus put forward the hypothesis that farmers instead of buying goods produced by manufacturers and vice versa, could all start saving.[51] But this would result in a spiral of under-consumption: "If the transformation of wages into capital, pushed beyond a certain point, would, by decreasing the effective demand for goods, leave the working classes without work, it is evident that parsimonious habits pushed too far would be followed, first of all, by the most disastrous effects and then cause a severe and permanent decline in wealth and population."[52] Keynes would later use this intuition to develop the idea that the lack of the propensity to consume could bring about a structural crisis.[53] Nor did Malthus rely on the big landowners, although they were very rich and had considerable savings. Had they contributed to the effective demand, England would not have experienced a situation of under-consumption; but since they were essentially interested in hunting and in raising game and did not show any interest in manufactured goods, their consumption habits were unfavourable to economic growth.[54] This was a shortcoming from which all quasi feudal countries suffered (e.g. Ireland and New Spain). Other sources of the demand for labour were domestic and international trade, which stimulated the desire to consume by offering new products, and finally "unproductive" persons in the sense that they did not contribute directly to agricultural or industrial production but had an income. Malthus placed in the last category the big landowners and persons employed in public or private service. Finally, much before Keynes, he gave thought to the financing of public works through budgetary allocations: in 1815, at the end of the Napoleonic Wars, England had to face the "disasters of peace" and Malthus believed that the unproductive classes were large enough to constitute an effective demand. Paradoxically, this Whig who opposed government intervention as a matter of principle recommended that public works be financed by the budget

---

[49] *Principles*: 349–350.

[50] *Principles*: 379.

[51] *Principles:* 260–265. Regarding this point, see Rashid, 1977: 373.

[52] *Principles*: 369.

[53] The resemblance between Malthus and Keynes was shown by Lambert, 1962. This article is useful in that it recalls the positions of Harrod, Robbins, Corry, Hansen, Schumpeter and Blaug on this point.

[54] *Summary View*: 246–247. See Rashid, 1977: 379. Regarding the consumption habits of the nobility, Cannadine (1986: 98–100) and Mingay (1986: 92–93) have different viewpoints, but Mingay seems more correct in his appraisal of the economic fallout of their consumption.

deficit. Thus the maintenance of public buildings, the construction of bridges, roads, canals and railway lines would come out of the government budget.[55] Finally, it was the consumption of manufactured goods by the greatest number that constituted the effective demand most advantageous for growth: "it is the diffusion of luxury therefore among the mass of the people, and not the excess of it in a few, that seems to be most advantageous, both with regard to national wealth and national happiness."[56]

England in Malthus's Time

Since the lower classes could not constitute an effective demand, what about the other potential sources mentioned by Malthus? His insistence that rural areas and unproductive classes should and could constitute an effective demand can undoubtedly be traced to his early years. Stapelton reminds us that Malthus lived in a house bought by his father in the parish of Albury in 1787 and that the background from which his first *Essay* emerged was that of a comfortable middle-class family in the heart of rural Surrey. Malthus himself described this background of rural nobility, persons of rank and members of the clergy, as "the middle regions of society [which] seem to be best suited to intellectual improvement", unlike excessive wealth or extreme poverty.[57] On the other hand, the peasants of Somerset, among whom he lived, were better off than the Scottish peasants and the workers of Warrington he had seen when he was sixteen. For example, at Abinger, not far from the place where Malthus lived, the price of bread had come down from 6 shillings 4 pence to 4 shillings 4 pence between 1650 and 1750. Also, noticing the spread of pasturelands and the growth of large agricultural farms as a result of the "enclosures movement", Malthus could only conclude that the surplus population was absorbed by industry and its "unwholesome occupations" in socially disastrous conditions, which explains his distrust of commerce and industry in the first model. It may be recalled that in the span of one century the population had increased at a slower pace than agricultural production, but things became worse later when, according to the figures provided by Wrigley, the real wage decreased by 28% between 1750 and 1801.[58] Malthus was thus bound to think that English peasants led a more comfortable life in the past and that their condition had deteriorated subsequently. As a Whig, he felt he had to defend the social objective of restoring their earlier standard of living.

In 1798, the second model was focused on agriculture but in the later editions of the *Essay*, Malthus did not give it the same importance and it became just one of the sectors in a comprehensive model. To assess the relevance of this theoretical and

---

[55] *Principles:* 315–328, 335–337, 355. Public expenditure: *Principles*: 511–512; *Essay,* 7th edition, I: 59–60. On these points see Spengler, 1945: 97–98; Lambert, 1962: 811–814; Cocks, 1986: 230–231.

[56] *Essay,* 7th edition, II: 253.

[57] *Essay*, 1798: 207.

[58] This information has been obtained from Stapleton, (1986:22–23) and Wrigley (1983).

doctrinal choice, it is necessary to reflect on the place of agriculture in English economy or, to put it in the terms of economic analysis, on the importance of rent in the economic circuit. The physiocrats held the extreme view that only agriculture could create wealth and that the net product supplied the entire economic circuit while Malthus assessed its role more on the consumption side. Fearing that the farmers' mode of consumption would be disadvantageous for production and that it would not suffice for a strong and sustained effective demand, he ended up by recognizing that industry, which he distrusted in the *Essay* of 1798, was more advantageous for effective demand. At the same time, he classified the big landowners and their servants among the unproductive classes having purchasing power. The contradiction is obvious, unless we extend our field of study and take into consideration the *inductive* effect of income from land in terms of the creation of wealth and employment. According to Dean and Cole, at the beginning of the nineteenth century land represented more than half of England's national capital and rent contributed 20% of the national income.[59] Landowners who did not farm their lands held 80–90% of the land and invested in improving rural property by maintaining verges of roads and hedges, canals, drainage of surplus water, access roads and construction works of different types. However, even though the return from these investments was lower than the returns from trade or financial speculation or urban property, only land brought social and political prestige. The low level of income from land can also be explained by the landlord's role as a social protector. Mingay points out that some nobles used their supplementary income (from coal mines or from the commercial operation of canals) to rehabilitate their tenant farmers.[60] Such are the socio-economic aspects of rent and it is essential not to underestimate their induced effects. Mingay estimates that in 1811 landowners employed one third of England's active population and that income from land was invested in both agricultural and non-agricultural sectors, not forgetting that a large part of this wealth was squandered on ostentatious and completely useless expenditure.[61] In short, although it is true that Malthus did give thought to these induced effects, the growth of manufacturing and trade benefited from a prosperous agricultural base. But what about the other sectors?

The aggregate data available on international trade makes it possible to complete this rapid assessment of Malthus's theory. As far as imports are concerned, Malthus's defence of the Corn Laws was based on the belief that protection, by raising the price of cereals, enriches agriculture and promotes effective demand from this sector; the purchasing power thus created may be limited to agriculture or it may extend to industry and trade. Vamplew believes that changes in the price

---

59 In this regard, we have followed Mingay, 1986.

60 When Malthus denounced their predilection for hunting and raising game, he either deliberately ignored or forgot that this activity was possible only because the lord compensated the peasants for the losses caused by hunting by lowering their rent.

61 A lively description of this behaviour is found in Cannadine, 1986: 97–100.

Table 2.1 Average price of cereals

	Wheat	Barley	Oats
1775–1784	45.06	23.03	16.06
1785–1794	47.26	26.14	18.19
1795–1804	75.26	38.31	25.19
1805–1814	83.51	46.58	31.38
1815–1824	68.75	36.26	25.33
1825–1834	60.07	33.74	25.53
1835–1844	56.82	32.39	22.28
1845–1854	51.52	31.36	21.58
1855–1864	53.72	35.76	23.73

Source: Vamplew, 1986: 135.

of wheat and the principal cereals confirm Malthus's point of view: these prices remained high until free trade was established in 1846 (Table 2.1).

It should be noted that according to Mingay the rise in prices between 1795 and 1815 cannot be explained by the difficulty of importing cereals, because wheat continued to come into the country even during the continental blockade. This involves a different type of mechanism which brings to mind the second model because with a demographic growth of more than 2 million persons 3 million acres of land were brought under cultivation; unfortunately, the efficacy of this response was partially nullified by a series of poor harvests responsible for the very high price of wheat and the increase of income from land.[62]

As for exports, the "the natural tendency of foreign trade is *immediately* to increase the value of that part of the natural revenue which consists of profits, without any proportionate diminution elsewhere (...) it is precisely this *immediate* increase of national income that furnishes both the power and will to employ more labour, and occasions the animated demand for labour, produce and capital, which is a striking and almost universal accompaniment of successful foreign commerce."[63] British exports (cotton, wool and metals) did not suffer, neither during the Napoleonic wars and the continental blockade nor due to the measures taken by Jefferson and Madison against the entry of British goods into the United States, because trade changed its course and found new markets (Portugal, Spain and their colonies). In 1783, they represented 8% of the national income as compared to 13% in 1821. The case of cotton is the most striking: exports increased in volume by 17% per year between 1792 and 1802 and 8% per year during the following decade. Malthus rightly attributed this development to mechanisation which made English manufactures very competitive.[64]

Finally, there remains the triple question of industry, accumulation of capital and the economic crisis in the 1820s. Malthus closely followed the development

62 Vamplew, 1986: 134–135; Mingay: 1986: 91.

63 Malthus, *Principles*: 460. Emphasis in the original text.

64 Quoted by Crouzet, 1986: 194.

of the British economy, especially the formation of capital, which he undoubtedly favoured, refusing to be compared to Sismondi who denounced mechanisation: "the three reasons that favour production the most are the accumulation of capital, soil fertility and inventions that save labour." The example of the cotton textile industry was quite conclusive: "The consumption of cotton cloth has increased so much within the country and abroad because it is cheap that the value of the total amount of cotton cloth and yarn presently exceeds extraordinarily their former value."[65] It is well known that the gross formation of fixed capital was very rapid in industry and even more in the cotton and metal industries. For the entire industrial sector, the annual rate which was between 4 to 13% around 1790 rose to 22% to 26% towards 1815.[66] Also, the relative share of agriculture decreased in favour of industry and transport. It is not worthwhile to dwell on this point of England's economic history which is well known, but on the other hand, we are directly concerned with the connection that Malthus established between the accumulation of capital and the analysis of the crisis during the 1820s.

He often analysed the situation in England since 1815 in the *Principles*. His analysis is interesting as it is based on the short and medium-term and combines factors linked to the demand for labour with those related to its supply, particularly population growth. As a matter of fact, the war years had stimulated demographic growth and several generations of workers appeared on the labour market. The good harvest in 1815 and 1816 led to a fall in agricultural income and to growing unemployment among agricultural labourers. At the same time, the end of the war (1815) threw into the labour market demobilised soldiers, thus increasing the downward pressure on wages, while farmers and merchants, whose earnings had decreased due to the low price of cereals, could not employ this plentiful labour. This caused a severe imbalance between the supply of labour and its demand: "For the four or five years since the war, on account of the change in the distribution of the national produce, and the want of consumption and demand occasioned by it, a decided check has been given to production, and the population, under its former impulse, has increased, not only faster than the demand for labour, but faster than the actual produce; yet this produce, though decidedly deficient, compared with the population, and compared with past times, is redundant, compared with the effectual demand for it, and the revenue which is to purchase it."[67] Was Malthus right to fear a glut in the markets? The crisis which followed the return of peace in 1815 proved him right. Censuses indicate that the population of England and Wales rose from 9,172,980 in 1801 to 11,978,875 in 1821. At the end of the Napoleonic wars, taxes

---

65 *Principles*: 413; cotton textile industry: 402–403.

66 Figures given by Pollard and Feinstein quoted by Anderson, 1986: 217.

67 Agricultural income and unemployment: *Principles*: 444–445. Interaction between factors: "the powerful stimulus which had been given to population during the war continued to pour in fresh supplies of labour, and aided by the disbanded soldiers and sailors and the failure of demand arising from the losses of the farmers and merchants, reduced generally the wages of labour, and left the country with a generally diminished capital and revenue." *Principles*: 494. Also see *Essay*, 7th edition, II, 62–63.

brought in £75 millions, a figure to be compared to the national debt which was estimated to be £860 millions, while in 1792 the figures were respectively £18 and 240 millions.[68] Given the rigidity of wages, a good harvest in 1815 led to a crash in the price of wheat which in its turn brought about a decrease in the availability of work and the purchasing power in the agricultural sector leading to a fall in the demand for industrial products. At the same time, the European markets, ravaged by years of war, proved to be incapable of absorbing the agricultural surplus, while two million soldiers were demobilised. Finding a remedy for this crisis takes us back to the question of capital accumulation: "What is now wanted in this country is an increase in national revenue (. . .). When we have attained this, which can only be attained by increased and steady profits, we may then begin to accumulate, and our accumulation will then be effectual."[69] The argument that reducing debt was an ineffective solution in a situation where there was excess capital and insufficient demand was therefore logical because if the state's creditors were paid back, there would be new capital in the market and the ensuing imbalance would evidently worsen considerably.[70]

In brief:

- according to Malthus, the means of subsistence were no longer a constraint for demographic growth because, with the coming of the industrial revolution, the people of Europe were no longer on the brink of survival;
- it was the demand for labour which controlled demographic growth, this growth translated into an effective demand which lead to the identification of social groups and, according to Malthus, the greatest effective demand emanated from the middle classes, both urban and rural;
- a rapid appraisal of England during the years 1800–1820 shows the *empirical* relevance of the theory of effective demand.

It is now a matter of integrating this conceptualisation of demo-economic growth into a more comprehensive model which shows the coherence of Malthus's doctrinal and theoretical views at the demographic, social, economic and religious levels.

A Comprehensive Model for Maximising Demo-Economic Growth

In Book III of the *Essay*, Malthus rejected several solutions to the problem of poverty such as equality, emigration and the Poor Laws. For example, he was in favour of amending the Poor Laws (the reform would come into effect in 1834)

---

68 Figures for 1884 quoted by Dome (1997: 284). Also see Cocks, 1986: 277.

69 Malthus, *Principle*: 505. Regarding this imbalance and discussions with Ricardo, see Hollander, 1969: 312–320.

70 Malthus, *Principles*: 505. Debt reduction: *Essay*, 7th edition, II: 61. Regarding this imbalance and discussions with Ricardo, see Hollander, 1969: 312–320 and Winch, 1996: 358–362.

since he believed that these laws released the poor from their responsibilities. Nor was emigration a real solution because in the long run, the land would be completely populated and the principle of population would continue to pose a threat. On the other hand, he was totally in favour of "manufactures", which is the subject of Chapter XIII of Book III of the *Essay*. Being a shrewd observer, Malthus successfully cut himself off from the eighteenth century rural society to which he belonged and understood clearly that everything would depend on industry in the future.

Social Doctrine

The justification of industrialisation is particularly interesting because it is theoretical and at the same time empirically based on the observation of the spread of prosperity. The aim is to improve the situation of the lower classes of society which "depends chiefly upon the conduct and prudence of the individuals themselves and is, therefore, not immediately and necessarily connected with an increase in the means of subsistence."[71] This distinction between necessaries, commodities and luxuries was analysed by the economist Nassau Senior, a contemporary of Malthus, in his *Outline of the Science of Political Economy*. It was often referred to in the nineteenth century, for example by Ricardo and by the liberal economists in France during the Second Empire, as an indicator of social progress.[72]

Malthus understood that the prices of industrial goods would come down as a result of mechanisation and the mass production of manufactured goods; consequently, the standard of living of the rural as well as the industrial population would fall due to the relative decrease of the price of industrial goods as compared to the price of agricultural products.[73] It may be recalled that the second model shows that the growth of agricultural production is followed by a *fall* in the price of the means of subsistence. If it is assumed that the higher price of wheat is a result of protectionist taxes, the model does not really change: it is just that the initial prices of wheat and the wage rates are higher. But what is more important is that the economic analysis is put in the proper perspective. Beyond the issue of economic and demographic behaviour (prudential restraint) the problem is essentially political with Malthus clearly establishing a connection between the aspiration for prosperity and prudential restraint. In a given population high wages can lead to high fertility or, on the contrary, they can be spent on the purchase of goods providing comfort; in the second case, there will be no increase in the population. So everything depends on the ability of the poor to stop living from day to day and to emulate those who know how to imagine the future, acquire the desire to become "respectable, virtuous and happy" and inculcate these qualities in their children. These two types

---

[71] *Essay*, 7th edition, II: 130.

[72] Ricardo: *Principles...*: 55. French liberals: see Chapter 6.

[73] *Essay*, 7th edition, II: 134.

of behaviour, in their turn, are largely determined by the political regime: in the first case, despotism, oppression and ignorance will not allow the poor to rise above their condition; on the other hand, education and civil and political freedom will encourage the second type of behaviour. This argument is constantly repeated, either with reference to certain countries, or in relation to the repercussions on the demand for labour.[74] These doctrinal positions are, as it can be seen, typical of Malthus's liberal ideas as a Whig and we are far from a mechanistic concept of the relation between the population and the means of subsistence which characterised the first *Essay*. Coming back to Malthus the economist, what form does the argument in favour of industry take?

Industry and Agriculture

The first *Essay* said almost nothing about industry except for condemning the high mortality among the urban population and the second model, which also appeared in the *Essay* of 1798, concentrated on agriculture and was purely a model of agricultural growth. So did Malthus finally give up this idea and turn to the industrial world once and for all? His position is ambiguous. From a theoretical viewpoint, he believed, unlike the physiocrats, that agriculture could not commercialise its net product if there were no industries; the complementarity of the two sectors was thus frequently reaffirmed.[75] However, in 1814 and 1815 he brought out two pamphlets in favour of maintaining import duties on foreign wheat as demanded by landowners, while almost all other economists, with Ricardo in the lead, were in favour of the industrialists and demanded the abolition of import duties so that the means of subsistence would be less costly and labour would become cheaper.[76] Among the arguments put forward by Malthus is the improvement of the lower classes. How can these potential theoretical and doctrinal contradictions be explained? It must be pointed out that they are no more than seeming contradictions that disappear under three conditions:

- the analysis of the effective demand should be conceived as a system of exchange between the two principal sectors, i.e. agriculture and industry, it being

[74] For example: "of all the causes which tend to encourage prudential habits among the lower classes of society, essential is unquestionably civil liberty (...) which cannot be permanently secured without political liberty." *Summary View*: 252. Also see *Principles*: 252; *Essay*, 7th edition, II: 74 (Poland, Russia, Siberia), 92, 140–141 ("the want of industry or the ill direction of that industry"); II: 194.

[75] *Principles*: 440. This argument is repeated in a letter published in the *Quarterly Review* in 1823, quoted by Bonar (1927: 276). Complementarity of sectors: see *Essay*, 7th edition, II: 76, 87–91, 99,128. Regarding this point, see Gilbert, 1980: 93–96 and Winch (1996: 272–273) who also quotes a letter from Malthus to Chalmers dated 6 March 1832 (ibid.: 383–384).

[76] The abolition of the Corn Laws came into effect in 1846 after a massive campaign launched by Richard Cobden.

understood that Malthus considered trade as a natural extension of industry and often dealt with it simultaneously,
- the big landowners should be distinguished from the other social groups living in rural areas, such as wage-earning agricultural labourers and all those whom Malthus included in the middle classes and described as "gentlemen",
- the consumption of the wage-earning agricultural labourers should have certain specific characteristics.

As for the first point, what really matters is the complementarity of the two sectors (Fig. 2.6) and this figure can be considered as a break-up of the straight line representing the demand for labour in Fig. 2.4. As a matter of fact, agricultural production will produce an income which will be partly used for paying production costs (labourers' wages, maintenance of fixed capital and cost of other inputs) and the net income will be used for the farmers' and landowners' expenditure on consumption. The labourers' wages and other income from agriculture will be spent on the purchase of *industrial* goods. They thus constitute an effective demand for the industrial sector and will stimulate the growth of industrial population (which is essentially urban) in response to the increase in the demand for labour. At the same time, the fall in the price of industrial products will lead to a rise in the standard of living of the rural masses and they will be able to access goods providing comfort and even luxury goods that were earlier beyond their means. On the other hand, wages disbursed by industry will be partly allotted to the purchase of food articles (cereals and vegetables, and meat by those who are wealthier) and thus constitute another effective demand for the *agricultural* sector, which will also stimulate demographic growth, but this time among the rural population. Evidently, *within* each sector, wages cannot constitute an effective demand because entrepreneurs, like farmers, cannot rely on a purchasing power that exists before investment.

As for the second point, the rural population, which was larger than the urban population in Malthus's time, constituted a much bigger market for consumer goods and constituted a much larger effective demand than that of a few hundred thousand industrial workers. Also, it is not surprising that he should have insisted on the one hand on the existence of an effective demand for industrial goods in rural areas and, on the other hand, anticipated favourable "consumption habits" in rural areas which

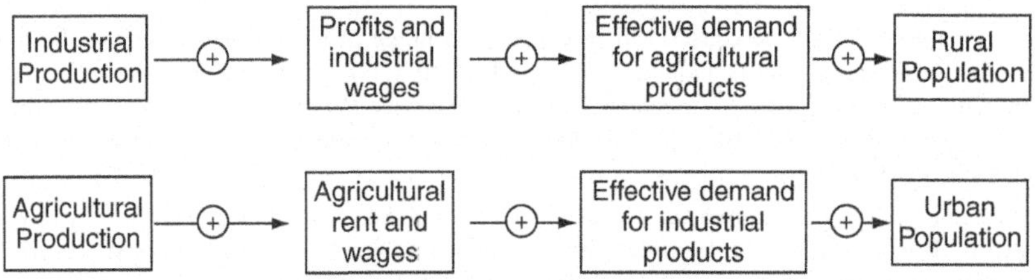

Fig. 2.6 Exchanges between sectors and demographic growth [Note: + indicates a positive relation: when industrial production rises, the *wage* bill rises (but not necessarily at the same rate as wages)]

would be very different from those of the big landowners, who were more interested in "hunting and raising game", because of which the latter seem to be an exception.

Finally, the type of expenses incurred by agricultural labourers would have the same effect. As a matter of fact, Malthus believed, on the basis of Frederick Eden's calculations, that about 40% of the wages were spent on the purchase of cereals. Only this part of the wages would normally increase exactly in proportion with the rise in the price of cereals. According to him, the other items would only partly reflect the rise in the price of cereals: this applies to the 20% spent on the purchase of meat, milk, butter, etc., and *a fortiori* the remaining 40% spent on the purchase of leather, linen, cotton, soap, candles, etc.[77] Given these conditions Malthus was right to recommend protective duties on the import of cereals. Since landowners were being paid a higher price for wheat, they could pay higher wages to labourers and as this rise would absorb only up to 40% of the nominal wage in the labourers' budget, it would result in an increase in the real wage and create a purchasing power which would allow labourers to buy commodities and even luxuries produced by the industrial sector. This argument is frequently repeated in his *Inquiry into the Nature and Progress of Rent*, published in 1815, in the seventh edition of the *Essay* and in *Principles* with reference to the United States, Flanders and France: "this high price of corn and labour has given great facilities to the farmers and labourers in the purchase of clothing and all sorts of foreign necessaries and conveniences."[78] Again in the *Principles*, as well as in the *Essay*, he remarked that inversely the lower price of wheat, contrary to appearances, gave less purchasing power and "ought to produce less effect on the increase of population".[79]

An objection that immediately strikes the reader is that all this assumes that landowners would automatically increase the wages of their labourers following a rise in their own income. Evidently, this happened only when agricultural labourers received a minimum living wage, because when the price of the means of subsistence went up, the simple need to reproduce their labour force made it necessary to raise their wages proportionately. But that was not the case, because only 40% of the wages were actually spent on the purchase of wheat. And since agricultural labourers were not in a position to negotiate, nothing could oblige the employers to reduce their own profits by raising the wages above the minimum living wage. In spite of the lack of clarity in his thinking and even though all we have are often incidental remarks, it is possible to reconstitute Malthus's answers to this objection. His arguments changed over the years. In 1798, in the first *Essay*, he maintained that the true cause of the rise in wages was "an act of compassion in favour of the poor".

---

[77] *Observations on the Effects of the Corn Laws*.... Quoted by Dow, 1977: 309. Also see *Essay*, 7th edition, II: 103.

[78] *Principles*: 167. On the other hand, Malhus claimed that the Irish peasants' misfortune was a result of their dependence on the potato as a staple food and wages were low because the price of potatoes was low. *Principles*: 232–233, 399. Also see *Essay*, 7th edition, II: 73, 228. Regarding this point, see Grampp, 1974: 282.

[79] *Principles*: 258. *Essay*, 7th edition, II: 135. Regarding this point, see Dow, 1977: 315.

The argument advanced in the *Principles* in 1820 was hardly more realistic. He said that if employers did not want to loose their labour force, they had to at least raise the wages proportionately to the increase in the price of wheat. This argument is not convincing because everything depends on the labour market: if the supply is higher than the demand for labour, employers have more room for manoeuvre. When he wrote these lines, the population of England had increased by two millions. It may therefore be assumed that industry did not absorb all the surplus rural labour or that labour was still plentiful in rural areas and therefore not in a position to negotiate. But this amounts to ignoring another market, viz. the capital market. Malthus wrote in the *Essay* and in *Observations on the Corn Laws* that following the rise in profits, capital would be invested in agriculture. It could at least be assumed that landowners would have to turn to the available labourers in order to take advantage of the new investment opportunities and that this would work in favour of the workers.[80] The entire hypothesis about the purchasing power of rural labourers is obviously weak and constitutes the Achille's heel of his argument, because no purely economic argument is foolproof (how can one define the exact point at which employers will react to the influx of capital by hiring more workers or by increasing wages?). In the final analysis, it is the workers' ability to negotiate their wages, essentially a sociological and political factor, which will have a decisive influence, but Malthus is silent on this point.

Except for this reservation, he can finally claim that the high price of grains is compatible with the growth of industrial consumption and the betterment of the working classes, especially those living in rural areas. We are thus far from the popular caricature depicting him as a shameless advocate of the landed aristocracy. Marx was not the only one to promote it: for example, Mac Culloch wrote to Ricardo in 1826 that *Principles* was "the text book - the very gospel indeed - of a few landlords."[81] There is no doubt that it was the price Malthus had to pay for his position on the Corn Laws, although the opinions he actually expressed were very modern since he advocated a society consisting largely of the middle classes as being the most favourable to effective demand. His microeconomic analysis of effective demand was logically followed by a comprehensive macroeconomic judgement, which is extremely important from the point of view of the social doctrine. He condemned non-egalitarian rural societies as being unfavourable to the happiness and prosperity of the people: "if in the best cultivated and most populous countries of Europe the present divisions of land and farms had taken place, and had not been followed by the introduction of commerce and manufactures, population would long since have come to a stand from the total want of motive to further cultivation, and the consequent want of demand for labour"[82] In support of this statement, Malthus cited as counterexamples Poland, Russia and Turkey where there was a feudal system

[80] *Principles*: 195;*Essay*, 7th edition, II: 104.

[81] Quoted by Rashid (1981). Cannadine quotes Hollander and Gregory in 1928, and more recently Meek, Semel, Pollard and Perkin (1986: 101).

[82] *Essay*, 7th edition, I: 104.

accompanied by poverty.[83] And all the arguments about the theoretical complementarity between agriculture and industry fit into his vision of the ideal society.

As Bonar points out, Malthus always chose the middle path between purely agricultural economies subjected to the risk of food shortages and commercial and industrial nations that were economically too unstable: "The countries which thus unite great landed resources with a prosperous state of commerce and manufactures, and in which the commercial part of the population never exceeds the agricultural part, are eminently secure from sudden reverses. Their increasing wealth seems to be out of reach of all common accidents; and there is no reason to say that they might not go on increasing in riches and population for hundreds, nay, for almost thousands of years."[84] Populationism is a natural result of this economic theory.

Malthus the Populationist

Let us return to Malthus's demographic and social doctrine. What measures did he recommend to improve the condition of the lower classes? "The object of those who really wish to better the condition of the lower class of society must be to raise the relative proportion between the price of labour and the price of provisions, so as to enable the labourer to command a larger share of the necessaries and comforts of life."[85] It is therefore essential to increase the real wages. A careless reader will conclude from this statement that the standard of living can be improved only by reducing fertility. That was the opinion of nineteenth and twentieth century Socio-Democrats radically opposed to Marx who favoured high fertility as it increased the industrial reserve army and accentuated the contradictions of capitalism. Would Malthus side with the neo-Malthusians on this point? This is certainly not likely and the social objective that he proposed was undeniably oriented towards populationism. Raising the standard of living of labourers does not in any way imply that their number is lower, contrary to the current interpretation of Malthus's thinking: "We are not, however, to relax our efforts in increasing the quantity of provisions, but to combine another effort with it; that of keeping the population, when once it has been overtaken, at such a distance behind as to effect the relative proportion which we desire; and thus unite the two grand *desiderata*, a great actual population and a state of society in which abject poverty and dependence are comparatively but little known; two objects which are far from being incompatible." However, this is not a vague generality as Malthus claimed that this objective was applicable to the England of his time: "I can easily conceive that this country, with a proper direction of the national industry, might, in the course of some centuries, contain two or three

---

[83] *Essay*, 7th edition, II: 74.

[84] *Essay*, 7th edition, II: 91; regarding Hamburg and Holland see II: 99. He was convinced that the mainly industrial and commercial nations had been more "short-lived" in world history than nations based on agriculture (*Essay*, 7th edition, Book III, Chapter X in particular).

[85] *Essay*, 7th edition, II: 171.

times its present population, and yet every man in the Kingdom be much better fed and clothed than he is at present."[86] In the *Essay* and in the *Summary View*, the same logic is applied to big developed and populous countries, which could have been two or three times in number and to many other countries (meaning less developed) which could have had a population ten or even hundred times higher if their social institutions and their people's moral habits "had been for hundred years the most favourable to the increase of capital, and the demand for produce and labour."[87]

A brief detour into the 1980s will be useful to assess the originality of Malthus's thinking. What are known today as structural adjustment policies are based on the so-called Malthusian idea that economic development and social progress are possible *on condition* that family planning programmes reduce fertility and control demographic growth. For Malthus, the three dimensions of the development equation, viz. economic, social and demographic, are on the contrary perfectly compatible and the populationist nature of his thinking is incontestable: he condemned - in the case of non-egalitarian feudal societies - the risk of a social structure where the population was less than the potentially available means of subsistence but also higher than the employment opportunities available.[88] In brief, his analysis of the demand for labour is actually a blueprint of the theory of demo-economic development according to which demographic growth depends on production growth. For this to happen there must be an effective demand or the willingness and the ability to buy a given product. The more egalitarian is a society, the higher is the demand for labour and hence production. From the social viewpoint, Malthus bet on industry because it could bring about a considerable improvement in the standard of living of the poor by providing greater access to consumer goods that were accessible until then only to the better off social groups.

Moral Restraint, the Principle of Population and Demo-Economic Growth

It remains to be understood why Malthus believed that *prudential restraint*, which prevented people from sinking into poverty was *socially desirable*, even though he was convinced on the *theoretical* level that *moral restraint was indispensable*. In reality, moral restraint was indispensable for several reasons that Malthus built up into a plea covering many different levels all through the first five chapters of Book IV of the *Essay*. On the moral level, we are obliged to practise this virtue because we must control our passions, be it the sexual instinct, anger or the craving for food and drink. On the religious level, chastity before marriage is certainly difficult to practise, but on the one hand, there will be greater passion between the spouses after marriage and, on the other hand, this form of abstinence is in conformity with Christian values. On the contrary, continuous warfare is a result of "old doctrines"

---

[86] Quotations: *Essay*, 7th edition, II: 172, 174.

[87] Quotations: *Essay*, 7th edition, II: 172, 174. *Summary View*: 249.

[88] See for example *Principles*: 371.

and even more of the religion preached by Mohamed, writes Malthus, which believes that procreation is necessary for the glory of God. Further, utilitarian moral philosophy teaches us that moral restraint is more effective than aid or an arbitrary increase in wages for the person desirous of improving his standard of living, because procreating when one does not have the means goes against one's own interest, not to mention the burden imposed on society as a whole; moral restraint is thus the best way of avoiding the evils ensuing from the principle of population. He concludes by emphasising the political responsibility of the ruling classes, and what he regards as a totally unacceptable populationism: the poor man "has always been told that to raise up subjects for his king and country is a very meritorious act. He has done this, and yet is suffering for it; and it cannot but strike him as most extremely unjust and cruel in his king and country to allow him thus to suffer, in return for giving them what they are continually declaring that they particularly want." The argument is developed into a fervent warning to rulers about their responsibilities towards the poor and goes to the extent of accusing them of being "criminal", a quite astonishing statement coming from an author considered to be conservative by his adversaries: "That it is always the duty of a state to use every exertion likely to be effectual in discouraging vice and promoting virtue, and that no temporary circumstances ought to cause any relaxation in these exertions is certainly true. The means therefore proposed are always good; but the particular end in view in this case appears to be absolutely criminal. We wish to force people into marriage when from the acknowledged scarcity of subsistence they will have little chance of being able to support their children. We might as well force people into the water who are unable to swim. In both cases we rashly tempt providence. Nor do we have more reason to believe that a miracle will be worked to save us from the misery and mortality resulting from our conduct in the one case or the other."

It is precisely at the end of this long argument that he came out with two forceful statements defining his own populationism: first and as noted above, an improvement in the standard of living of the masses was perfectly compatible with rapid demographic growth. He immediately went on to point out that the rich could not therefore claim to improve the lot of the poor and simultaneously complain of excessively high wages. Second, in the absence of moral restraint, poverty was unavoidably followed by famine, high mortality, sexual depravity, criminality and finally despotism in societies where poverty reigned. These lines figure in the 7th edition, but even in 1798, his liberal ideas made him condemn the extremely non-egalitarian nature of property: "it must certainly be considered as an evil, and every institution that promotes it is essentially bad and impolitic" (*Essay*, 1798: 177). And under the existing Poor laws "the whole class of the common people of England is subjected to a set of grating, inconvenient, and tyrannical laws totally inconsistent with the genuine spirit of the constitution."[89]

However, prudential restraint can also bring about an improvement in the people's standard of living. So what did he have against it as compared to moral restraint? For example, he wrote in 1817 on the subject of contraception: "Indeed, I

---

[89] *Essay*, 7th edition, II: Chapters 1–5. See in particular: 152, 161, 165–171, 171 (quotation), 174. *Essay*, 1798: 100, 177.

should always particularly reprobate any artificial and unnatural modes of checking population, both on account of their immorality and their tendency to remove a necessary stimulus to industry. If it were possible for each married couple to limit by a wish the number of their children, there is a certainly reason to fear that the indolence of the human race would be very greatly increased; and that neither the population of individual countries, nor of the whole earth would ever reach its natural and proper extent. But the restraints I have recommended are quite of a different character. They are not only pointed out by reason and sanctioned by religion, but tend in the most marked manner to stimulate industry."[90] As it can bee seen, the ethical argument is much less developed than populationist considerations which stress the economic advantages of moral restraint. Or, to be more precise, Malthus's populationism is inspired by his religious convictions, which confirms Nathan Keyfitz's penetrating observation, quoted in the first chapter of this book: "It is a strong injury that posterity has inflicted on Malthus when it calls contraception 'Malthusian' or 'neo-Malthusian'."[91] We must therefore try to reintegrate demography, economics, sociology and religious ethics in a comprehensive model, and through them, the population theory and doctrine.

According to the third model, the effective demand emanating from rural areas is the driving force behind the process of growth and the absorption of purchasing power by the supply of industrial goods is more desirable from the social view point. Let us dismiss a first objection. According to Ricardo's theory, the scarcity of land is an absolute limit which necessarily pushes every economy towards a stationary state: due to the law of diminishing returns, wages increase with the rise in the price of agricultural products because of the increase in the cost of the means of subsistence; profits are eroded, further investment is not profitable, the demand for labour stops and in the end population stops growing. Since Malthus was the author of the theory of diminishing returns borrowed by Ricardo to formulate his theory of the stationary state, the following contradiction arises: how could Malthus simultaneously propose a model of *uninterrupted* growth? It is easy to solve it as Malthus himself provided the answer: he was convinced that technical progress constantly slowed down agricultural production and kept it from reaching its upper limit thus delaying the inevitable rise in income from agriculture. This is the meaning of the above quotation regarding England.

Although long-term growth is possible thanks to the proposed strategy, nothing can be deduced about its *effectiveness*. For example, what will be the pace of the demographic growth brought about by industrialisation? Malthus clearly affirms that a "great and continued demand for labour" is necessary. But how is it achieved? As shown above, Malthus conformed to the classical economic theory: since population only reacts to the stimulus of production and has no driving force of its own, prudential restraint can only be a *response* to the fluctuations in demand. Worse still, it may even curb demographic growth: nothing can contribute more to the spread

---

90 Annex to the 5th edition of the *Essay*. Quoted by Winch, 1996: 285.

91 Keyfitz, 1984:5

of prudential restraint, writes Malthus, than the taste for comfort. And as early as 1798 he remarked that due to utilitarianism the middle classes delayed marriage while the lower classes tended to be content to satisfy their most immediate needs and were not prepared to work more to improve their living conditions.[92] In the later editions, he clearly moved to the level of moral philosophy and expressed his belief in the catchy and oft-quoted formula of "the great machine": a society founded on charity instead of personal interest "would from the inevitable laws of nature, and not from any fault in human institutions, degenerate in a very short period into a society constructed upon a plan not essentially different from that which prevails in every known state at present ; a society divided into a class of proprietors and a class of labourers, and with the self-love for the main-spring of the great machine."[93]

So moral restraint and the principle of population would together provide the necessary stimulus for growth and maximise it as indicated in the quotation in which he condemned the risk of "indolence": if he produces all the children that God gives him, the individual will be compelled to work. The model can now be completed by considering moral restraint and the principle of population as two *exogenous* variables which, unlike others, are not subject to any feed-back effect (Fig. 2.7).

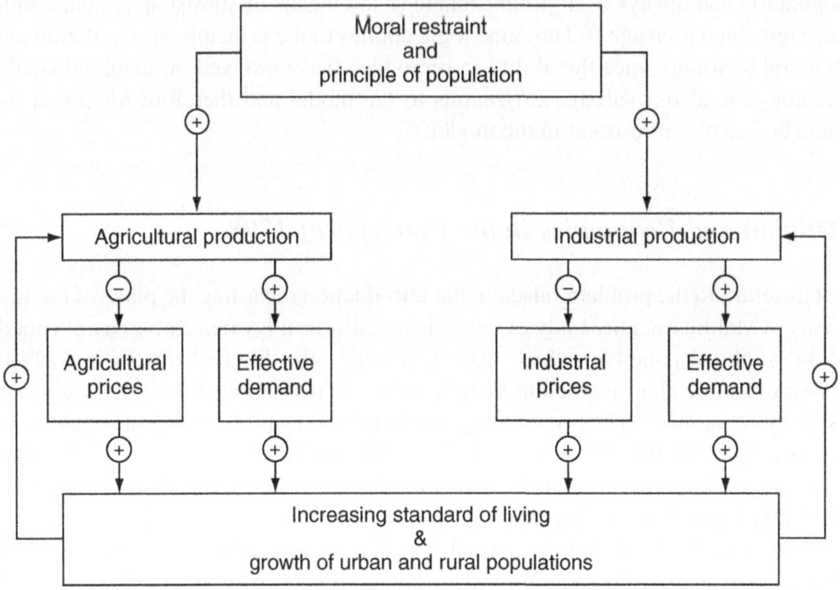

Fig. 2.7 Comprehensive model for maximising demo-economic growth

---

[92] *Essay*, 1798: 91.

[93] *Essay*, 7th edition, II: 21.

This is totally justified at the epistemological level. Moral restraint being essentially different from the other variables in the model, it is neither demographic nor economic, but it is a moral necessity that corresponds to the Creator's intentions, it being understood that the Divine Order transcends the world of human affairs. What would happen if moral restraint were not practised? People would indeed have a satisfactory standard of living thanks to prudential restraint, but the growth desired by the Creator would not be certain because individuals, to maintain their standard of living, would tend to restrain their progeny.

Let us now turn to the role of the principle of population. It has been seen that its role was becoming increasingly marginal in Malthus's writings, as if he were willing to give up this central idea. Far from it being the case, it is necessary to return to the first *Essay*, whose last chapter but one provides the key to the system's functioning: "to urge man to further the gracious designs of Providence by the full cultivation of the earth, it has been ordained that population should increase much faster than food. This general law (as it appeared in the earlier part of this *Essay*) undoubtedly produces much partial evil, but a little reflection may, perhaps, satisfy us, that it produces a great overbalance of good (...) It keeps the inhabitants of the earth always fully up to the level of the means of subsistence; and is constantly acting upon man as a powerful stimulus, urging him to the further cultivation of earth, and to enable it, consequently, to support a more extended population". Further, if population had always been proportionate to the means of subsistence, man would have remained a savage.[94] The same logic applies to the principle of population and to moral restraint: since the ability to reproduce was bestowed on mankind by the Creator, it is also a variable exogenous to the model and therefore figures in the same box as moral restraint in the model.

Religion and Economics in the Concepts of 1798

Let us return to the problem raised in the introduction regarding the place of the first *Essay* in Malthus's entire body of work. Is it really, as it is often carelessly affirmed, a philosophical pamphlet which was abandoned after his first travels in 1799 in favour of a more empirical scientific reflection in which moral philosophy was swept aside by economics? The principal argument in this regard is the suppression of the last two chapters which develop a line of thinking based on religion while other arguments, which are much more fundamental, make the opposite plea. Firstly, most of Malthus's theoretical contributions can be found in the first *Essay*: as early as 1798, he clearly delineated the central concepts of our comprehensive model, and all the elements indispensable for the formulation of a theory of growth are present. Let us begin with moral restraint. One of Malthus's most profound contributions to

[94] *Essay*, 1798: 205–206. On the "salient" importance of the concept of natural indolence see Levin (1996: 100) and LeMahieu (1979). Relation between indolence and agriculture: Winch, 1996: 367–368.

population thought – though mostly unknown and unappreciated by specialists of demographic thought – is undoubtedly the resolution of the contradiction between the evil caused by the principle of population and his absolute certainty of divine kindness, which has been called Malthus's theodicy.[95] This is the central idea of the last two chapters, the ones that contain the essence of his theological beliefs.

It has been argued that the religious heterodoxy of his opinions undoubtedly explains why these beliefs were suppressed in the second edition published in 1803.[96] Malthus did not give up his religious convictions but he had to stop arguing on this level and be satisfied with frequent references to the Creator's designs while repositioning himself in matters related to economics. By affirming in the first *Essay* that "Evil exists in the world not to create despair but activity", he could ensure an effective linkage with economic utilitarianism. In this he is not particularly original because it was common in the seventeenth century for great minds like Newton and Leibniz to proclaim that all discoveries, needless to say including their own, were no more than a revelation of a particular aspect of the Creator's greatness, wisdom and kindness by a humble human being.[97] Malthus believed that because God wanted man to be happy, population growth is the most obvious sign of a state's happiness and prosperity. Only through this dual utilitarian and teleological perspective can we understand the astonishing argument he advanced in support of the Poor Laws, claiming that if the Poor Laws had not existed, there "might have been a few more instances of very severe distress, but the aggregate mass of happiness among the common people would have been much greater than it is at present."[98] As Pullen very aptly puts it, "Malthus set out to write on human perfectibility, not just on the wealth of nations."[99]

If the religious dimension is left out from Malthus's thought, the insistence on moral restraint becomes incomprehensible, prudential restraint seeming more consistent with the utilitarian component of Malthus's ideology. It is then possible to understand better why he gave his utilitarianism a teleological dimension as Bonar and later scholars pointed out: by controlling their passions, men "add to the sum of human happiness and fulfil the apparent purpose of the creator."[100] All passions as well as hunger, thirst and other needs should be regulated by experience and

---

[95] This neologism (which brings together two Greek words meaning *God* and *just*) was coined way back in 1696 by Leibniz. It is found in the title of his work which brought him fame in Europe (*Essays of theodicy on the goodness of God, the freedom of man and the origin of evil*) published in 1710. Regarding Malthus's theodicy, see LeMahieu (1979), Santurri (1982), Pullen, (1981, 1986) and Harvey-Phillipps (1984) Waterman (1991).

[96] Pullen, 1981: 49–51; 1987: 137–140; LeMahieu, 1979: 470; Waterman (1983: 200–203), who has also analyzed with great exactitude the contradictions in Malthus the theologian. Harvey-Phillipps (1984: 599–607) opposes this thesis about the pressure exerted on Malthus: the latter simply gave up his religious arguments in favour of others drawn from political economy.

[97] Quotation: *Essay*, 1798: 217.

[98] *Essay*, 7th edition, II: 51.

[99] Pullen, 1981: 52.

[100] *Essay*, 7th edition, II: 217.

frequently subjected to the test of experience, without which they would run counter to their purpose. As Lemahieu puts it, "For Malthus, as for other liberals, the road to happiness was paved with the repression of the natural instincts".[101] Utility is therefore the moral principle that should rule men. But from the theological angle, he rejected the idea that man is forever condemned to suffering and poverty because they are temporary and affect only a portion of mankind. If it were not so, how could one believe in the Creator's goodness?[102] On this basis, Malthus was able to write that the utility principle makes it possible for human passions to be "suited to our state, or conformable to the will of God."[103] Finally, moral restraint also ensured the coherence between economic theory and social doctrine. Making the access to comforts and even luxury the social objective meant pleading in favour of industrial development, because recommending moral restraint to the lower classes amounted to guaranteeing an improvement of their standard of living, while maintaining a high level of fertility.

That the principle of population played a crucial role in refuting Godwin's utopia is a banal observation which refers to the rational argument developed by Malthus on the basis of the postulates and the progressions. But Godwin's idea can also be refuted on the basis of Malthus's religious beliefs. Waterman proposes a model which establishes logical links between the different philosophical concepts found in the first *Essay*. God is at the origin of Nature (including human nature) and he has full power to change its laws, some of which may certainly cause "partial evils". Santurri however observes that God is unlikely to repeal the laws of nature "because such an abrogation would render science, and consequently the development of mind impossible".[104] Besides, human nature is dual being both spiritual and carnal. The human mind is capable of reasoning while the body tries to fulfil its carnal desires (this is the second postulate) and may produce negative effects, particularly poverty combined with excessive fertility. In Chapter 10 of the first *Essay* of 1798, Malthus defends the idea that benevolence and kindness cannot have the upper hand over interest and egoism because hunger and the defence of private property lead to the victory of egoism. Waterman's conceptual figure thus expresses the relationship between utilitarianism and the teleology of Newtonian inspiration. In short, if the moral philosophy underlying his first *Essay* had the effect of refuting Godwin, the introduction of economics and the principle of population enabled him to demolish the Godwinian system *as a utopia* firmly embedded in political philosophy.

The introduction of the third major concept, viz. prudential restraint, shows how right from 1798 onwards Malthusian ideology was able to use economics to oppose Godwin in two ways: the first was a Tory-oriented anti-Jacobinic defence of the status quo, while the second, more Whiggish in spirit, was better suited to explain the dynamics of industrialisation witnessed by Malthus during his early years. Why

---

[101] Ibid. LeMahieu, 1979: 471.

[102] *Essay*, 1798: 214–215.

[103] Regarding these points, Pullen (1981) completes Bonar's analyses (1927).

[104] Santurri, 1982: 317

did Malthus opt for the Whig path, as confirmed by his later position on the reform of the Poor Laws, the importance of spreading education among the lower classes, the recognition of the widespread practice of prudential restraint and his tolerance towards it?[105] Waterman rightly proposes a dual interpretation based on the one hand on arguments of a biographical nature and, on the other hand, on the assumption that he could again choose between an economic option favourable to the landowners and a more liberal option. Two biographical elements may be mentioned. Firstly, the intellectual training Malthus received in Cambridge was clearly alien to the anti-Jacobinic rhetoric. Further, the recognition of the practice of prudential restraint in England can be explained by the fact that Malthus, who was then thirty-two years old, could not marry his cousin Harriet, aged twenty-two, because his earnings were not enough to permit him to lead the life of a "gentleman". He therefore understood fully that prudential restraint enabled individuals to attain a certain level of comfort. It should be recalled that even in 1798 the social groups that served as a reference were the rural middle classes, half-way between extreme wealth and extreme poverty, and he clearly had in mind their practice of prudential restraint, as proven by several quotations in the first *Essay* referring to the behaviour of the middle classes in English society.[106] This biographical interpretation can be considerably reinforced by an analysis of the social model chosen by Malthus. Waterman thus contrasts two alternative options for sharing wealth which Malthus faced as a political economist. In the first case, landowners, by keeping the wages low with the "complicity" of the principle of population, could control the social surplus and redistribute it if they so desired, thus influencing the rise in the demand for consumer goods. This brings us back to the analysis of rent. In the second case, where the sharing of wealth follows a more liberal pattern, prudential restraint, by neutralising the principle of population, results in an increase of the nominal wage, and particularly the real wage, thus leading to the transfer of a part of the landowners' wealth to wage-earning labourers having no possessions.[107] So all Malthus had to do to complete what we have identified as the second model was to integrate the industrial sector to obtain a comprehensive model. But the basic essentials were in place and the social doctrine was supported by the theory of economic growth.

If we try to put the specific stakes involved in each of the three main concepts in proper perspective, we come to the famous conflict between Malthus and Ricardo over the nature of political economy, which runs through their voluminous correspondence. It is hardly surprising that the religious dimension of Malthus's thinking, far from contradicting his economic theory, incorporated it because "'science' and 'theology' in eighteenth-century England (and particularly in Cambridge where Malthus was educated) were so closely intertwined as to be almost a single discipline".[108] This education was undoubtedly responsible for his conception of

---

105 Levin 1996: 107; Waterman, 1991: 29; Harvey-Phillipps (1984) may also be consulted.

106 *Essay*, 1798: 90–91. *Summary View*: 263–264.

107 Waterman, 1991: 56–57.

108 Waterman, 1998: 308.

economics, radically different from Ricardo's: "the science of political economy bears a nearer resemblance to the science of morals and politics than to that of mathematics." Hence, as noted by Morley, a breadth of historical and classical references in Malthus, as opposed to their paucity in, for example, the work of Senior or Ricardo. Malthus' political economy was embedded in history and moral philosophy, whereas the latter "abandoned the ethical questions which had concerned Smith and Malthus in favor of an ethically neutral science and they changed from an inductive method which drew on historical and comparative evidence to a system of hypothetical deduction from logical principles".[109] But this initial divergence refers to another of a much more fundamental nature. As Winch writes, for Malthus it was a matter of "sustain(ing) a Christian alternative to the secular version of the science associated with Ricardo".[110] This "Christian political economy" was also different from the Christian political economy promoted in France in the first half of the following century by Villeneuve-Bargemont and the Social Catholics. The latter essentially judged on the moral plane the social evils created by industrialization and looked for a solution to the problem of poverty in the teachings of Christ and particularly in charity. But unlike Malthus and the English Christian political economists, they did not propose the kind of synthesis between facts and values that has been described in this chapter.

At the end of this reconstruction of the Malthusian system, it is necessary to remark on the scope and the finesse of the synthesis achieved by Malthus, who succeeded in reconciling his own religious beliefs with his economic theory on the basis of sociological observations and analyses of demographic mechanisms to come up with recommendations that were truly pragmatic from the political viewpoint.

Contradictions and Unity in Malthus's Writings

The three models thus express the progressive passage of a biological vision towards a real analysis lying in the domain of human and social sciences. Due to the regulation of population by mortality, the first model is based on a mechanistic conception of demography and very little importance is given to man's ability to control his living conditions or – more accurately – to ensure his own survival. The second model is undoubtedly embedded in classical political economy; as Adam Smith stated, population, just like corn or any manufactured good, can be negotiated in the market and its price or the wage rate is determined by the necessary adjustment of the demand for labour to its supply. The third model is based on the mechanism of effective demand, but it separates the problem of population from that of the means of subsistence. The model as a whole is quite original. Firstly,

---

[109] Morley, 1998: 107–108.

[110] Winch, 1996: 286–287, who quotes Malthus. And according to Waterman (1991: 7) the *Essay* "is an anti-Jacobin defence of property rights embedded in the religious world-view and theological framework of eighteenth-century Anglican Christianity."

Malthus manages to achieve a synthesis between economic theory and a correct analysis of the different fertility and nuptiality patterns prevalent in England at the time of the industrial revolution. But even more important, unlike Ricardo's classical model characterized by convergence towards a point of equilibrium, he proposes a dynamic of uninterrupted growth. This is quite remarkable as it is inspired, not by the object of achieving social well-being in the sense it is understood today, but by this clergyman's obsession to remain true to the Creator's objectives. In other words, the only truly independent variables in the third model are moral restraint and the principle of population, precisely because of their origin. Their justification is of a divine nature.

The objective of finding an internal coherence in Malthus's thinking by looking behind the apparent contradictions has been accomplished, but there are still some problems to be solved.[111] Let us first return to the statement mentioned in the introduction to this chapter that there were in reality two works bearing the same title and to a paradox that is often remarked upon: "In its first form the *Essay on Population* was conclusive as an argument, only it was based on untrue facts; in it second form, it was based on true facts, but it was inconclusive as an argument."[112] It is easy to point out that the transformation of a polemical pamphlet into a scholarly piece of writing inevitably compelled Malthus to verify the facts. Malthus's opponents as well as his supporters have almost always taken this stand, both during his lifetime and after his death. Hence endless controversies over the reality of this principle that was frequently cited but never verified, the acknowledgement of the fall in fertility due to the spread of contraception in Europe and last the social well-being and progress brought by the industrial revolution, all of them as unquestionable empirical refutations of the Malthusian theory of population. There is no epistemological problem as such but only the usual difficulty of analysing a work that has been thoroughly revised by its author, partly in the light of new data. The fact that there are two books is just a warning that we must look at it simultaneously from a religious, philosophic, demographic and sociological viewpoint, which calls for a thoroughly multidisciplinary approach. The real epistemological problem is different: if there are contradictions, it is because the focal distance is wrong or because we are confined within the limits of too small a number of disciplines, as we have seen in Plato's case where the flagrant contradictions between *The Laws* and *The Republic* disappear as soon as his so-called demographic indicators are taken for what they are, a simple illustrative quantitative cover-up. The unity of the work lies in its philosophical content, since Plato was trying to solve the problem of Justice and find a solution to the conduct of politics in the City. On the contrary, in Malthus's case, if we set aside the ideas pertaining to his religious convictions, no single level of analysis is more *fundamental* than any other. His thinking is therefore genuinely interdisciplinary and his demographic sociological and economic

---

[111] Regarding incoherence within the same discipline, see Charbit, 1998.

[112] Walter Bagehot (1889), as quoted by Coats (1984: 311), and Himmelfarb, according to Waterman (1991: 41).

observations have the same epistemological value. That is why the contradictions mentioned – is Malthus a Malthusian or a populationist? – disappear when one takes his entire work into account.

As for his population theory, that is to say a generalisation and an abstraction on the basis of observed facts, it has been seen that Malthus was capable of integrating facts relating to his times and of proposing appropriate doctrinal measures on this basis. What about the facts that came into existence after he wrote his book? It was stated in the first chapter of this book that an idea cannot be rejected on the grounds that it did not take into account facts that the author could not have known in any case. So it is futile to start a discussion on the predictive abilities of the theory regarding future changes and more precisely about the validity of the law of population and the two progressions as a regular occurrence that can be verified later. This is so for two major reasons. Firstly, demography is neither theoretical physics nor is it mineralogical chemistry, but it is a human science whose specialists base their theories on social and economic factors *peculiar* to a given context. The very idea of verification at a later date, in the sense of reproducing results obtained in the original experimental conditions, does not have any meaning. Further, the implicit separation of demography and economics with reference to "Malthus's population law" lends itself to criticism. Demographers, apart from some rare exceptions, are not in the least concerned about the arithmetical progression of the means of subsistence and the law of diminishing returns, which they leave to agronomists and specialists in economic history. Having put aside arithmetical progression, they concentrate on geometrical progression and mention Malthus particularly with reference to the "population explosion" in the Third World after 1945, thus committing ipso facto two related errors: anachronism and simplification. It is not because the average annual growth rate in some Central American countries has been about 3%, a ratio higher than the 2.8% representing the doubling of the population in twenty-five years corresponding to the geometrical progression, that the Malthusian theory can be claimed to be proven in its entirety. What has been observed is no more than a quantitative *indicator*, the much wider context being simply ignored. Demographic thought is thus artificially disconnected from economic conceptualisation even though Malthus was always intent on taking into account both the long term and the short term, the individual and his environment, against a utilitarian background and within a teleological system. Waterman is therefore right in denouncing the "Victorian view" prevalent even today that there are two Malthuses – the demographer and the economist.[113] This observation by Waterman leads us to a final reflection. The demographer is known universally undoubtedly because of the burden of history. He waged a battle against egalitarian ideologies and laid the trap of double progression that they could not get out of. The argument was used all over Europe in the nineteenth century and it met with a great deal of success in the Third World after 1945. But history cannot explain everything. Why was Malthus generally ignored even though he was the first theoretician of demo-

113 Waterman, 1998: 299, 321.

economic growth? The answer is simple; on the basis of his analysis of effective demand, he vigorously challenged Jean-Baptiste Say's law of markets and therefore the liberal credo according to which behind short-term economic crises there is a natural order which all economic systems should strive to reach. Malthus had witnessed the poverty brought by the Napoleonic wars, the difficulty experienced by entrepreneurs in selling their goods and the "under-employment" of almost one and a half million workers, if the number of poor helped by parishes can be taken as an indicator. Consequently, he could not but believe that the general glut in the market was the result of a structural crisis and under-consumption.[114] One cannot avoid one's destiny and it is easy to understand why Ricardo criticized Malthus, Marx acclaimed him and Keynes considered him the first of the Cambridge economists.

[114] Barber, 1967: 70; also see Winch, 1996: 26–27.

Chapter 3
From Malthusianism to Populationism: The French Liberal Economists (1840–1870)

The Economists as a Sect

Of the large number of writers interested in population in France in the mid-nineteenth century, the liberal economists deserve special attention.[1] Like the English free-trade economists, they organised in 1841 an opinion and pressure group to press for the abolition of protectionist laws which had become increasingly stringent since the seventeenth century.[2] They did not, however, succeed in giving rise to a mass movement in support of free trade like their counterparts across the Channel and their adversaries did not fail to denounce them as a "sect of economists" obsessed by the idea of free trade. This sect was nonetheless quite active. The economists spread their ideas through their publications. Thus, in 1841, they established the periodical *Le Journal des Economistes* and in 1846, the weekly *Le Libre-échange* to support their anti-protectionist campaign; in 1860 *L'Economiste français* and *Journal de la Société de statistique de Paris* were set up. The economists also wrote regularly in dailies (*Le Journal des débats*) and in periodicals (*La Revue des Deux Mondes*).[3] Moreover, they held almost all the chairs, both public and private, in economics and related disciplines. In addition to having a firm footing in many learned societies like the *Académie des Sciences Morales et Politiques*, they founded several *Sociétés d'économie politique*, initially in Paris in 1842 and later in Marseille, Lyon, Bordeaux, Saint-Etienne and Douai and the *Société de statistique de Paris* in 1860. Thanks to political support from Napoleon III, these ardent believers

---

[1] This chapter is largely a summary of Charbit: *Du malthusianisme au populationnisme : les Economistes français et la population 1840–1870*. Very few recent studies have dealt specifically with the ideas of economists on population, but *L'économie politique en France au XIXè siècle*, (Breton and Lutfalla ed.,1991) takes stock of several important aspects of the situation and also the major debates on this topic. As regards demographic factors, Volume 3 of *Histoire de la population française* (Dupâquier ed.,1988), provided new information in 1988 which has confirmed, and at times amended, the contribution of earlier works on this period covered in this chapter.

[2] Regarding the historical background of the question, Levasseur's *Histoire des classes ouvrières en France* (1859) provides useful information.

[3] We will use the following initials to denote the above publications: *Jde, Rddm, Ef, Sep, Asmp, Le, JSsP, Dep (Dictionnaire de l'économie politique).*

Y. Charbit, *Economic, Social and Demographic Thought in the XIXth Century*,
DOI 10.1007/978-1-4020-9960-1_3,

in free trade witnessed the success of their ideas after 1860 following the signature of several trade treaties, particularly with England. The period between 1840 and 1870 marked the height of their glory. But this period should be studied for another reason. Unlike in the previous decades, their traditional adversaries, the protectionists who were influenced by neo-mercantilism, were first and foremost industrialists and no front-ranking figure had yet formulated a social doctrine or even taken part in the debate on the population question. As for the Social Catholics, closely studied by Duroselle (1951), they dealt only incidentally with the population question and mostly in relation to the problems of charity and abandoned children. Finally, except for Proudhon, the Utopian Socialists, who were violently anti-Malthusian, were reduced to silence during the Second Empire by means of severe police repression.

In two papers published in 1936, Spengler has firmly established the contribution of French economists to the demographic theory and more precisely to the inclusion of population as one of the factors of production in the framework of classical economics.[4] Spengler however stresses on its purely theoretical aspect and consequently neglects two important dimensions of the ideas on population. In the nineteenth century, these ideas were derived as much from the social doctrine as from economic theory and constituted a very effective ideological weapon, as proved by the success of the first edition of Malthus's *Essay on the Principle of Population*. Further, like Malthus, the French economists were extremely interested in demographic facts and their ideas on population were based, at least partially, on an empirical approach. Since one of the rigid criteria for membership of the group was belief in the free-trade doctrine, it was possible for them to adopt much more flexible positions on the population question without facing the risk of being excommunicated by the group. Hence they were able to readjust their population doctrine constantly according to the ongoing structural and short-term changes. This is reflected in the topics chosen for the after-dinner debates of the *Société économie politique de Paris* between the years 1842 and 1870, which were regularly reproduced in the *Journal des économistes*. These reports constitute a most valuable record of the evolution of ideas.

The period 1840–1870, which would give them the opportunity to compare their ideas with facts, was marked by radical changes. Firstly, there were demographic changes: in a situation where the total population grew at a slow pace as a result of a regular fall in the birth rate since the beginning of the century, in 1853–1854 there was such a steep rise in the death-rate that for the first time a natural deficit was recorded. On the other hand, France was going through an unprecedented phase of urbanisation as a direct result of the growing need of labour for its industries. This demographic change took place at a time when the economic, social and political situation was particularly favourable. The July Monarchy was swept away by the severe economic, social and political crisis of 1845–1848. The short-lived Second Republic (1848–1851) which followed was swept away in its turn by the coup d'état

[4] Titled "French Population Theory since 1800". Also see Spengler's *France Faces Depopulation* (1938), particularly Chapters V, VI, VII and VIII.

carried out by Prince President Louis Napoleon Bonaparte in 1851. The Second Empire (1851–1870), on the contrary, seemed to be a period of economic expansion, rising prices and comparative social peace, at least till the mid-1860s. It was also under the Second Empire that the building of the French colonial empire began. But after 1860, social and political problems obliged the government to become less authoritarian as it was facing a series of setbacks at the international level. Let us mention these problems briefly. At the domestic level, the right of coalition, which was recognised in 1864, gave a new impetus to social unrest while free trade, established in 1861, was opposed by industrial circles who favoured protectionism; finally, the Catholics withdrew their support while the Republican opposition became more powerful. At the international level, the disastrous Mexican expedition from 1861 to 1867, the Polish question as well as those of the Danish duchies of Schleswig, Holstein and Lauenbourg from 1863 onwards, the Roman problems in 1867 and the failure of the compensation policy in 1867 due to Prussia's claims proved to be serious disappointments or blunders. It was in these circumstances that a radical about-face occurred a few years later in both the population theory and doctrine of the free-trade economists.

While Malthusianism won unanimous support from 1840 to 1850, several well-known Malthusians clearly became populationists during the 1860s. First, it appears that such a change could only be the result of the pressure exerted by circumstances, because no theoretical work capable of bringing about such a drastic change in ideas was published during this period. Secondly, when the comments provoked by the results of two censuses (1856 and 1866) are compared, it is impossible to claim that the change in ideas on population was caused solely by demographic factors. If, on the contrary, the totality of social, economic and political changes are taken into account, it is easier to understand why Malthusianism occupied a central position in the social doctrine and also why it was *progressively* abandoned. Although, Malthusianism was the principal doctrine behind the refutation of socialistic ideas during the 1848 revolution, under the Second Empire a powerful synthesis of urban and industrial changes partially questioned the Malthusian doctrine. After 1864, this synthesis in its turn weakened under the pressure of facts and there was a decisive doctrinal upheaval as a result of which Malthusianism was abandoned in favour of populationism.

A Double Paradox

The censuses of 1856 and 1866 led to the publication of a large number of articles and books by members the group. Comparing the changing demographic facts with the evolution of ideas reveals a double paradox: the objectively disquieting demographic situation between 1851 and 1856 did not seem to perturb these specialists. The 1866 census did not raise any serious problems and yet they were admittedly pessimistic.

The 1856 Census: Demographic Crisis and Economic Prosperity

The 1856 census recorded a very low rate of annual population growth: 0.14% between 1851 and 1856 (against 0.22% between 1846 and 1851), resulting from a deficit of births as compared to deaths in 1854 (−69, 318) and 1855 (−35, 606). The continuation of a long-term fall in the birth rate was confirmed (26.1 per thousand between 1851 and 1855 as compared to 30.5 per thousand between 1826 and 1830). The census also revealed a steep growth of the urban population, which rose between 1851 and 1856 from 25.5% to 27.3% of the total population. The average annual growth rate in the intercensal period (1.52% from 1851 to 1856 and 1.59% between 1856 and 1861) is the highest recorded in the nineteenth century. The growth was particularly high in the industrial suburbs of the major industrial and commercial centres like Paris, Lyon, Le Havre and Lille: in Paris it went up by 13.5%, but in the suburbs of Montrouge, La Chapelle and Belleville it rose respectively by 122%, 78% and 66%; in Lille it rose by 4% against 39.5% in Wazemmes. These facts should have been considered disturbing as this conjunction between the concentration of population in urban areas and a high death rate gave rise in the first half of the nineteenth century to the theme of "working classes, dangerous classes" as shown by Chevalier (1958) in the case of Paris. With just one exception, the members of the group were almost unanimously satisfied by the demographic changes and particularly by the exodus from rural areas. The problem then is to explain the reasons for this surprising optimism going against the traditional analyses and the pessimism that reigned around 1848, as we shall see later.

The reasons for the exceptionally high death rate in 1854 and 1855 were the high price of cereals in 1853 following a poor harvest, the cholera epidemic in 1854 and the Crimean War in 1854–1855. The cholera epidemic in 1854, which caused some 150,000 deaths, was even more severe than the ones in 1849 (110,000 deaths) and in 1832 (102,700 deaths). However, the former head of the Statistical Bureau, Moreau de Jonnes, did not hesitate to write that "public health has not been affected by the cholera epidemic". This declaration and the underestimation by all economists of the seriousness of the epidemic are explained by the second component of the demographic crisis of 1854–1855, viz. the rise in the price of wheat in 1853. However, this was nothing compared to the serious food crisis during the period 1846–1848, some aspects of which were reminiscent of the crises during the Ancien Régime. But generally speaking, the economic context was different: France had developed remarkably due to the influx of gold and silver from California and Australia since 1850 and the economic policy adopted by the Second Empire (building of public works and development of railways). In these conditions, it is not surprising that Wolowski should have claimed that "the economic fact that strikes us in France is the increase of wealth and the means of subsistence".[5] And according to the economists,

[5] Moreau de Jonnes (*Jde*, T. 18, 1858: 230). Chevalier (1958) has brought out the social significance of the 1832 epidemic, which created havoc in districts crowded with a poor and itinerant population. This led to a wave of panic among the bourgeois population. See the opinions of Wolowski (*Jde*, T. 13, 1857: 331) and Legoyt (*Jde*, T. 18, 1858: 361). Wolowski was a professor

the rural exodus was the logical result of the need for labour in industries and for major public works.

Some economists called for the use of Malthusian adjustment mechanisms. In the absence of major destructive checks – a position which was easily justified by underestimating the gravity of the cholera epidemic and by the fact that the high price of wheat did not lead to a famine – a low demographic growth proved that preventive checks had effectively prevented the principle of population from producing all its effects: "it is quite possible that this fact coincided (...) with a more definite and better regulated tendency in the birth rate, that is to say in the management of pressing interests which determine this rate". According to Villermé, author of *Tableau de l'état physique et moral des ouvriers*, the fall in the number of births reflected a decrease in fertility among the working classes who were traditionally supposed to be more fertile. This change, he felt, was very satisfactory because it resulted in a lower infant mortality. In all, economists based their optimism on non-demographic considerations by laying stress on the overall economic situation and by minimising the importance of the crisis of 1854–1855.[6]

The 1866 Census: The Decreasing Fertility and International Outlook

According to the official commentator of the census, the rural exodus was less severe than in earlier times and the short-term economic crises did not slow down demographic growth. But there was no mention of the long-term decrease in the birth rate.

Slow Growth and Low Fertility

Economists were interested above all in the long-term decrease in the birth rate, while in 1856 they were more concerned about the rural exodus. However, all said and done, opinions on the rural exodus were by and large positive and reflected the awareness of the need for change as a result of industrial development. But when the rural exodus slowed down, the fall in fertility became inevitable. It became clear that there was no more hope of a demographic revival after the disappearance of the temporary causes of the slowdown because the extraordinary reasons for mortality had almost disappeared after 1856: there was no food-shortage despite poor harvests and

of political economy and industrial law in the *Conservatoire des Arts et Métiers* from 1839 and a member of the *Académie des sciences morales et politiques* from 1855. He was also a member of the National Assembly from 1848 to 1851 and again from 1871 to 1875.

6 Quotation from Dunoyer (*Jde*, T. 13, 1857: 229). A native of the Lot department Dunoyer was one of the most important liberals during the Restoration; his newspapers, *Le Censeur* and *Le Censeur Européen*, were taken to court. He became interested in political economy after 1825 and was appointed Prefect from 1830 to 1837 and then member of the *Conseil d'Etat* (1838–1851). Villermé, in Fayet (1858: 42).

the 1865 cholera epidemic was not very serious as compared to previous epidemics. Hence it was the low fertility that was slowing down demographic growth, and that too excessively, considering the economic and political needs of the time. This was the conclusion drawn by the statistician Block after studying the departments in which population had decreased between 1836 and 1866: the reason was the fall in the number of births and not the high rate of deaths caused by epidemics. Better still, the wealthiest departments had experienced the heaviest losses. Normandy was a perfect example of this, observed Hippolyte Passy and his nephew Louis Passy, who claimed that the reason for the drop in the population of Normandy was not the rural exodus but the low fertility of married couples in rural areas, and only in rural areas. Given the economic situation, this observation could not be explained by the traditional Malthusian models: "What makes it remarkable is that it happened at a time of great prosperity and showed to what extent Malthus's doctrine is baseless." This statement takes us back to the first edition of the *Essay* in which only mortality (the destructive check) plays a role in population control. But by ignoring the possible role of preventive checks, it reduced Malthus's theory to the first model, thus revealing that the Malthusian system was no longer regarded as relevant to France under the Second Empire. Hippolyte Passy's opinion suggests that traditional Malthusianism was on the decline as the dominant tone of the article is one of pessimism resulting from the consequences of demographic changes: "If the population continues to decrease, it will ultimately lead to (...) a reduction of the forces required by nations to increase their power and industrial activities."[7]

International Stakes

Unlike the preceding period, fertility in France was seen from an international viewpoint: "The average annual growth for thirty years is only 0.43%, lower than in most other European states."[8] This change of view can be explained in the first place by Prussia's unexpected victory over Austria at Sadowa on 3 July 1866, which rudely revealed the existence of a new, well-organised and well-armed European power on France's doorstep. While public opinion suddenly became aware of the military handicap represented by a low demographic growth, economists were caught in a contradiction: for these free-traders, the safety of international trade was crucial; but as pacifists, they could not recommend an increase in the size of the army to safeguard it. They therefore had no choice but to denounce the disastrous economic consequences of wars while stressing anxiously that fertility in France was

[7] Block (*Jde*, T. 7, 1867: 423–427); L. Passy (*Jde*, T. 36, 1862: 421–427); H. Passy (*Jde*, T. 5, 1867: 314–315). The reason for the fall in fertility was, according to Passy, the fear of having too many children. H. Passy, deputy from Louviers from 1830 and a Peer of France from 1843, was a friend of Thiers. Considered as a financial expert, he joined the government in 1848 but he resigned in 1851 after the *coup d'état* of Louis Napoleon Bonaparte.

[8] *Jde*, T. 5, 1867: 423.

insufficient to face such dangers.[9] On the other hand, the rivalry with England in the colonies inevitably led to the problem of having adequate human reserves to populate the territories controlled by France. In fact, for the first time it was recognized that the colonial question was explicitly linked to demographic changes. Due to the low demographic pressure, it was difficult to encourage emigration and therefore colonisation, which explains why France lagged behind other European countries in the race for colonies: "These emigrants, these colonisers are either large families moving out together or youngsters. It is they who have been pioneers in America and populated Australia and, what a miracle, these people grow and multiply much faster than us who send abroad only a few representatives of our nationality." At the time these lines were written, England could support its industrial development with its vast Empire on which the sun never set.[10]

A comparison of the reactions to the results of the censuses in 1856 and 1866 leads to an epistemological problem: it is impossible to explain the shift in ideas on population by simple demographic facts and it is necessary to widen this analysis and relocate it in the overall context of France during the Second Empire, also keeping in mind the ideological corpus of liberalism. As we shall see later, the economists succeeded in maintaining the coherence of their economic doctrine (that free trade is necessary for economic prosperity) as well as social doctrine (social peace is possible in France) by taking into account the demographic and socio-economic changes which they had closely followed. And since demographic facts were obviously not properly analysed, it is necessary to deduce that scientific discipline in terms of ideas on population was subordinated to maintain this coherence. In other words, it remains to be shown that the contradictions noted so far on the objective level are only apparent contradictions and that they conceal a strong ideological coherence.

Poverty of the Working Class and the Dangers of the Revolution

The 1840s were a period of intense ideological activity because the beginning of industrialisation and the birth of a working class seriously raised the problem of social peace. However, the figures do not justify the shift in ideas because industrial growth under the July Monarchy (1830–1848) was very modest as compared to the following decades. But it must be remembered that France was essentially rural during the reign of Louis-Philippe: in 1836, the population of two of the largest cities, Lyon and Lille, was respectively only 150,814 and 72,005. Unlike in England, the rural areas had not changed much as neither the agricultural revolution nor any "enclosures movement" had given rise to a rural proletariat. On the other hand, the geographical concentration of a few hundred thousand workers constituting the first industrial force did not fail to strike such sharp observers as the economists,

[9] For example H. Passy (*Jde*, T. 5, 1867: 317); F. Passy (s.d.). F. Passy received the Nobel Prize for Peace in 1901; Block, Bénard and Lavergne also adopted this position, (Ibid.: 309, 310, 429).

[10] Block (*Jde*, T. 5, 1867: 426); Duval (*Jde*, T. 5, 1867: 318–319).

especially since England had shown to what extent industrialisation could spread: would Lille become another Manchester? Would the proletarianisation of the English working classes with its attendant troubles and agitations also occur in France?

It is in this context that the 1845–1850 crisis broke out. It started with a disease which affected the potato crop: attacked by phytophtora, the crop was as poor as in 1832. In 1846 again, the wheat crop was poor in the whole of France. The price of wheat, which had reached its maximum in February 1847, was the highest recorded in the nineteenth century except for 1812 and 1817. As it often happens, it fell drastically later on, bringing down the farmers' purchasing power. In 1847, the crisis reached the industrial sector. With the skyrocketing of the stock market due to heavy speculation on the railway, a one-point increase in the interest rate by the Banque de France immediately put the banking sector in a precarious position leading to the collapse of the largest private bank, *Caisse du Commerce et de l'Industrie*. In 1848 and 1849, the crisis was certainly an industrial and commercial crisis affecting the whole of France, except for Marseille and the Var region. In Paris, production collapsed and unemployment ranged between 50 and 75%; in Rouen, port activity came down by one third; in Lille, Roubaix and Tourcoing, the situation was disastrous: of the 50 cotton-spinning mills that existed in 1832 only 34 remained in 1848 and 27 in 1849. After a partial revival in 1849, the economy collapsed again in 1850–1851. The crisis would end only during the Second Empire. The population suffered a great deal and poverty was particularly severe in the countryside. In the West, the government had to take action against troops of beggars and trouble broke out all over France. The reduction of the peasants' purchasing power affected the demand for industrial goods. In Northern France, for example, where the crisis affected the textile sector in 1846, unemployment grew severely while wages fell drastically: in Roubaix, among the weavers living outside the city walls, 4,800 were unemployed in February 1847, 6,000 in mid-March and 7,000 at the beginning of May. In the Calvados region, lace-makers, who earned 1 franc per day in 1845, earned no more than 0.10–0.30 franc in 1848–1849.[11]

Industrialisation and Its Demographic Implications

The interest shown in the 1840s in analysing the social differentials in fertility and mortality corresponded, as in England, to the need to understand the working class population created by industrialisation. Their harsh living conditions were in sharp contrast with the relative prosperity of the majority of the population and average figures could not evidently serve as a satisfactory statistical tool: "This contrast between the constant increase in the life span of the overall population and the bleeding wounds of poverty can have but one explanation. It must be concluded that the average figures expressing general facts are high due to the exceptional

[11] This information has been taken from various contributions to Labrousse ed., (1976). Also see: Markovitch (1965).

prosperity of the bourgeois classes, a prosperity which is quite noticeable as it compensates for the misery of the proletariat." Detailed demographic data was therefore necessary to combat poverty and social suffering and the economists could, in fact, base their analyses of the extent and gravity of the economic and social situation on the remarkable differential statistics that they had sometimes helped to collect. As was the case in Paris, working classes were formed in towns by the immigration of the rural population attracted by industrial jobs and generally speaking, the growth of the Seine department and the city of Paris can only be explained by immigration.[12] The economists, who were fully aware that this rapid movement did not allow for a proper assimilation of the immigrants, connected the demographic growth with the rural exodus and social problems. And when the revolution broke out in 1848, the problem assumed political tones: "It is desirable more than ever before that the urban population should not increase at the cost of the rural population. Anything that encourages the concentration of a large number of workers at a particular point is not only bad for public order but also worsens the workers' condition."[13]

Even though some of the analyses deal with the food shortage between 1846 and 1848, most articles and books published before and after the 1848 revolution deal with the growth of the factory system and its consequences, which were very lucidly analysed: the technical and capitalistic concentration of labour, chronic crises of overproduction and their disastrous human consequences. In Lower Normandy, wrote Jérôme-Adolphe Blanqui, the brother of the famous revolutionary, "This is the novelty and the crux of the present manufacturing system: wherever a big factory comes up, a population of labourers gathers around it and grows in a disorderly fashion; it is badly housed, badly fed and is subjected to every likelihood of instability of profits and wages." Even after the turmoil of 1848, he was pessimistic about the future of social peace – "The centres of sedition have not been wiped out" – and cities like Lyon and Paris still contained many young and unstable people, who became trouble-makers and disturbers of the social order. This bourgeois notion of danger related to the age structure of the working class population has been stressed by Chevalier in relation to crime in Paris in the first half of the nineteenth century. His book stops before the 1848 Revolution: it is clear that when the revolution broke out, the social problem assumed a political colour. According to Villermé, for example, working-class housing projects, often built by employers, were likely to aggravate social antagonisms by giving rise to social segregation.[14]

---

[12] Chevalier, 1950. Also see Le Bras and Garden (1988: 142).

[13] Faucher (*Rddm*, novembre-décembre 1843: 794). The quotation is taken from Léonce de Lavergne (*Rddm*, April 1849: 55).

[14] Quotations from Blanqui (*Mémoires de l'Asmp*, T. 7, 1850: 743 and 730. Also see: 730, 743, 769, 805, 821); Villerme (1850: 9).

Responses to the Problem of Poverty

Despite the social evils ingrained in industrial cities, none of the economists advocated that the "excessive" urban working-class population should return to the countryside. This solution went against all their analyses of mechanisation, which required a large labour force: in a country where the population increased very little and where deaths exceeded births in the cities, the industrial labour force could be strengthened only by immigration from the rural areas. Further, since the beginning of the nineteenth century, landowners had joined hands with the owners of ironworks and textile mills to enforce protectionist barriers. In these conditions, these economists who favoured free trade were not in the least interested in advocating a return to the land for the benefit of the landowners who complained about a shortage of labour in the agricultural sector. Charity too was condemened as an inadequate solution to the problem of poverty. Private charity, often advocated by Social Catholics, had a major disadvantage in that it weakened the sense of responsibility among individuals and hence "foresightedness" and favoured in the long run an inordinate increase of the poor population and, therefore, misery. As for assistance to the unemployed, characteristically described as "public charity", it was associated with the unfortunate experience of the *Ateliers nationaux*, the useless public works undertaken to reduce unemployment. The right to work, inspired by the socialist doctrine (the decree of 15 February 1848 was issued under the influence of Louis Blanc) was vigorously opposed by the economists during debates in the National Assembly. In the first place, it violated the sacrosanct right to work and consequently the right to property. In the same vein, they rejected Proudhon's thesis: though it was true that the right to property and the right to work were contradictory and hence could not coexist, it was wrong to claim, as Proudhon did, that going beyond this contradiction would ensure progress. Further, the right to work, like the English Poor Laws, led to an increase in the number of poor under the guise of alleviating poverty. Finally, it was refuted with reference to the wage-fund theory: since it was impossible to increase the overall remuneration of labour, what was given as aid to unemployed workers was actually taken from the wages of the employed ones. These are in fact traditional Malthusian arguments. Having rejected these solutions, how did they propose to solve the problem of poverty?[15]

The Malthusian Weapon

Demographic arguments were advanced to solve the social and political problems created by the 1848 revolution. They were reduced by de Colmont to a pithy formula at the height of the revolutionary turmoil: "One of the principal causes of the poverty of the working classes is that they have too many children", and this was due to two reasons. Workers as consumers could escape poverty and even starvation only if they

---

[15] The speeches were immediately compiled by Garnier in *Le droit au travail à l'Assemblée nationale*, published in 1848.

reduced their fertility; as producers, their excessive fertility increased the supply of labour and brought down wages. The Malthusian argument was thus used to ignore the social problem of poverty and bring the debate down to the individual and biological level. But it had a much more interesting ideological function according to Garnier, an orthodox Malthusian and chief editor of the *Journal des Economistes*, "Malthus was content to recommend moral restraint and he only asked the poor classes to imitate the affluent classes who always abide by it." Since they had thoroughly analysed the social differences responsible for fertility and mortality, writing that workers could avoid their sad fate by adopting a prudent and therefore bourgeois type of behaviour amounted to denying the fundamental difference between social classes. In 1848, when an open class struggle was in progress, this argument proved to be extremely important: to restore social peace, it was necessary that everybody became bourgeois and that was possible only if the workers reduced their fertility by following Malthus's advice. The generous socialist claims for equality were caught in the Malthusian trap.[16]

Protectionism and Free Trade

The existence of conflicts was also denied at the economic level. At the height of the social and political crisis, Horace Say proclaimed the solidarity of labour and capital: "We should stop considering the interests of capital and labour as being opposed because they are really identical. Capital, which is formed by the savings of workers, becomes the most useful instrument for production; its destruction would be a public calamity." This delightful statement could simply mean that capital is created only by workers' savings. Though it is true that savings banks were a great success, it is surprising that Jean-Baptiste Say's own son should believe that all the capital invested in France came from them. Even more important, it has a bearing on the significance of the ideological legacy of the 1789 revolution according to which capital is accumulated labour and capitalists are also workers and members of the Third Estate like all workers.[17]

The economists cleverly used another argument: those responsible for the workers' poverty were the protectionists who, by defending the privileges of industrialists, increased the cost of living for the masses. Frédéric Bastiat, chief editor of the weekly *Le Libre-échange*, combined Malthusianism with free trade: "Ultimately, Death takes care, after much suffering, to bring the population down to a level that can be supported by the reduced wages and combined with the high cost of living." The free-trade argument had a dual purpose. First, by rising to the defence of consumers, they identified their cause with the general interest and set themselves

---

[16] Quotations: De Colmont (*Jde*, T. 20, 1848: 197); Garnier (*Jde*, T. 23, 1848: 151). Chevalier claimed that foresightedness would spread among the people when reason gained an upper hand over instinct (*Jde*, T. 22, 1849: 352); du Puynode (*Jde*, T. 23, 1849: 149); Garnier (*Jde*, T. 15, 1846: 127, 129); Chevalier (*Jde*, T. 16, 1847: 221); Reybaud (*Rddm*, April 1846: 56).

[17] Horace Say (*Jde*, T. 20, 1848: 23).

up as defenders of the masses and hence of the workers. On reading the weekly *Le Libre-échange*, it is seen to what point they believed – or wanted to show that they believed – that the Republic would adopt their doctrine for the good of the people. But between February and April 1848, when the last issue of *Le Libre-échange* was published, the disillusionment increased week after week because instead of supporting free trade, the Republic became socialistic and they denounced its folly. The second purpose of the free trade argument was to blame protectionism for the economic and social crisis as if the customs regime were solely responsible for the workers' misery: "The restrictive system is one of the most direct causes of the excessive competition, of the concentration of workers in cities and of pauperism which worries and troubles them. When the storm broke out over our country in February, we saw how fragile and inadequate the protective edifice was."[18] In his well-informed report on the working classes, Blanqui systematically opposed the industries in the North, in the East and in Normandy, which were the strongholds of protectionism, to the social stability in Marseille, Bordeaux, Dunkirk and in ports as a whole. It is worth noting that Blanqui was one of the members of the national legislature representing Bordeaux, a city which supported free trade. In short, by turning the protectionist industrialists into scapegoats, it was possible to exonerate the bourgeoisie as a whole from the evils created by the anarchic capitalism which prevailed in the early years of industrialisation.

The economists thus waged a dual ideological struggle around 1848 – against the socialists on the one hand and against the protectionists on the other. Demographic arguments played a key role because the Malthusian vulgate suited the situation perfectly, but it was modified to take into account the peculiar nature of French society: the solidarity of the various social classes was stressed much more than in England in conformity with the main principles of 1789 and the urgent need to restore social peace.

The Second Empire: Social Peace

It was under the Second Empire that France stumbled into the modern world: development of the railways (from 3,010 km in 1850 to 17,929 km in 1870) as well as the improvement of the road network and river transport contributed to the "expansion of the national market" characterised by a marked growth in the circulation of coal, raw materials for the textile industry and food products. Generally speaking,

[18] Blanqui's report is titled *Classes ouvrières pendant l'année 1848.* Quotation from Bastiat: *Le*, 29 août 1847: 318. Regarding the changes during the Second Republic, compare *Le*, 5 March 1848: "The last revolution, while preparing for an unlimited extension of the electoral base, has greatly facilitated the success of our cause... No one would dare today to proclaim loudly that the high cost of food stuffs is a good thing" (p. 77) and *Le*, 26 March 1848: "The government has undertaken the implementation of this excessively regulatory, anti-liberal and monstrous programme that goes under the name of organisation of labour." (p. 89). Also see Blanqui (*Classes ouvrières...* in *Mémoires de l'Asmp*, T. 7, 1850: 791).

the Saint-Simonians (Talabot, the Péreire brothers, Guéroult, Chevalier) played a decisive role as they convinced the Emperor that the state had to intervene in the business sector. Thus credit was reorganised according to their ideas to support industrialisation and tap savings at a time when there was an influx of precious metals in France from Australia and California which facilitated banking operations while industrialisation, by producing more consumer goods, checked inflation. There is no doubt that Napoleon III's interventionist policy promoted economic growth. His coming into power reassured the ruling classes as pointed out by Labrousse and Marczewski and the overall economic policy, especially at the beginning of the Second Empire, contributed to the economic revival. Demand was sustained by undertaking large-scale public works and the introduction of free trade gave a boost to the economy. It should be remembered that the treaty of 1860, which boosted the economy, was signed against the wishes of the majority of industrialists. The total exports increased from 16 in 1848 to 92 in 1875 (the base being 100 in 1890), almost at the same pace as the imports. As for industrialisation, the movement, which had begun in the 1840s, expanded considerably. A few figures will support this statement: the number of machines operated by steam, which had gone up from 2,591 in 1840 to 5,322 in 1850, reached 27,088 in 1870. The industrial production index calculated by Crouzet, which fluctuated between 5 and 7 in the 1840s (the base being 100 in 1913), shot up from 9.7 to 30.6 between 1851 and 1869. There was progress also in the agricultural sector due to a decrease in the area of fallow lands, better crop rotation and improvement of tools; for example, the number of steam-operated threshing-machines rose from 81 in 1852 to 6,000 in 1873. This led to an increase in the yield of the two major cereals (wheat and rye), sugar-beet and grape-vines in the South of France. There was also an improvement in cattle rearing with a larger number of cattle-heads as well an increase in the yield of milk and meat.[19] The progress in the transport, agricultural and industrial sectors promoted the development of consumption and brought down the prices of cotton and woollen fabrics and also iron and steel goods which benefited the consumers. The diversification of consumption is confirmed by qualitative studies such as Duveau's thesis on the condition of the working class under the Second Empire. Available statistical series show that the nominal wage rose continuously but the real wage suffered during some years, partly because of the sharp rise in house rents in all the cities where large-scale public works were undertaken under Hausman's urban development scheme. Labrousse concludes that the average factory-owner saw his profits double between 1850 and 1880 while it took 60 years for agricultural income to double. As for the workers, it was during the 1860s that "the anxiety about bread" disappeared and consumption became more diverse. In other words, the standard of living improved and changed.[20]

---

[19] National market: Léon (1993: 275–304). Exports: Broder (1993: 311–312. Agriculture: Laurent (1993: 680–685, 698–707). Daumard (1993: 897–929). Industrial production: Crouzet (1970).

[20] Duveau (1946: 333, 336, 363–368); Singer–Kerel (1961); Léon (1993: 275–304, 598). Series of prices and incomes: Bruhat (1993: 797–798). Assessment by Labrousse (1993: 1018–1022).

So this was the economic and social situation observed by the economists and as a rule they all analysed it with considerable insight. Better still, they managed to summarise the demographic, economic and social changes by focusing on two groups – peasants and workers. However, this choice was not objective as it involved essential ideological stakes. When dealing with the "working classes", the economists always looked at them from the viewpoint of the factory system, workers being above all a labour force whose present and future availability was of primary concern to them. However one of the most innovative ideological responses to industrialisation was the "standard of living argument", which cannot be separated from the problem of social peace. And that is precisely what constitutes the profound ideological link between the analyses of the rural masses and the analyses focused on workers. The economists succeeded in putting together an original thesis based on the economic and social changes that took place between 1850 and 1860 and proved that social peace was possible, and had perhaps even been achieved, both in the countryside and in cities.

The Peasants: Small Holdings and Rural Exodus

The Problem of "Parcellisation"

Although the existence of "parcellisation" was proved only in a few regions, it is agreed that there was a progressive fragmentation of land holdings in the first half on the nineteenth century. The reasons for this are quite uncertain and the traditional argument that the law of succession was directly responsible is not very convincing: the fragmentation had started before 1789 and in some regions local customs and practices just managed to circumvent the law.[21] Nonetheless, the problem of fragmentation had demographic implications: if the property was divided with each successive generation, the same area had to support a larger number of families and the small size of the holding hindered agricultural development. In this way, a whole argument could be built on the relationship between the laws of succession, small land holdings and overpopulation. Malthus claimed that the predominance of small land holdings in France encouraged the growth of population, refusing to admit that the system of equal distribution of property introduced by the Napoleonic Code was really responsible for the fragmentation of land holdings and that this fragmentation was the principal cause of poverty and impeded any improvement in agricultural practices.[22] Several writers (Clément, Léonce de Lavergne, F. Passy,

---

[21] The best proof of fragmentation is provided by Vigier with reference to the Alpine region. Vigier then extends it to the whole of France (1963: 172–178). Barral, who deals with the Isère region, is more ambiguous (1962: 89). Corbin gives more importance to temporary migrations in the Limousin saying the introduction of paper currency permitted the purchase of lands (1975, I: 606–615). Regarding fragmentation in Alsace before 1789, see Leuillot (1959, I: 44).

[22] "In France, there have always been a lot of small farms and small landowners. This state of affairs is not very favourable to the increase of the net product or the available national wealth,

Legoyt and Levasseur) misunderstood Malthus and remarked that since fragmentation had started well before 1789, the Napoleonic Code could not be considered as its cause. Malthus's refutation was also based on a comparison between the changes in the number of *cotes foncières*[23] and the total size of the population. Since the two were not comparable, the economists deduced that the growth of population had nothing to do with the fragmentation of land holdings and that Malthus was wrong. Actually their painstaking calculations are not of much interest because they ignored other factors. For example, the fragmentation of land holdings can occur simply as a result of the urbanisation of rural areas. Further, since each *cote foncière* corresponds to the totality of pieces of land owned in a particular commune, if the same landowner acquires small holdings in another commune, the number of *cotes* will increase. Generally, properties can be sold or bought (and consequently the number of *cotes* can increase) with a total absence of demographic growth. When reference is made today to the fragmentation of land holdings, it is to explain the decreasing fertility towards the end of the nineteenth century – a causal relationship not yet proved; the peasants are supposed to have offset the harmful effects of the equal distribution of inherited lands by reducing their fertility and by marrying their only son to the neighbour's only daughter in order to combine the two properties in the next generation. This is just the opposite risk that preoccupied the economists, but no more than today, they could not explain the real relationship between land and fertility with reference to fragmentation. On the other hand, looking at it from the angle of the liberal ideology, the problem turns out to be particularly heuristic, as we shall now see.

Foresightedness

The economists unanimously rejected Malthus's opinion about the demographic consequences of small land holdings having partly misunderstood, as we have pointed out, Malthus's thinking: "The event has proved that in France the inheritance law does not have the disastrous consequences foreseen by Malthus and it does not in particular discourage prudential restraint with regard to population." In support of their defence of the French inheritance laws, they analysed at length the ways in which small land holdings slowed down demographic growth. They encouraged foresightedness and a sense of responsibility precisely because the inheritance law demanded the equal distribution of the inherited property: it encouraged the peasant to limit the number of children in order to avoid the fragmentation of his land after

---

but sometimes it increases the gross product and it always has a strong tendency to encourage population growth." *Essay*, 7th edition, I: 219. Similarly, the equal distribution of land among the heirs tended to encourage the growth of population among the Greeks and the Romans (*Essay*, 7th edition, I: 139).

[23] Each landlord has one *cote foncière* in a given commune, whatever be the number and the type of property or the pieces of land: e.g. his house, a separate barn, one or more pieces of land, a wood, etc. However he would have another *cote foncière* for his properties located in another commune.

his death.[24] At a time when the Malthusian doctrine was still predominant in their group, the economists were against Malthus only on the question of the inheritance law. How can this tough stand be explained? They believed that Malthus was a staunch supporter of big landowners and of the "aristocratic" English inheritance laws, while the right to property and its corollary, the law of succession, were praised as the most important achievement of the revolution of 1789. The bourgeois social order rested on these two pillars as Lavollée openly declared in 1861: "The law of succession, as established by the Civil Code, rests on principles that cannot be easily undermined and which will be defended, should the need arise, by the strongest forces of democracy and French society." To understand the solemnity of this warning, we must go back to the late 1840s. The 1848 revolution, which disrupted the social order, also established universal suffrage and it was obvious that the bourgeoisie faced imminent danger as the lower classes could seize power democratically. Nevertheless, the peasants, who voted for the first time in 1849, proved to be overwhelmingly conservative. So there was no more risk on that account and it was even proved that the French succession law constituted a major political advantage: by averting the creation of a rural proletariat (because each child inherited a part of the father's land), it ensured the continuance of political conservatism. Moreau de Jonnes could thus write in 1851 that the number of small holdings multiplied: "The number of citizens, defenders of the motherland and of the social order, [who] rose above the level of the proletariat because of their purer mores and their attachment to their father's land; and it is there, much more than in the cities, that the nation lies."[25]

The Underestimation of Push Factors in the Rural Exodus

Almost all the authors referred to here studied the causes of the rural exodus without concerning themselves too much about the scale of the phenomenon. The most noteworthy exception is the book by A. Legoyt, *Du progrès des agglomérations urbaines et de l'exode rural* (1867). But the purely statistical research covers only 70 of the book's 260 pages. A possible explanation is that the rural exodus was a well recognised fact, which the figures published in various volumes of *Statistique Générale de la France* made it possible to analyse it satisfactorily.[26] As for value

[24] Quotation: de Molinari (s.d: XXXVIII). As early as 1846, when the first French edition of *Principles of Political Economy* was published, the translator pointed out Malthus's mistake in a note. Also see H. Passy's demonstration (1853: 184–193, 213) which concluded: He is thrifty, he is foresighted: "He simultaneously suffers from the fear of becoming poor by producing an excessively large family and the desire to leave a larger inheritance for his children." The very same opinion was stated by Baudrillart (*Jde*, T. 13, 1857: 27), who was a journalist and a member of *Asmp* as well as a professor in the Collège de France.

[25] Moreau de Jonnes (*Rddm*, January 1861: 79); de Parieu, article titled "Succession" (*Dep,* 1853, II: 676). Also see Rossi (1865, II: 49, 55); Moreau de Jonnes (*Jde*, T. 23, 1851: 321).

[26] See in particular the following volumes of *Statistique Générale de la France*: *Résultats généraux du dénombrement de 1861* (p. XIII) and *Résultats généraux du dénombrement de 1872* (pp. XV–XXI) for the general results of the censuses of 1861 and 1872.

judgements on the rural exodus, they were the exact opposite of those pronounced at the time of the 1848 revolution. Urbanisation, which was considered socially and politically harmful, became normal and even desirable after 1850: "The increased movement of workers, their tendency to emigrate and gather in large numbers in big production centres [are] inevitable consequences and according to us beneficial for industrial progress."[27] In fact, industrial expansion under the Second Empire resulted in intense urbanisation and when France opened its doors to international competition, these semi-official ideologues could not denounce the growth of cities because of the dire need for labour. But more than anything else, the political climate had changed and during the Second Empire, police repression was used to maintain public order under the pretext of keeping the "socialist threat" at bay.

Surprisingly, the economists were unanimous about the causes of the rural exodus. They all agreed that pull factors were responsible for the massive movement from the rural areas to the cities: industrial wages were higher, life in the cities was more attractive and the need for labour in the cities increased after the adoption of the policy of building large public works and the development of communication networks. But no one suggested that there could also be push factors in the countryside: miserable living conditions, low wages, partial or total unemployment, absence of relief in times of difficulty, etc. The official agricultural survey conducted in 1866 clearly described the technical progress in the agricultural sector and it was well known as seen, for example, in this extract of the report of the agricultural survey of 1866: "One factor beyond all doubt, already observed for several years and most positively confirmed by all the results of the survey, is that the progress made by agriculture since the last thirty years or so is extremely significant... The improvement of cultivation methods, the progressive decrease of fallow lands, the intelligent modification of cropping patterns, the spread of fodder crops, increasing improvements in the production of cattle and manure and the introduction of industrial crops have had the effect of giving a strong impetus to our trade by creating elements conducive to it and whether within the country or in relation to foreign countries, and finally, as a natural result of all these factors, of increasing in a large measure the legitimate benefits and the well-being of our agriculture."[28] What do we know today? There were significant increases in productivity, which freed rural labour for good, as indicated by the figures calculated by Toutain: the final product per active agricultural male worker increased faster than the number of active male workers, the number of persons dependent on agriculture for a living and the final product itself (Table 3.1).

It is impossible here to go beyond this initial observation and, to be more precise, to contextualise these data by assimilating in a comprehensive model the numerous factors likely to have contributed to the transformation into permanent migration of what had earlier been seasonal or temporary migrations. In the case

---

[27] De Molinari, Article titled "Emigration" (*Dep*, I: 676).

[28] Known as *Enquête agricole de 1866*. Ministère de l'Agriculture, du Commerce et des Travaux publics, 1869: 1ère série, I: 223.

Table 3.1 Indicators of progress of agriculture

Period	Final agricultural product*					
	Total product		Per person dependent on agriculture		Per active male farmer	
	Francs*	%	Francs	%	Francs	%
1815–24	5152	0.2	275	0	1120	10
1825–34	5805	12.6	305	11	1209	8
1835–44	6719	15.7	348	14	1344	11
1845–54	7475	11.2	381	9	1410	5
1855–64	8586	14.8	432	13	1608	14
1865–74	9312	8.4	503	16	1764	10
1875–84	9267	0.5	508	1	1694	4

Source: Toutain, 1961: tables 138, 139 and 140.
*: Final product and not gross product, to account for self-consumption of agricultural products.
*: In francs 1905–1914.

of agriculture, it is necessary to take into account the improvement of agricultural techniques and productivity, the size of agricultural holdings, the microeconomic logic of family holdings, the absence of a rural proletariat and regional specialisation in agricultural production. Other contextual factors are the slow demographic growth and the elimination of rural craftsmen by the crisis of 1846; and among the pull factors, the development of the railways, the demand for labour in industries and in cities, and last the exogenous impact of the introduction of free trade in 1860. These different factors and their possible interactions are discussed at length in the annex, but given the prevailing state of knowledge, to put it briefly, it was the push factors that played a decisive role in the depopulation of rural areas.

Considering this situation, it is truly astonishing that almost none of the economists, who were the best specialists of their time and also the most informed, expressed the opinion that push factors could explain the rural exodus. Consequently, we must necessarily look for ideological reasons for this "error" of analysis. The two apparently distinct issues of small holdings and the exodus are actually complementary. The economists were not prepared to admit the existence of push factors because it implied that small holdings were the cause of latent overpopulation and disguised unemployment from which the French countryside suffered. And if this were the case, there is no doubt that this objective data confirmed Malthus's opinion and weakened their defence of the right to property. The only problem would be that the rural exodus posed a challenge to social peace, in which case there would have been a contradiction at the ideological level. But as we have seen, the economists, unlike earlier, were happy about the rural exodus. In these conditions, there was total ideological coherence and the general situation in the countryside was clearly regarded as satisfactory. But from the viewpoint of the history of ideas, one observation is necessary: when they contradict the very basis of the bourgeois ideology, and particularly the right to property, ideas on population are necessarily sacrificed to maintain coherence because of their secondary position in the ideology.

The Urban Working Classes

Considering that in the 1840s factory workers were the main threat to social peace, the industrialisation of France under the Second Empire should have been a source of even greater anxiety because urbanisation increased throughout the two Bonapartist decades. Let us quickly recapitulate the facts as they appeared to the economists. Between 1851 and 1872, the urban population rose from 25.5% to 31.1% of the total population, the main contribution to the overall urban growth being that of towns with a population of over 50,000 and those with over 100,000 which more than doubled in size.[29] However, a closer look at the results reveals that contrary to the statement of the commentator of the 1861 census, the pace of growth did not depend on the size of the town but on the degree of industrialisation. For example, there was a sharp increase in the population of the Pas-de-Calais department following the discovery of coal deposits and it rose by 19.8% between 1851 and 1856 as compared to 2.7% between 1841 and 1846. Also, between 1856 and 1861, industrial towns grew much faster than others: Le Creusot (18.2%), Montluçon (8.9%), Saint-Nazaire (7.7%) and Mulhouse (6.8%). Finally, growth was highest in the suburbs with Paris, Lyon and Lille (though limited by its walls) being the most striking examples (Table 3.2).

Table 3.2 Growth of cities and their suburbs

	% of growth between 1856 and 1861	
	City	Suburbs
Paris	1.5	19.3
Lyon	1.1	5.1
Lille	0.4	8.2

Source: *Résultats généraux du dénombrement de 1861* (p. XV).

At the end of the Second Empire, the most urbanised departments (Seine, Bouches-du-Rhône, Rhône, Nord, Seine-Inférieure, Loire and Pas-de-Calais) were also the most industrialised except for some departments in the South (Var, Hérault and Vaucluse) where the traditional concentration of population increased the rate of urbanisation.[30] There was a close relation between urbanisation and industrialisation because the two principal industrial sectors, viz. metallurgy and textiles, experienced an unprecedented financial, technical and geographical concentration. Gille, who has studied the process in the metallurgy sector, points out that the 1848

---

29 From 5.4% to 11.6% and from 4.1% to 9.1% respectively. Source: Toutain, 1963: Tables 16 and 17. For the figures for 1872, see *Statistique de la France*, 1873: 7.

30 Source: *Résultats généraux du dénombrement de 1872* (p. 21).

crisis was an important landmark and in 1869 large-scale enterprises had superseded smaller ones once and for all. This is confirmed by Léon in his thesis on the Dauphiné where industrial growth kept pace after 1848–1852 with the concentration of production. The effects of the treaty of 1860 were treated as favourable or unfavourable according to the degree of modernisation.[31] The textile industry, studied by Fohlen, clearly reveals the influence of the factors mentioned in the introduction to this chapter, viz. development of transport, introduction of free trade and reorganisation of the financial structure after 1848. However, unlike the other sectors, one crisis followed another, encouraging technical and financial concentration in the spinning sector (Normandy, the North, the East and isolated areas such as the Aube department or the town of Cholet) and to a lesser degree in the weaving sector (persistence of hand looms due to the lack of technical progress).[32] Local studies such as Léon's study of the Dauphiné or Pierrard's study of Lille confirm Fohlen's opinion. In Lille, for instance, the concentration and modernisation of cotton and linen spinning and the manufacture of yarn sustained the economic growth.[33]

The social consequences of this technical and geographical concentration have been analysed by Duveau. Though the tendency to increase the working hours was not observed during the Second Empire, workers were subjected to a strict discipline under the factory system due to the new working conditions. Even in Lille, the solidarity between employers and workers disappeared in spite of a long tradition of charity and paternalism. This change in working conditions was accompanied by changes in urbanism. We have taken note of the growth of industrial towns and the creation or increase of working-class suburbs, sometimes because of the large public works undertaken by the Empire and certainly because of the rise in the price of land in the cities. Paris is the best known example, but Lille, Saint-Quentin, Rouen, Lyon, Elbeuf and Roubaix went through the same changes. The day-to-day interaction and the solidarity between the different social classes disappeared.[34] The

[31] Iron and steel industry: Gille, 1968: 67–71, 118,169–194, 198; Léon, 1993: 484–489. Regarding the Dauphiné see Léon, 1954: II, 658–662, 680–683 (the same changes took place in the mines). Regarding the Treaty of 1860 see Dunham 1930: 177; Vial, 1968: II, 209–220; Thuillier, 1966: 310–312; Léon states that the 1860 treaty did not have a harmful effect on the Dauphiné (1954: II, 814–817), nor in France as a whole (1993: 334). Fourchambault should be considered separately: the decline started in the 1860s, but it cannot be attributed to causes that are traditionally considered fatal. Neither the treaty of 1860 and international competition, nor the lack of a spirit of enterprise, nor an unfavourable geographical position were responsible for the decline, but an unfortunate investment policy. Regarding Fourchambault see Thuillier, 1959: 93–94, 103, 106–107, 117, 167–170.

[32] See Fohlen, 1956: 139–142 (transport), 292 and 442–444 (free trade), 125 (financial aspects). Regarding the consequences of free trade, also see Dunham, 1930, 213–214, 235, 251 and 275. Regarding the impact of these factors on an enterprise (Méquillet-Noblot), see Fohlen, 1955: 69–92. For the entire sector, see Fohlen, 1956:253–268 (crises), and 445–449; Léon, 1993: 484–563.

[33] Léon, 1954: 501–507, 667–670, 663–664 (on Dauphiné). Pierrard, 1965: 65–75 (on Lille).

[34] Duveau, 1946: 246, 258. Regarding the increased working hours, see Pierrard, 1965: 163–164, 167. Tradition of charity and paternalism: Pierrard, 1965: 181–191. Regarding the suburbs of Paris, see Chevalier, 1950: 243, 248, 259; Pinkney, 1958: 165–166. Lille: Pierrard, 1965: 56–65,

change in the working and living conditions strengthened the feeling of being a separate group among the workers. Blanchard and Thompson have maintained that the Emperor's policy was responsible for the new awareness of the working class, but these factors undoubtedly played a much more decisive role. And as we shall see, contemporaries, or at least the economists, were perfectly aware of this situation.[35] Since urbanisation, industrialisation and social change cannot be dissociated from the Second Empire, we may expect ideological answers comparable to those formulated during the July Monarchy, if not even more pessimistic analyses, due to the severe destabilisation of society. But far from ignoring industrialisation, the economists included it in their analyses of social changes and succeeded in developing an optimistic synthesis at the end of which it was shown that social peace was possible thanks to industrialisation.

The Industrial Labour Force

The economists described with great precision the replacement of rural crafts and scattered small industries by the large mechanised units of the factory system and correctly analysed some of the consequences for the labour force: mechanization, far from doing away with jobs, created new ones and machines reduced physical labour. Feeling obliged to apologise for the factory system, they concluded that the machine "freed" the worker; however, they kept silent about the greater economic dependence that it led to. Anticipating criticism, Baudrillart talked of the general interest, embodied as usual by consumers. The majority of the nation would benefit by mechanisation: "Manufacturing produces more and it produces at a lower cost. It is protected by the spirit of democracy though it may appear aristocratic due to the accumulation of capital that it requires and the type of powerful and centralized government in the hands of a single leader." The change in the attitude towards the factory system was brought about by the introduction of free trade after 1860. Earlier, the major industrial sectors, particularly the textile industry, were protectionist; after 1860, since the main reason for the industrialists' hostility had disappeared, the economists could extol the merits of the factory system, which alone was capable of facing competition from England. Also, they did not fail to emphasise the improvement in the working conditions in factories.[36]

It was equally necessary to raise the workers' level of education, not to promote social peace, as during the 1848 revolution, but because of international competition: "If we want all the French factories to bravely face foreign competition, we must remember that we will always be beaten on account of raw materials and coal

---

102–107. Saint-Quentin, Rouen, Lyon, Elbeuf, Roubaix: Duveau, 1946: 219–221, 225, 349, 351. Interaction between social classes: Chevalier, 1950: 240–241; Duveau, 1946: 207.

[35] Blanchard, 1950: 150. Thompson, 1954: 237–238.

[36] Creation of jobs: F. Passy (1866: 74); Reybaud (1867: 117); Garnier, article titled "Machines" (*Dep*: 119–122). Regarding the "freeing" of workers: Reybaud, in his study of the silk industry (*Mémoire de l'Asmp,* T. 10, 1860: 894–895); Baudrillart (1860: 559; quotation: 552).

(. . .) let us prepare in advance strong and educated workers." This argument implied that the workers had given up political agitations or that the government was capable of controlling them. It is significant that Reybaud in his detailed survey of the woollen industry quoted the notables of Reims who were convinced that "The workers are very calm being under the control of a strong and respected government." Last but not least, the workers were not fundamentally opposed to the bourgeois social order, but they had been "corrupted" by external agitators and their strikes certainly were not of a political nature.[37]

Marginal and Temporary Suffering

Under the Second Empire, even the demographic arguments were different. Rather than study the characteristics peculiar to workers, the economists gave up their differential analyses in favour of arguments pertaining to the bulk of the French population, such as the average life span. Baudrillart interpreted the observed increase in life expectancy as follows: "The increase of life expectancy is the result of better nourishment, healthier lodgings, more hygienic clothing, the practice of temperance, a more reasonable behaviour, higher savings and greater order. The increase in life expectancy is the result of the fact that more persons are free from poverty and more souls have been weaned away from crime and vice; it is a guarantee for the state of assured security, more charity, a widespread feeling of responsibility and a more equality." This lyrical insistence on average characteristics is not accidental; it refers to the liberal credo that the consumer personifies general interest because, according to the economists, the increase in life expectancy corresponded to the greater well-being of the masses. It followed that the workers' suffering and poverty would only be marginal and temporary because the average living conditions were better on the whole. A major debate took place on this issue in early 1851 in the Academy of Moral and Political Sciences, after a meeting of the Legislative Assembly during which a member wrongly quoted Blanqui's figures on juvenile mortality in Lille. In the course of the discussion, Blanqui himself and Faucher drew attention to the improvements that had occurred in Rouen and Lille since the survey conducted by Blanqui in 1848. As for Villermé, he remarked that the mortality of abandoned children was unprecedented while Faucher, Villermé and Moreau de Jonnes observed that in 1848 the situation was quite abnormal amounting to a state of crisis. In short, one of the eminent Academicians suggested that Blanqui had undoubtedly allowed

[37] Quotation: Simon (*Rddm*, décembre 1863: 734); to be compared to a more conservative viewpoint like Garnier's: "Education provided by enlightened men to the workers dispels socialistic utopias and prejudices against capital and makes them aware of the eternal laws of political economy." (*Jde*, T. 15, 1846: 127); quotation from Reybaud (1867: 343). Regarding external agitators: Audiganne (*Rddm*, November 1851: 741, February 1852: 693, January 1853: 345); Reybaud (1867: 129–130 and 213), on the non-political nature of strikes.

himself to be carried away by his emotions. Altogether, a fine example of the a posteriori re-interpretation of both qualitative and statistical data.[38]

Well-Being, Free Trade and Malthusianism

It is true that the condition of the working classes improved under the Second Empire, even though inflation created a gap between the monetary wage and the real wage after the 1860s. Nevertheless, a large number of consumer goods became affordable for the masses. In keeping with the populist policy of Napoleon III, the well-being of the masses, and particularly the workers, was considered an important factor for social peace and, during the 1850s and 1860s, a great deal of writing rightly described the improvements in the workers' housing, clothing and food habits. Thus Jules Rapet wrote, "If the worker cannot achieve this well-being, his condition will be lower than that of all his fellow men and his existence will be miserable (...) envy and jealousy will assail him, they will add (...) to his woes caused by the inferiority of his position and will perhaps make him an enemy of a society in which he finds himself badly treated."[39] The subject of housing is particularly interesting because the few cases where workers had access to property, notably in the working-class districts of Mulhouse, acquired a great symbolic value: by owning his house, the worker became more bourgeois and his conduct became more moral.[40] In short, the economics of poverty was replaced by the sociology of well-being.

The introduction of free trade in 1860 came at the right time as a decisive factor allowing people access to a condition of well-being due to the availability of cheaper goods.[41] Garnier developed a very complete analysis which has the advantage of assimilating some Malthusian elements: "Free trade can be practised with a definite advantage if it is done on a sufficiently large scale by increasing its markets, stimulating production and consumption, increasing wages in proportion to the demand for labour or, indirectly, by lowering the price of goods, bringing comforts to the people and, with the coming of comforts, the conditions needed for a feeling of dignity so that foresightedness arises among the poor classes and the preventive check on population and competition maintain them in a situation that is morally and spiritually superior." This model is still Malthusian in the sense that individual responsibility remains indispensable because without it the principle of population would wipe out the benefits of free trade. And, of course, the problem of social

---

38 Baudrillart (*Jde*, T. 20, 1858: 374). The debate in *Asmp* was reproduced in *JdE* (T. 28, 1851: 281–286).

39 *Jde*, T. 28, 1851: 378–379.

40 Regarding housing: Levasseur (*Jde*, T.4, 1866: 230); Simon (*Rddm*, March 1861: 96–105); Reybaud (*Mémoire de l'Asmp,* T. 10, 1860: 943, 1011); Audiganne (1860, II: 308–325). Regarding consumption: Levasseur (*Jde*, T. 4, 1866: 235–236); F. Passy (1868: 28–31). Regarding clothing: Baudrillart (*Jde*, T. 20, 1858: 370); Block (1869: 232).

41 Baudrillart (*Jde*, T. 20, 1858: 371).

peace was at the heart of the Garnier's argument: according to him, foresightedness and free trade were the only two means of improving the condition of the people.[42] Another step towards the abandonment of Malthusianism was the "standard of living argument".

The Standard of Living Argument

Under the Second Empire, the economists developed a rather original ideological synthesis, in so far as it was based on demo-economic arguments. In substance, the standard of living argument states that the desire for well-being is the principal reason for controlling fertility and it is no longer necessary to practise prudential restraint because an improvement in the standard of living strengthens the individual's desire to better his condition which leads almost automatically to birth-control: "A certain degree of comfort, which absolves a man from worrying about his most immediate needs, makes him think about the future and creates in his mind the fear of demeaning himself in his own eyes and those of his family. Malthus's so-called law is ineffective in such a case." As it was to be expected, the orthodox Malthusians in the group reacted strongly against this fundamental questioning of the Malthusian theory. However, it was widely accepted as it was obviously compatible with the other elements of the social doctrine, particularly free trade and mass production and also with the demographic slow-down observed under the Second Empire. And above all, the standard of living argument allowed a dynamic analysis: following economic progress, luxury goods became comforts and even essentials and their use spread in the different social classes, including the working classes, so that class differences became blurred and society became more homogeneous.[43]

It is here that the socio-demographic implications of the standard of living argument come into play. The economists described the behaviour of the bourgeoisie with regard to fertility and, in accordance with their own ideological models; they claimed that it was a suitable model for all classes. Only the bourgeoisie maintained a satisfactory balance between fertility and the standard of living while aristocratic families were disappearing as a result of excessive sterility and the proletariat, on the contrary, were suffering from an equally excessive fertility as compared to their resources. They also stressed the fact that the working class's access to well-being was turning its members into bourgeois. The fact that the middle classes were becoming more numerous despite the low fertility of the bourgeois and the aristocrats, necessarily implied that more workers were becoming bourgeois. In other words, this upward social mobility was the result of access to well-being as well as of the decline

---

[42] Garnier (1857: 128–133, 206).

[43] The quotation is from Wolowski (*Jde*, T. 37, 1863: 349). See the reaction of the Malthusians during a debate in *Sep* in 1863 (*Jde*, T. 37, 1863: 330–357). Regarding access to new consumer goods, see Dameth (1872: 397, 407). Regarding English nineteenth century writers, see Eversley (1959).

of fertility among the workers.[44] It is necessary to stress the ideological implication of the argument: workers wanted to merge with the middle-class population because they adopted the bourgeois model of maintaining a balance between well-being and fertility. There is no doubt that this involved only a minority, but according to Paul Leroy-Beaulieu, this was the vanguard: "The workers at the top of the scale of well-being and education have (...) become bourgeois in this respect. Almost all of them systematically distance themselves from the burden of a large family." Some economists even tried to prove the existence of this upward social mobility: there were many workers who became independent small entrepreneurs thanks to the very bourgeois virtues of perseverance, thrift, hard work and, of course, foresight. For maintaining social peace this was crucial: more than just passive participation in the social order of the Second Empire due to the access to consumption, there was evidence of an active desire to cooperate with this social order and that too at the most basic level of the sexual instinct and procreation. The political importance of the argument can be gauged from the fact that it was taken up word for word by Emile Ollivier when he defended the bill tabled by the government in 1864 which would lead to the right of coalition, itself a prelude to the right to strike recognized twenty years later.[45]

In the case of both peasants and workers, the economists succeeded in assimilating the demographic, economic and social changes in their social doctrine by developing a coherent ideological synthesis, which showed that thenceforth nothing would oppose the permanent establishment of social peace. This explains the optimism expressed in the comments on the 1856 census: more than a simple change of the economic situation, the main factor was the compatibility between the new demographic, social and economic data on the one hand and the ideological stake of social peace on the other.

Towards Populationism

It would be an exaggeration to claim that at the end of the Second Empire there was a unanimous feeling in favour of populationism. However, after the years 1862–1864 a change of direction occurred which would lead to the total abandonment of Malthusianism in the following decades. The fear of depopulation was only partly a result of purely demographic factors: as we have seen, the reactions to the results of the 1866 census suggest that greater anxieties on the domestic and international front were behind the economists' pessimism.

---

44 Differences in fertility between different classes: Baudrillart (Paris, 1872, II: 440) ; H. Passy (*Jde*, T. 37, 1863: 335); Villiaumé (1867, I: 307, 313).

45 Leroy-Beaulieu (1868: 101–102). Social mobility: Courcelle-Seneuil (1858, I: 161–169, 367, 378, 383). Le Play stressed the fact in his monographs (1879, IV: 194–195, 339–340, 345–346, 379 and V: 311, 375, 386, 430). According to Chevalier, social mobility was possible among Parisian craftsmen (1950: 224–236). Bruhat and Daumard are more prudent (1993: 807, 905).

The New Socialism

After the 1860s, a series of strikes raised doubts about social peace. The Parisian typographers' trial in 1861–1862 was followed by the carpenters' strike at the end of 1862 and later by the conflict between the bronze-casters and their employers in 1865–1867. In the provinces, in 1867–1868 agitations spread among the miners of Saint-Etienne and Carmaux; strikes broke out in the spinning mills of Elbeuf in September 1869; finally, widespread strikes hit Le Creusot in early 1870. The economists astutely analysed the growing class-consciousness among the workers. Molinari spoke of a revival of socialism and Dameth made a distinction between the "old" socialism, which was bourgeois, and the "new" socialism which was genuinely proletarian. Reybaud's survey of the iron industry, which took him to Le Creusot, Commentry, Fourchambault, the Loire and the Cévennes, contains commentaries that became more and more pessimistic as the years passed: France "was divided into two camps". The economic consequences of the strikes did not escape their notice: by paralysing industrial activity, these strikes caused serious losses because of the large amount of capital invested in big production units and international competition, particularly since the introduction of free trade.[46] Faced with this situation, the economists formulated new ideological answers which opened the way for a new type of labour relations. Paul Leroy-Beaulieu thus developed a productivist theory of wages: when the level of education rises, the per capita productivity also rises, which in its turn leads to a rise in wages. This was in fact the best way to increase wages and reduce working hours. In other words, workers alone could bring about an improvement in their conditions and the capitalist system was not to be blamed.[47] In a more classical fashion, Anselme Batbié, who held the chair in political economy in the Law Faculty in Paris, reaffirmed the importance of education in 1867 in the following words: "The question of education underlies all social problems. This is not surprising because most of the evils arise from ignorance (...) If the relationship between capital and labour were understood better, antagonism between the two would be rare because the two adversaries would be separated by enlightenment." This amounted to endorsing the failure of the standard of living argument: social peace was not just a problem of well-being as everything depended of the attitude of workers as producers. Hence it is not surprising that for the first time the subject of the association between labour and capital, in the form of financial interest in the profits or the enterprise's turnover, came up. Three

[46] De Molinari (*Jde*, T. 14, 1869: 349); Dameth (1869: 20–21, 97); Reybaud (*Mémoires de l'Asmp*, T. 12, 1872). Comparison of his first impressions of the Creusot region (p. 567), Commentry (p. 604) and Fourchambault (p. 630), to those of the Loire and the Cévennes regions (p. 795), which he visited later. Regarding strikes: see Chevalier (*Jde*, T. 17, 1870: 82); Leroy-Beaulieu (1868: 47).

[47] Leroy-Beaulieu (1868: 37, 189). Regarding this point, see Spengler (1936: 758–759). Wolowski (*Jde*, T. 18, 1868: 127); Simon (1863: 127).

discussions were held in the Society of Political Economy in 1870 and the principle of profit-sharing was discussed from the point of view of social peace[48].

Demographic Conditions: Infant Mortality and Fertility

Due to unsatisfactory health conditions, infant mortality had not decreased in spite of economic progress. In fact it was considered to be alarming, not because of what it revealed of the health conditions of the working classes but because of the need, according to the head of the Statistics Bureau, to "protect in the country a large number of precious lives which would later add to its strength and security." Simon was even more explicit. Infant mortality was worrisome in view of the observed demographic growth: "everybody is obliged to admit that in England and in Prussia the population increases at a much higher rate than in our country (. . .). M. Brochard is right to warn that mortality among the new-born is one of the most active causes for this inferiority." Similarly, the social consequences of illegitimacy were analysed: due to their illegitimacy, these children were excluded from society and, according to Legoyt, they were turned into "enemies of the state". This moralistic viewpoint becomes meaningful when it is compared with the same author's observation that illegitimate births were particularly high among the working-class population in industrial departments like the Seine, the Rhône and the Bouches-du-Rhône. With the social climate in a state of severe deterioration, the demographic data acquired a very precise meaning for the "demoralisation" of the working classes constituted a social danger. Eighteen years later, Bertillon would be even more categorical: "it is in our interest to watch over the lives of all our children" for military, economic and cultural reasons. When the birth rate was at its lowest, each child became precious.[49]

The results of the 1866 census gave rise to several articles describing the psycho-sociological consequences of low fertility. Block in particular described brilliantly what Alfred Sauvy would later call the "Malthusian mentality": children in small families, who are sure to inherit a fortune, take pleasure in idleness or lack a spirit of enterprise which means economic stagnation for the country. This analysis was certainly a rationalisation and theorisation based on the counter-example of England where the law of primogeniture forced the younger sons to emigrate or earn their living by some other means. But it was clear that it was no longer possible to confine oneself to the boundaries of France and it was necessary to take into account the international consequences of low fertility. In 1867, Duval affirmed that the practice of coitus interruptus corresponded to the corruption of mores and a decline of society and he became an advocate of an increase in legitimate fertility. But

---

[48] Batbié (*Rddm*, June 1867: 981). The most significant contributions of the debates are in the *Sep (Jde*, T. 18, 1870: 129–136, 292–293, 441–462).

[49] Legoyt (*JSsP*, 1867: 236); Simon (*Mémoire de l'Asmp*, T. 17, 1869: 51). Also see the opinion of Levasseur and Cochin (Ibid.: 61). Brochard was a doctor who wrote a pamphlet to draw attention to the disastrous consequences of the common practice of engaging a wet-nurse for infants. Illegitimacy: Legoyt (*JSsP*, February 1867: 64, 76). (Bertillon, 1885: 26–35, 126).

apart from these moralistic considerations, often supported by economic arguments, the economists' pessimism was caused essentially by the labour-supply problem.[50] Leroy-Beaulieu's analyses are particularly interesting because his book *De l'état moral et intellectuel des populations ouvrières*, written to justify the accumulation of capital at a time when the social climate had deteriorated considerably, studies several economic issues from this angle. For example, he held that an increase in productivity as a means of restoring social peace could also compensate for the insufficient labour force. Leroy-Beaulieu was not unduly worried about the changes in the total population, but he drew an interesting conclusion from the standard of living argument, viz. the striking contrast between the workers who had become bourgeois and those who continued to multiply thoughtlessly. His conclusion deserves to be quoted: "Since the educated and capable workers systematically have no children or only one or two, this class does not increase and it is with difficulty that one can find new recruits among it; as a result of which it cannot meet the needs of artistic production which grows constantly. If this trend continues over a long period, there would be an abundance of labour in the lower levels of production but a lack of skilled workers in the higher levels. This is a step that goes directly against the progress of civilisation."[51] This astonishing remark is interesting for more than one reason. In the first place, Leroy-Beaulieu pointed out that the problem was not necessarily global but sectorial and there could be bottlenecks even if the overall labour supply was sufficient. Secondly, when he talked of "artistic production", he probably referred to the industries manufacturing luxury goods, such as the *articles de Paris*, which were very favourable to free trade. Finally, as we have seen, it was in these industries that there was upward social mobility among workers having few children. Given these conditions, it is easier to understand that Leroy-Beaulieu, as a free-trade economist, expressed his anxiety on this point while remaining optimistic about the overall demographic growth.

The economists' pessimism became even clearer when they compared France to its European neighbours. Between 1800 and 1850, the population of France had grown by 29% (from 27.3 to 35.8 millions), of Great Britain by 47% (from 15.25 to 22.5 millions) and of Germany by 42% (from 24.7 to 35.7 millions). However, it was only in the 1860s that some of them became aware of the relative weakness of the French demographic growth. The most spectacular change that occurred was in Legoyt, the head of the Statistics Bureau. In 1847, he expressed his satisfaction about the low rate of population growth because "the states where population is growing most rapidly, like England, Ireland, Prussia and Saxony are precisely those where poverty is making the most formidable progress." Eighteen years later, in 1865, the same demographic indicator, viz. the average annual growth rate, which had remained unchanged, gave rise to a radically different comment: "France and Austria rank the lowest (. . .). But whatever the reason for the considerable differences that we have just pointed out, they still demand our serious attention because

---

50 Block (*Jde*, T. 5, 1867: 425–426); Sauvy (1966, II: 171); Duval (*Ef*, 30 May 1867: 168 and 6 June 1867: 211).

51 1868: 99–100: "We have no reason to wish that the French population should become much larger." Quotation: 103.

in a span easy to calculate the present ranking and strength of the European states will be seriously disturbed as a result of the inequality (...) in the growth rate of their populations." We cannot go into the details of the strictly demographic analysis proposed by Legoyt, whose incoherences indicate a difficulty in assessing the political and socio-economic consequences of demographic data such as the age structure, infant and general mortality and legitimate fertility.[52] How can this complete reversal be explained?

Military Problems and Pacifism

As mentioned above, the moment the results of the 1866 census became known, the victory of Sadowa came as a real psychological shock to the French public. It also affected the group of economists and some of them perspicaciously described the changes in the European equilibrium: a great and powerful nation, so well organised and having a vast scientific and military potential, had just been born, an observation that gave rise to diverse reactions. According to Legoyt, the relatively low fertility in France implied a more favourable age structure from the military viewpoint: with an equivalent population, France could line up more men on the battlefield. This purely static analysis did not take into account the long-term effects: thirty years later, due to the aging of the generations that were meant to bear arms, fewer men would be available for recruitment and, what is even more important, the newer generations would be even less numerous. It is, to say the least, surprising that the head of the Statistical Bureau should not have thought of this argument. He was probably guided by his Bonapartist convictions and his anxiety not to go against the optimism prevalent in official circles. Other opinions were more nuanced. Thus Cochut was pleased about the qualitative improvement of the population: fewer men were exempted for reasons of physical disability, fewer recruits were illiterate; unfortunately "This is the type of progress that was sought twenty years ago; but despite this improvement there is still cause for sorrow and France still lacks the vitality that should have been the normal condition of a great nation." This contradiction could not have been explained more clearly: the optimum well-being had been achieved but not the optimum from the military viewpoint.[53]

---

[52] Legoyt (*Jde*, T. 17, 1847: 174–175). Same opinion expressed by Villermé (*Jde*, T. 14, 1846: 239) and A. Clément (*Jde*, T. 3, 1843: 95); Legoyt (*Jde*, T. 46, 1865: 378). Regarding the incoherences in Legoyt's writings, see the second part of the article which appeared in the *JSsP* (1867: 166, 169–172, 174–179, 221); Cochut (*Rddm*, Februray 1867: 653). Block's writings (1861 and 1869) are characteristic of this awareness; see Lavergne's opinion on Block's writings (*Séances et travaux de l'Asmp*, 1861, T. 5: 275–281).

[53] Sadowa and Prussia (*JSsP*, 1866: 282–284, unsigned article); de Laveleye (*Rddm*, February 1867: 769); Cherbuliez (*Rddm*, November 1869: 263); Cochut (*Rddm*, August 1866: 715); Legoyt (*JSsP*, 1867: 223). Quotation from Cochut (*Rddm*, February 1867: 654).

Faced with this contradiction, a strong pacifist tendency developed within the group. For example, Garnier gave the title "Europe at the Height of Barbarism" to his economic column which appeared on 14 July 1866. A committee was set up on 30 May 1867 to form a "Permanent and International League for Peace". The economists and industrialists who supported free trade such as Jean Dollfus dominated the committee. The pacifism of the economists can be explained by their defence of free-trade interests: war paralysed all trade-related activity, reduced the labour force and destroyed the economic infrastructure. Block believed that nationalism was responsible for all the wars during the preceding fifteen or twenty years. Some economists tried to estimate the economic and demographic consequences of the wars that had been fought since the beginning of the century. The final argument was that France would only benefit from the existence of a great industrial nation. And they had good reasons to put it forward: a free trade treaty had been signed with Zollverein.[54]

Emigration and Colonies

Unlike England, France had few colonies in 1848 apart from Algeria which it controlled only partially. Under the Second Empire, France had an active colonial policy: in 1858 a Ministry for Algeria and the colonies was set up. Faidherbe colonised Senegal, which between 1850 and 1860 became an important colony specialised in the production of groundnuts. In the Far East, Cambodia and Cochin China were conquered between 1859 and 1867. Finally, the island of Madagascar was annexed to France in 1868. This situation explains the revival of interest in the colonies during the 1860s as it was very frequently associated with emigration and consequently with the question of population. The previous generation of economists, under the influence of Jean-Baptiste Say and Rossi, were hostile to both emigration and colonisation for three reasons. The failure of the earlier colonial policy had amply demonstrated that the colonies were more costly than profitable and could not provide markets for France. In addition, colonisation was associated with the Colonial Pact, based on mercantilist principles that went against the very essence of the liberal economic doctrine based on the free circulation of goods and men. Finally, the first popularisers of Malthus in France went back to his argument that colonisation could not solve population problems because the space created by emigrants was filled immediately in accordance with the population principle.[55]

---

[54] Regarding the denunciation of war, see the articles by Reybaud and Block (*Jde*, T. 3, 1866: 5–12 et 249–257); Garnier (ibid.: 167); F. Passy (1869: 53); de Laveleye (*Rddm*, February 1867: 809). Estimates of the cost of war: Courcelle-Seneuil (*Jde*, T. 5, 1867: 185); also see F. Passy (1869: 39) and Block (1869: 73).

[55] Say (1832, III: 411–426); Rossi (lecture given in 1848, published in 1865. See I: 200–256 and II: 206–238).

From Anti-colonialism to Colonialism

Under the Second Empire, the question of colonisation gave rise to spectacular reversals of opinion, especially in the case of Molinari, Pautet, Garnier, Baudrillart and F. Passy. Let us consider the last. In 1855, he was against colonisation because of its demographic consequences for the country of origin and he criticised de Watteville, who claimed that the migrants should be skilled and hard-working: "Such men constitute the wealth of a country and it is difficult to understand the advantage of making them leave the country. As for the poor, it costs more to send them out than to feed them in their own country." This is an allusion to the "disastrous" results of the Decree of 23 September 1848. The Second Republic had spent 50 million francs on transporting colonisers and settling them in Algeria. By the end of the Second Republic, half of the 2,100 emigrants had come back. Passy therefore concluded that it was impossible to solve the social problem by colonisation. In 1867, his opinion was quite different. Though he continued to declare that no country had ever profited by its colonies, he admitted that is was necessary to have reliable markets: "The canon is not the best way of opening up markets. I certainly admit that we should want civilisation to prevail over barbarism; but (...) it is not through terror, it is through enlightenment, through capital, through example, that this result must be obtained."[56] These humanitarian justifications are undoubtedly the forerunners of the rhetoric of the white man's burden, but henceforth the very principle of colonisation, whatever its methods, was accepted. F. Passy's about-face can be explained by two factors. In the first place, he had taken part in the debate on the decadence of France, a direct proof of which is a lecture he gave in 1867. But to fully explain his reversal, it is necessary to refer to his deep involvement in the pacifist movement: faced by growing perils, this pacifist, then the Secretary General of the Committee that set up the International League for Peace, did not fail to contrast the advantages of colonisation with the harmful consequences of war: "That is not (...) true patriotism, true ambition; that is not how one can occupy a larger part of the globe (...). Populating the numerous countries in which the human race has not yet set foot, calling for the flowering of intellectual and moral life of these fellow-beings whom we call barbarians (...) these are the victories that remain to be achieved."[57]

Emigration and Colonisation

Quite conceivably, the emigration problem could have been treated *independently* of the colonial question. From the Malthusian viewpoint, for example, emigration is considered to be the wrong solution for relieving the excessive pressure of popula-

---

[56] (1855: 171, note). He referred to Spain and France but was silent about England. Also see (1867: 13).

[57] *Conférence sur la paix et la guerre donnée à l'Ecole de Médecine de Paris* (1867: 47).

tion on resources. However, even an orthodox Malthusian like Garnier justified his hostility to emigration, not in Malthusian terms but by citing the evils of the colonial system inspired by protectionism. But it was more of a rear-guard action because the objection did not have a valid reason any more. The Law of 3 July 1861 abolished the Colonial Pact and the colonies became open markets and a source of raw materials for metropolitan France, while the introduction of free trade made it necessary to think in international terms. As a result, the argument changed as competition in trade became more difficult. Colonisation made it possible to open up privileged markets at a time when colonial politics and expansion gained an unprecedented importance and emigration became the means and colonisation the goal to be attained. And when they were compared to the slow demographic growth, the two intertwined themes of colonisation and emigration inevitably raised questions about the validity of Malthusianism. Due to excessive prudential restraint, the population of France grew too slowly to satisfy the needs of colonisation: "In France, the problem is not one of keeping a better watch on oneself; perhaps it is done excessively, if we take into account the balance to be maintained between the territorial influences (. . .). All things taken into consideration, up to now there has been no shortage of land, but rather a shortage of men, and on this point as in everything else, they must complete their mission within the time assigned to them."[58]

Attention must be drawn to some factors which can explain the revival of colonisation. Reybaud referred to "territorial influences". In his *Histoire de l'émigration européenne, asiatique et africaine au XIXème siècle* Duval, chief editor of the *L'Economiste français* which had taken up the cause of the French settlers in Algeria, was much more explicit: "While France stagnates with its 36 million inhabitants, England is nearing 30 millions, and, advancing at a quick pace, it will have equalled and even overtaken France in a few years whose number can be easily calculated. During this time, it will have populated fifty colonies which will add to its power and the Anglo-Saxon race will have taken possession of half the globe. On the day of the fight, it is inevitable that France will succumb due to a great inequality of forces. Patriotism will therefore suffer due to the stagnation of French population."[59] This fervent populationist analysis focuses attention on the problem that preoccupied the economists who were in favour of colonisation: how to oppose British imperialism, which was far ahead of France in the domain of colonisation? Algeria seemed to be a major asset: situated on the opposite shore of the Mediterranean, it would be an excellent base for extending French influence in the entire Mediterranean basin and counterbalancing England's predominance. In 1867, during a meeting of the Senate, Chevalier declared, "We need to turn Algeria into a warehouse for European and

[58] Quotation: J. Garnier (*Jde*, T. 15, 1869: 131); Reybaud (*Rddm*, April 1868: 987); Chevalier (*Ef*, 5 October 1869: 318).

[59] It appeared in 1862; quotation: 445. The same opinion was expressed by Chevalier (*Annales du Sénat*, 1863, II: 290 and *Ef*, 5 October 1865: 318).

American trade with the rest of the African continent", closely preceding Prévost-Paradol's *La France nouvelle* (1868) and his famous pre-Gaullist view.[60]

It is therefore not very surprising that the question of "acclimatising" Europeans to Algeria was raised quite often. For example, Bertillon observed in 1863 that after a period of thirty-five years of excessive deaths, mortality seemed to go down and more births were being registered.[61] Algeria held out another advantage: the "cotton famine", which followed the American war of secession, made the free-traders aware how dependent French industry was on countries producing various raw materials: "If the cultivation (of cotton) is sufficiently developed in Africa to offer serious competition to America, our colonisation will have done a lot for setting European industry free." Some industrialists in favour of free trade like Jean Dollfus, the leader of the *Société industrielle de Mulhouse*, attempted to spread cotton cultivation in Algeria. Generally speaking, the introduction of free trade and industrial development led the economists to advocate colonial expansion for creating new markets for French manufactures and also as a source of raw materials for French industry. And England, a constant point of reference and the principal rival of France, was often at the centre of the argument: "Has anyone imagined what England would be today if it did not have any colonies (. . .) Great Britain's industrial development and Holland's trade would have been stifled in their early stages if they had not been able to spread beyond the narrow confines of Europe and find inexhaustible resources for expansion in America and Asia."[62]

These circumstances cast light on the reasons why the normal demographic growth recorded by the 1866 census seemed unsatisfactory: the population of France was no longer sufficient to defend the country and satisfy its needs as regards labour and colonial expansion. The peculiarity of the period lies in the growth of a pessimism having two sources, domestic and international: the question of social peace was reopened with the revival of class consciousness among the workers while international problems raised their head suddenly. An optimistic synthesis would be possible only when domestic problems prevailed. And such a synthesis became impossible once the contradiction between various economic, military and colonial needs became apparent.

Malthusianism and the Bourgeois Ideology

Let us cast a quick backward glance at the period from 1840 to 1870 and take a look at the study of ideas on population before coming to a conclusion on the

---

60 Chevalier (*Annales du Sénat,* 1867: 167); Prévost-Paradol, 1868: 415–416 and 419.

61 Bertillon (*JSsP*, 1863: 168–180). Legoyt (*JSsP* 1865: 7–13, 93–105). Outside the group: de Quatrefages (*Rddm*, April 1861: 635–731; Boudin, *JSsP*, 1860: 30–50 and 121–131, and his two books (1852: 51–56 and 1860: 33–41).

62 Batbié (1866, II: 316–317). Regarding Dollfus, see Fohlen (1956: 347–355). Quotations taken from Lavollée (*Rddm*, February 1863: 883, 905).

central place of Malthusianism in the ideology of the French economists and its subsequent decline. The period lends itself particularly to a comparison of facts and ideas, firstly because the writers who have been studied here had at their disposal a large amount of factual demographic data, which gave their doctrine a firm base in reality, unlike the utopian socialists whose writings were not so well documented. Better still, secondary sources enable us to assess to what extent their writings deviate from reality as we have interpreted them on the ideological level. On the other hand, we have to deal with a veritable school of thought and not isolated writers. Consequently, the dynamics of ideas and facts proved to be much more effective than if the intellectual exchanges had depended exclusively on scholarly reviews. In such a lively group, the assimilation of facts into the doctrine and doctrinal modifications under the pressure of facts were naturally much faster. Historically speaking, the period was rich and also conducive to the formulation of doctrines. Industrialisation, though it was on a modest scale as compared to the subsequent decades, caused as profound an upheaval in the social sphere as the revolution of 1789 which brought about a complete transformation in the ideological and political framework. And just as industrialisation under the Second Empire was an integral part of the official social policy and doctrine, it is not surprising that the group's ideological activities regarding the workers' question was stimulated by it. As for free trade which triumphed after 1860 thanks to a series of bilateral treaties, we have seen it being used fruitfully as a social doctrine. But it was abolished once and for all by the Méline Law of 11 January 1892: the free-trade experiment imposed by the imperial power against the wishes of the majority of business circles had lasted for thirty-two years and the economists had lost their *raison d'être*. It is not surprising, therefore, that after 1870 the group weakened and saw its influence waning. Top-level thinkers like Emile Levasseur and Paul Leroy-Beaulieu distanced themselves from the group; other trends appeared, particularly the one which led to the creation of the *Société d'économie sociale* and from 1896 onwards the National Alliance for the Growth of French Population having Bertillon at its helm stood out. Finally, at the end of the 1890s, Gide and Gonnard questioned the pre-eminence of the *Journal des Economistes* through the pages of the *Revue d'économie politique*.

As compared to the following decades, these thirty years lend themselves particularly well to an ideological interpretation of the relationship between facts and ideas regarding population for two final reasons. On the one hand, in the middle of the nineteenth century demography had not yet acquired the status of an independent science and still came under economic theory as well as social doctrine. Facts relating to population were therefore naturally interpreted in economic and social terms. The subsequent progress of statistics, at a time when the populationist ideology established itself with much fanfare, would accelerate the separation of demographic theory from demographic doctrine. Like other social sciences, demography gradually acquired some measure of "scientific" autonomy. Certainly the demographic argument, now considered scientific, would be used in debates on doctrine, but the extraordinary limpidity of the discourse on population disappeared. On the other hand, the mid-nineteenth century is characterised by a rare ideological transparency, which considerably facilitates research. In most cases it is enough to allow the economists to speak. The trauma caused by the Commune and the rise of the *nouvelles couches sociales* so dear to Gambetta would change the shape of the social discourse: it would become more prudent and therefore more opaque, and the victorious conscience of the liberal bourgeoisie would become more discreet at a time when Marxist criticism would denounce the mechanisms of the dominant ideology.

In a situation so favourable to the formulation of a socio-demographic doctrine solidly rooted in facts, what was the position of Malthusianism in the bourgeois ideology? Even on a strictly demographic level, the economists showed a certain amount of originality in relation to Malthusianism: their arguments were based on a twofold conviction, viz. the scientific validity of their analyses of individual behaviour and their profound belief in the universality of bourgeois values. If individual foresightedness was socially moral and praiseworthy, it was because it was practised by the bourgeoisie. The bourgeois behaved rationally because they managed to maintain a satisfactory balance between their resources and their expenditure by controlling their fertility. This "proof" of the rationality of bourgeois behaviour strengthened in return their belief in the universality of bourgeois values. By making reason triumph over the procreative instinct, bourgeois behaviour conformed to the natural and beneficial order of things which governs the physical world and human society. That is why workers were told in 1848 that foresight was the only way to escape poverty. Formulas and words should not mislead us for, no matter to what class they belonged, the "peasant", the "industrial worker" and the "capitalist" were above all regarded as free and equal citizens and, thanks to the revolution of 1789, privilege could no longer prevent them from pursuing a productive activity. When a social crisis of the magnitude of the one in 1848 broke out, it was essential to reaffirm the solidarity between the bourgeoisie and the proletariat, and the simplest thing for the economists was to insist on a strictly legalistic argument even though they themselves recognised the economic and social differences between individuals. The same logic underlies the accusation against the protectionists that they were responsible for the workers' sufferings. But this position was ambiguous because it meant identifying the workers with the general interest as opposed to the liberal assumption that consumers embodied the general interest. This ambiguity was soon removed: the revolution of 1848 obliged them to take up the defence of the bourgeoisie and abandon their quarrel with the protectionists. However their belief in free trade led them to put forward an argument that was promising and perfectly coherent with the liberal axiom, namely "cheapness of goods". It reappeared under the Second Empire in a more sophisticated form as the standard of living argument.

Under the Second Empire, the distortion between social facts and ideology was quite striking: industrial labourers gave rise to a literature whose volume does not match up to their number, especially as compared to the rural masses. The new situation created by the development of the factory system inspired such an abundant literature on industrial workers because it was important to assess this major structural change and, even more important, to interpret it. It could be said that the economists concentrated on the workers because social problems had been solved and interpreted satisfactorily. But this is only partly true: for various reasons, the rural masses inspired a literature that was far from negligible. Firstly, they could not ignore this social group which represented three quarters of the French population. Secondly, the escalation of the rural exodus gave rise to anxiety because it increased the number of industrial labourers while reducing the number of agricultural workers. Thirdly, as a logical outcome of the spread of the communication network, the economists had to consider the possibilities offered by the opening of the national market at a time when traditional small-scale production was swept out by industrialisation. Fourthly, a simple comparison between the living conditions of urban industrial workers and peasants ended in speculation on the social and political stability of the two groups. Finally, universal suffrage was introduced in France for the first time in 1848. It was a new situation which was worth reflecting on even though the 1849 elections brought to light the widespread conservatism of the rural population. It is therefore unrealistic to maintain that the economists concentrated only on industrial labourers in their writings. It would appear instead that the arguments they developed were often quite original because the growth of the factory system was a unique and unprecedented development.

On the contrary, the economists sometimes stressed the ideas developed about peasants during the period prior to the 1840s, as for example in the case of small holdings. But they also strove to integrate some socio-economic factors like the rural exodus whose magnitude was in no way comparable to the growth of the factory system. Nevertheless, these two themes are not independent of each other. The analyses of the causes of the rural exodus present a bias which can be explained only by taking into account the arguments related to property. It is easy to explain why the economists were so determined to refute Malthus on the question of small holdings. These liberal bourgeois were writing at the end of a period marked by a series of attempts to return to the inheritance system of the Ancien Régime as several bills were tabled in the 1820s, during the Restoration, to put an end to the equal division of property. They believed that equal division of property was essentially a victory of the bourgeoisie over the aristocracy and the very symbol of the revolution of 1789. The insistence on the demographic consequences of small land holdings should therefore be interpreted not from the viewpoint of a fertility theory but as an indication of an ideologically fundamental debate: if Malthus was right, then small holdings were a factor of overpopulation that favoured the constitution of a rural proletariat and weakened the possibility of social peace in the rural areas. The defence of this keystone of the bourgeois ideology, therefore took precedence over Malthusianism. In other words, Malthusianism, unlike during the years of the revolutionary turmoil, was no longer indispensable for the bourgeois ideology.

It is indeed surprising that the very specialists who claimed to be orthodox Malthusians should recommend prudential restraint to workers although Malthus had always rejected prudential restraint at the doctrinal level and strongly advocated moral restraint. Actually, it was the anxiety for immediate results that drove the economists, who were fully aware of the contradiction: how to condemn, on the one hand, the excessive fertility of the workers and, on the other, praise moral restraint, that is to say the absence of any control over fertility after marriage? The implications of this doctrinal divergence deserve to be stressed: the main point was that the workers should control their fertility following the example of the bourgeoisie. When it came to the crunch, the means hardly mattered, they could, if the need arose, be "prudential" and therefore immoral. What was offered to the workers, who were the victims of the social system, was the possibility of escaping their miserable condition by emulating bourgeois behaviour. But there are deeper reasons for the ideological decline of Malthusianism. It was in a way a defensive doctrine because it tirelessly affirmed that the demand for goods could not exceed their supply. During the1850s and 1860s, the economists, under the influence of Saint-Simon, formulated a radically different doctrine based on their belief in industrialisation, which was in perfect accord with the official social doctrine of the Second Empire. Despite the poverty of the working class, the industry held out unlimited possibilities of well-being thanks to mechanisation which permitted low-cost production and mass consumption. The standard of living argument provided the bridge that was missing earlier between demography and economics, but at the cost of giving up the Malthusian dogma of the need for individual responsibility.

Finally, due to new domestic and international preoccupations, the end of the Second Empire can be looked upon as a period characterized by a revival of mercantilism, since the French population ran the risk of being insufficient to satisfy the requirements of labour, the needs of military recruitment and to ensure France's influence in the international domain. Malthusianism certainly had its uses in the debate on social peace. Due to the impossibility of reaching an ideologically satisfactory synthesis of the contradictions mentioned above, and because the problem of social peace ceased to be the driving force behind the evolution of ideas on population after 1870, the decline of Malthusianism was inevitable. The end of the Second Empire was in fact a key period during which several components of the Third Republic's bourgeois ideology came of age. A couple of decades later, when the run on colonies escalated and the colonial policy became a matter of national interest, the ideologues were able to get away from the contradiction which consisted of hoping that a low demographic growth would simultaneously populate the mother country and the colonies by advocating a firmly populationist policy aimed at increasing the birth rate.

Annex: The Causes of the Rural Exodus

All through the nineteenth century, there were a large number of temporary migrations and Chatelain's thesis, published posthumously (1967), describes their extreme diversity. Unfortunately, it is impossible to assess the magnitude of the permanent rural exodus, since the distinction between the rural and urban population appeared only in 1846. It is generally believed that though it was not very common during the first half of the nineteenth century,[63] some French departments

[63] Pouthas (1956) should be used carefully. Chevalier (1950: 23) underlines the weaknesses in the analyses of intercensal periods. Toutain (1963: 53–54), has attempted to establish a complete series

did lose a considerable part of their population. But these departments were situated in mountainous or semi-mountainous regions (Ain, Jura, Basses-Alpes et Hautes-Alpes, Cantal, Lozère, Ariège, Ardèche and Puy-de-Dôme) or in regions where the birth rate was too high as compared to their resources (Bas-Rhin, Meurthe, Moselle, Meuse and Creuse), or, finally, agricultural regions (Haute-Saône, Saône-et-Loire, Aveyron, Lot, Aude and Drôme).[64] Although it is not possible to overlook the migratory movements of a permanent nature which took place in the first half of the century because the towns were growing even as they generally suffered from an excess of deaths as compared to births, the 1850s and 1860s were quite unusual. The rural exodus became a permanent feature under the Second Empire when there was a large-scale decline in the population which cannot be explained by the natural deficit. In fact, the departments which recorded a *decline* in their total population between 1851 and 1872 continued to have a natural *positive* balance. Unfortunately and quite disappointingly, the recent *Histoire de la population française* does not take sides between contemporary specialists on the rural exodus, nor does it propose any conclusive contribution to the debate on the causes of the rural exodus. We may also note the contradictions between the different chapters of volume 3 of this collective work.[65] So what could have been the real causes for the permanent rural exodus?

It appears that the traditional temporary and seasonal migrations became permanent. Chevalier gives the examples of the Cantal, Creuse and Haute-Vienne regions while Chatelain points out that the workers employed for building the railways migrated permanently only after 1848, and he believes that on the whole migrations tended to acquire a permanent nature only after this date. Finally, Armengaud underlines the decisive importance of the crisis that occurred between 1846 and 1851 and reminds us that in spite of an excess of births, the rural population decreased while there was only a slight increase in the total population.[66] Subsequently, rural population continued to decline, going down from 26.7 to 24.8 millions between 1846 and 1872 (Table 3.3).

It is generally agreed that the French countryside was overpopulated.[67] Given these conditions, why is it that the rural population did not decline earlier? How can it be explained that the migrations became permanent only after the middle of the nineteenth century? These questions give rise to others. Rural crafts, which

---

on the basis of various estimates and on the reconstruction of French population by Bourgeois-Pichat.

[64] Pouthas, 1956: 126–128. According to Chatelain, in the Alps and the Massif Central, for example, the high birth rate was responsible for the temporary migrations in the first half of the century (1967: I, 92–95).

[65] Poussou, Lepetit, Courgeau, Dupâquier (1988: 167–227). Regarding the causes of the rural exodus, see p. 184. As for contradictions see for example maps 125 on p. 147 and 79 on p. 191 relating to the natural deficit between 1851 and 1872.

[66] Chevalier, 1951: 217–219; Chatelain, 1967a: 16–17 and 1967b: II, 1105. Armengaud, 1993: 223–224.

[67] Vidalenc, 1970: 38, 44, 139, 184, 293, etc.; Leuillot, 1959: II, 13, 31–32, 44–47; Armengaud 1993: 224–225; Agulhon, 1976: 66–79.

Table 3.3 Evolution of the rural population (1846–1872)

Census year	Population (in thousands)	% of total population
1846	26,750	75.6
1851	26,650	74.5
1856	26,190	72.7
1861	26,600	71.1
1866	26,470	69.5
1872	24,890	68.9

brought in extra earnings for the peasants, had contributed to the overpopulation of the countryside. Their decline began during this period. So was it a cause or a consequence of the rural exodus? Besides, what were the effects of the introduction of free trade in 1860? Finally, in a country with a low demographic growth, agriculture and industry necessarily compete with each other for labour. So what effect did the industrial expansion have on the rural exodus? All these questions are important because they lead to the debate on the "push" and "pull" factors.

It appears that there was an increase in productivity in the agricultural sector on account of technical advances such as the draining of swamps (in Dombes between 1863 and 1867 and in the Landes region thanks to the laws of 1857 and 1860), irrigation (in the South of France), clearing of lands (in Poitou after 1850) or, on the contrary, reforestation (in Sologne and Corbières), replacement of the swing-plough by the Dombasle plough, introduction of threshing-machines run on steam (81 machines in 1852 as opposed to 6,000 in 1873), use of natural phosphates and decrease of fallow lands. The higher yields of wheat, rye, sugar beet and especially the vineyards in the South of France bore witness to the advances in agriculture.[68]

This rise in productivity brought in larger incomes (agricultural rent, profits as well as wages increased under the Second Empire, although with a marked contrast between different regions), which can probably explain the following paradox: there was a continual complaint about the "shortage of hands" even though the figures do not indicate the existence of a bottleneck. If there was a shortage, it may at best have encouraged mechanization. As seen above, the final product rose considerably during the Second Empire and particularly during the years 1855 to 1864 and the final product per living person in the agricultural sector as well as the final product per active farmer increased substantially.[69]

Though agricultural productivity increased substantially during this period, it does not necessarily mean that the rural exodus was triggered by the freeing of labour. If the *same* rural population becomes more efficient and produces more, then the final product increases *faster* than the per capita product without stimulating a

[68] Regarding technical advances, see Specklin, 1976: 194–209; regarding results, Laurent, 1993: 671–697 (the figures given here correspond in most cases to those given by Laurent for the period from 1815 to 1880 and 1840 to 1880). The 1946 *Annuaire statistique* brought out by Insee gives the annual series.

[69] Table 2, based on Toutain, 1961.

rural exodus. A comparison of the growth rates shows that the final product increased faster under the July Monarchy than the two indices of productivity (see Table 3.1 above). On the other hand, under the Second Empire, the difference between growth rates declined initially and was reversed towards its end. This implies that the rural exodus checked the growth of the final product from 1850 onwards while technical progress continued to be translated into substantial productivity gains and freed the labour force suffering from disguised unemployment.

How to assimilate into this analysis the rural crafts which allowed peasants to earn an extra income during the off-season and could have helped to hold back in the countryside the labour that had become redundant due to technical advances? On the one hand, domestic crafts, for example in the Rhone valley, were one of the reasons for chronic overpopulation.[70] On the other hand, the crisis of 1846–1851 was, in Pouthas's words, a "liquidation crisis" which affected both rich and poor regions. In the rich regions, traditional industries, which had been a source of extra income, disappeared (small iron foundries in the South-West and the small-scale textile industry in Normandy) while the progress of communications encouraged regional specialisation (cattle-breeding and monoculture) in Normandy, Midi-Languedoc, Burgundy, etc. In the poor regions (mountainous areas and East Aquitaine), a veritable exodus of people took place because of a permanent breakdown in the demo-economic equilibrium.[71]

Thus under the Second Empire, the rise in agricultural productivity was accompanied by the disappearance of entire sectors of rural crafts. The problem here is one of causality. It can be claimed that the two changes were independent of each other, in which case the free trade treaty with England in 1860 must be regarded as an exogenous shock for the system. It encouraged greater concentration on the metallurgy and the textile industries which directly affected the rural crafts and had nothing to with the advances in agriculture. Conversely, it should be noted that the treaty of 1860 and the following treaties led to greater specialisation in agriculture by creating a new line of exports (sugar, wine and spirits, potatoes, butter, cheese and cattle), generally to Great Britain, and sometimes even by reviving inter-regional trade: the less rich areas supplied products to regions specialising in exports which were in a position to buy them by selling their own products to foreign countries.[72]

So it is doubtful if these two developments were really independent. It could be said that the disappearance of rural crafts was not the consequence but the *cause*

---

[70] Vidalenc, 1970: 299; Laurent explains that they continued till the middle of the nineteenth century due to the density of the population (1993: 746).

[71] Rich regions: Laurent, 1993: 698–712. Poor regions: Pouthas, 1956: 61. Corbin, 1975: I, 580.

[72] Regarding this point, see G. Désert, 1976: 233–234. Thus the export of butter and cheese rose from 25 million francs in 1859 to 78 millions in 1869. On an average, 1,540 hectolitres of wine were exported every year between 1855 and 1859 and 2,940 between 1865 and 1869. The inhabitants of Aveyron were able to sell "more fattened bulls to Languedoc because the prosperity of this region rose due to the growing export of wine. They began to send to the Parisian market 'choice products' from their cattle farms because the pastures of Normandy and the northern departments sold their own products to England." (quote p. 234).

of progress in the agricultural sector since the peasants decided to give up their crafts for good and compensated the loss of extra income resulting from the crisis and the opening of borders by improving their agricultural yield. However, many reasons militate against this viewpoint. Firstly, even if a part of the family labour were available, it would have been possible to increase the productivity of only some types of crops, for instance market gardening. It is in fact difficult to see children contributing effectively to improve the yield of one hectare of wheat. It is also difficult to imagine a peasant giving up his craft to devote all the labour at his disposal (himself, his wife, his children and, in rare cases, a helper) to a purely agricultural activity. In overpopulated regions where peasant families lived on the brink of poverty, this meant the immediate loss of an indispensable resource in the hope of an increase in resources at some future date. Finally, farming and crafts were not practised simultaneously, but they followed each other on a seasonal basis. It is therefore much more likely that agricultural progress was the cause and not the consequence of the decline of rural crafts.

This model is valid only with regard to family holdings where the decision to leave the land for good is determined by both the lack of additional resources and increased productivity. This was the case with small and medium-sized holdings farmed by their owners or through tenant-farmers or sharecroppers, which were predominant under the Second Empire. In 1882, the size of three quarters of the 5.5 million land holdings was between 1 and 10 hectares. Similarly, this model assumes the absence of a rural proletariat, which by itself could have provided the numbers for the rural exodus while the tradition of family crafts would have been maintained. But in 1862 there were hardly 1,400,000 day labourers out of a rural population of 26 millions.

Increases in productivity were therefore obtained by the spread of new agricultural techniques. It should be remembered that these techniques were developed at a time when agricultural prices were rising, when the advance of the means of communication made the marketing of products easier. Thus the possibility of transporting wheat from surplus areas rapidly to those suffering from shortages contributed to the disappearance of traditional reflexes. Thanks to the development of artificial grasslands, the areas devoted to pasture lands kept increasing while the area of fallow lands decreased and the area of ploughed fields remained stagnant.[73] The centuries-old fear of food shortages disappeared because it was now possible to buy food. In these conditions, the increased productivity and the growing demand for agricultural products, both at the national and international levels, brought about the collapse of the rural crafts with the crisis of 1846–1851 with the trade treaties acting as catalysts. It became possible from then on to maintain the family earnings at the same level without having to depend on an extra source of income.

It now remains to define the role of industrialisation. The development of railways or the wages offered by industries in towns and cities could not be considered

---

[73] Toutain, 1961: 212–215. Sorlin wrote regarding Brittany and the Vendée area: "towards 1860... turning fertile land into pasture no longer seemed a heresy" (1969: 33).

as the cause of the rural exodus because, had it been so, the exodus would have been permanent from the time industrialisation started in the 1830s and 1840s. But, as we have already observed, this did not happen. When the land could produce more with fewer hands, it "released" its human reserves and migration, until then temporary, became permanent. The case of the Limousin region is interesting: though the migrations continued to be temporary until 1880, it was so only because of the obsolete economic structures. It is therefore unlikely that the "shortage of hands" caused by the demand for labour in industry led to the mechanisation of agriculture as Désert claims.[74] This claim is not compatible with the existence of rural overpopulation, which this author admits. The socio-economic result of overpopulation is the continuation of disguised unemployment and not mechanisation which, according to contemporary economists, brought down the number of jobs. So it is necessary to admit that industry actually only offered an outlet for the surplus labour which the rural areas could not hold back any longer.

These are the facts that we must keep in mind to appreciate the analyses of the rural exodus by the economists.

[74] 1976: 223–227. On populating land, see Aghulon: 66 and following pages. On the importance of the push factor, see Aghulon: 80–86, who does not explain why temporary migrations became permanent.

Chapter 4
The Malthusian Trap: The Failure of Proudhon

A Thinker Who Cannot Be Classified

All through the nineteenth century, the two progressions of Malthus' *Essay on the Principle of Population* proved to be a dangerous trap for the social reformers nurtured by the heritage of the Enlightenment and the French revolution of 1789. It was believed that the pressure of population on the means of subsistence acted like a noose that becomes tighter when population grew too fast and all attempts to redistribute wealth in a more egalitarian manner came to nought. Such is the meaning of the allegory of the banquet figuring in the second edition of the *Essay* published in 1803 which was later dropped by Malthus because it seemed inhuman. "A man who is born into a world already possessed, if he cannot get subsistence from his parents on whom he has a just demand, and if the society does not want his labour, has no claim of right to the smallest portion of food, and, in fact, has no business to be where he is. At nature's mighty feast there is no vacant cover for him. She tells him to be gone, and will quickly execute her own orders, if he does not work upon the compassion of some of her guests. If these guests get up and make room for him, other intruders immediately appear demanding the same favour. The report of a provision for all that come, fills the hall with numerous claimants. The order and harmony of the feast is disturbed, the plenty that before reigned is changed into scarcity; and the happiness of the guests is destroyed by the spectacle of misery and dependence in every part of the hall, and by the clamorous importunity of those, who are justly enraged at not finding the provision which they had been taught to expect. The guests learn too late their error, in counter-acting those strict orders to all intruders, issued by the great mistress of the feast, who, wishing that all guests should have plenty, and knowing she could not provide for unlimited numbers, humanely refused to admit fresh comers when her table was already full."[1]

---

[1] A summarised translation by Joseph Garnier was available in the Guillaumin Edition of French version of Malthus' *Essay*. This is probably the translation that was read by Proudhon and most of his contemporaries. The allegory is quoted in full by Proudhon in his *Système des contradictions économiques*, I: 83.

Y. Charbit, *Economic, Social and Demographic Thought in the XIXth Century*,
DOI 10.1007/978-1-4020-9960-1_4, © Springer Science+Business Media B.V. 2009

This allegory caught the attention of Pierre Joseph Proudhon (1809–1865) who wrote at a time when the Malthusian doctrine and theory were accepted almost without question.[2] Like many other English radicals (particularly William Godwin, Thomas Paine, William Cobbett and Robert Southey) or French Utopians and Socialists (Charles Fourier, Pierre Leroux and Sismondi), Proudhon tried in vain to refute Malthus. This chapter analyses the causes of this failure because Proudhon's case is particularly interesting. Unlike other French critics, he refers to Malthus and the population problem all through his work. His own theory is explained in Chapter XIII of *Système des contradictions économiques* (1846), but important elements of his system, both doctrinal and theoretical, can also be found in his famous opuscule *Qu'est-ce que la propriété ?* (1840) as well as in *Carnets* (1843–1850), *Les Malthusiens* (1848), *De la Justice dans la Révolution et dans l'Eglise* (1858), *La guerre et la paix* (1861) and, finally, in his posthumous and incomplete work *De la Capacité politique des classes ouvrières* (1865). Proudhon's writings provide enough material to analyse the difficulties experienced by anti-Malthusians in escaping the malthusian trap, but one difficulty arises immediately.

As several commentators and specialists – even the most well-disposed – have remarked, his work eludes the most stringent analysis and it is difficult to circumscribe his thoughts because of the diversity of his views.[3] He was first and foremost a formidable polemist who attacked all his contemporaries, whom he criticised in general for their *esprit de système*. Socialists, revolutionaries, liberal economists and, finally, newspapers, which competed with those managed by him, were all victims of his scathing criticism.[4] Secondly, Proudhon was fascinated by statistics and economics. Like the classical economists he had read and sometimes commented on at length, he believed that population, and more precisely "population balance", was essentially a branch of economics. That he accepted this static vision without any hesitation partly explains his inability to extricate himself from the Malthusian model. However it is necessary to keep in mind a whole set of factors. Writing with his customary self-satisfaction, he says, "I am taking up science at the point where J.B. Say left it. Nothing important, nothing scientific has been achieved by his successors."[5] And when in December 1847 he was offered the editorship of the future *Journal de la navigation intérieure*, because of his experience in managing an inland navigation company, he observed in his *Carnets*, "It could be considered

[2] We have used what is known as the Marcel Rivière edition of *Oeuvres complètes de Pierre Joseph Proudhon* to which must be added the three volumes of his *Carnets*, brought out by the same publisher. Fréville has devoted one chapter to Proudhon (1956: 222–229). Also see: Spengler, 1936: 751–753.

[3] For instance, Augé-Laribé and Droz: "A piece of writing by Proudhon defies analysis", admits Augé-Laribé in his *Introduction* (see: 30) to *De la célébration du dimanche* (a dissertation for which he was conferred an award in 1839 by the Academy of Besançon).

[4] Successively, *Le Peuple*, *Le Représentant du Peuple* and finally *La Voix du Peuple*.

[5] *Carnets*, VIII: 100. Regarding his admiration for A. Smith see *Création de l'ordre dans l'humanité*, 292–301.

my practical speciality just as economics is my scholarly speciality."[6] It must be remembered that for him economics was the concretisation of philosophy. He further insisted that it was not possible "to understand anything about economics if one does not know or has not guessed the development of philosophical thought."[7] This is because Proudhon believed himself to be a philosopher more than anything else. So, when he published *La création de l'ordre dans l'humanité ou principes d'économie politique* in 1843, he "expected to be ranked as a thinker forever."[8] His hopes were fulfilled when, in 1845, the German socialist Karl Grün paid him a compliment by calling him the French Feuerbach. In the same year, the Russian socialist Alexandre Herzen credited him with grounding social action on speculative thinking, on a new philosophy.[9]

Being a polemist, philosopher and economist at one and the same time, his writing is characterised by frequent changes of level: he moves from empirical observations to fragmentary analyses based on what he retained of classical economics, to arguments on social philosophy or even purely moral considerations. Although it is impossible to ignore the protean nature Proudhon's thought processes, it is necessary to point out, and that precisely is the purpose of this chapter, that his refutation of Malthus on the basis of a radical social criticism fails to achieve its ends because of a very conservative moral code, which led him to frame astonishing doctrinal propositions regarding population. For the sake of convenience, we will begin with his demographic criticism of Malthus, since Proudhon often discussed the two progressions. Further, his views on production growth are shown to be at the basis of his anti-Malthusian economic theory, political economy ultimately leading to social criticism and moral philosophy. We will conclude with a brief comparison with Marx, who, unlike Proudhon, was able to avoid the Malthusian trap.

The Two Progressions

The Early Carnets: To Be or Not to Be a Malthusian?

While reading Droz, Rossi, Buret, Destut de Tracy, Simondi, Godwin, between 1840 and 1844, Proudhon inevitably encountered their own comments on Malthus'

---

[6] *Carnets*, VI: 173. He considered it as an "echo of *Peuple*", his own newspaper, ideal for propagating his ideas that would put him "on the same level as the bourgeois aristocracy and face to face with power."

[7] *Carnets*, VIII: 19. Also: "it is impossible to resolve even one of its problems if one is not convinced that the same solution can be applied to religious problems regarding the existence of God and the immortality of the soul."

[8] Quoted by Cuvillier, *Introduction* à *De la création de l'ordre dans l'humanité*, 8 and 26–27. See, for instance, Puech, *Introduction* à *Philosophie du progrès*, 16–20 and Cuvillier, *Introduction* à *De la création de l'ordre dans l'humanité*, 19–21. Scherer, Sorel, Halévy were highly critical of Proudhon while Renouvier, Bouglé, Fouillée, Sainte-Beuve had a more positive attitude.

[9] Cuvillier, *Introduction* à *De la création de l'ordre dans l'humanité*, 28–31.

Essay. In approving or rejecting these writers' opinions on Malthus, Proudhon inevitably revealed his own.[10] Although one could expect Proudhon to be a harsh critic of Malthus and his followers, he on the contrary sometimes backed Malthusians against his opponents, for instance approving of Rossi: "Mr. Rossi's principles mostly drawn from Malthus are very true and full of a sound philosophy." But against the anti-Malthusian Buret: "Buret attacks Malthus, but without shaking him. He did not understand Malthus. Indeed, the current misery causes disorder, but that does not prevent Malthus from being right. We may conjecture that if order is re-established population will immediately grow and we should think about checking it".[11]

The same defence of Malthus can be found in Proudhon's marginal notes on Droz' and Destut de Tracy's books, and in two unpublished letters he wrote to Joseph Garnier. Before trying to interpret this surprising standpoint, let us recall which "Malthusian" arguments Proudhon used. First of all, as shown by the above quotation on Buret, Proudhon perfectly understood the nature of the principle of population, namely a dynamic force reacting immediately to any increase in the means of subsistence. Secondly, when dealing with checks to the principle of population, Proudhon concentrated on what we described as the first model of Malthus, in which mortality plays a decisive role. Commenting for instance on Desttut de Tracy, he clearly alluded to Townsend's allegory of the Island Juan Fernandez, where an ecological balance was necessarily reached between goats, dogs and grass.[12] Moreover, he fully accepted Malthus' view that emigration and the colonization of empty land were not a real solution, the problem of the excessive population being only postponed because of the ultimate physical limits of the world. Finally, he clearly identified two possible checks to demographic growth, infant mortality and birth control, and agreed that they sometimes acted simultaneously.[13]

In view of the above, Proudhon could easily be classified as a convinced Malthusian. However, at least seven other instances can be found which qualify him as an anti-Malthusian. Let us begin with a pure demographic discussion. About the checks, Proudhon asserted, as noted above, that growth was curtailed by infant mortality and by the control of fertility. This logically implied that the principle of population would constantly exert its pressure. However he suggested that, should infant mortality be reduced by increased means of subsistence, it would induce a *lesser* fertility. Here, Proudhon is precisely hinting at the modern theory of replacement

[10] I wish to thank Edward Castleton who provided me with a transcription of the unpublished *Carnets* which he had spotted at the Bibliothèque municipale of Besançon (Fonds Proudhon), and among the *Nouvelles acquisitions de la Bibliothèque nationale* (hereafter NAF);

[11] Rossi, NAF 18259 (October 1841); Buret, NAF 18261 (July 1844).

[12] Dogs can live as long as they find sheep and sheep as long as they can graze. The limits to grazing areas (meadows) are the limits to the growth of all of them.

[13] Desttut de Tracy, NAF 18256 (s.d.). Colonies : *Inédit sur le économistes*, Fonds Proudhon, Ms. 2818. Rossi, NAF 18259 (October 1841).

births.[14] This interesting insight should have led him to adopt a non-Malthusian logic, whereas a Malthusian would reply that the children kept alive would surely increase the ratio of consumers to producers, thus reduce the amount of subsistence per head and worsen the condition of the population, and in any case the whole argument does not affect the validity of the principle of population. What Proudhon is saying is precisely the contrary: Reduced infant mortality resulting from a bettering of the condition of the poor would induce a decline in fertility, which logically eliminates the principle of population. Secondly, he refused to admit that population always exceeded subsistence, arguing that short-term relief to population pressure could occur even if Malthus' prediction was to be ineluctably fulfilled in the long-term. Per se, contrasting short term and long term is by no means contradictory. What is problematic here is his earlier strong approval of the long-term risk, especially if we turn to the third objection he raised against Malthus. Proudhon claimed that food can massively be increased, a question, which "Malthus did not ask himself". If so, it is Proudhon's belief in the long term risk of overpopulation which cannot be taken at face value. His fourth objection brings even more confusion. He objected to Malthus' limits of available corn by turning to the possibility to consume other foodstuff such as meat, wine and vegetables. This argument is drawn from his faith in the possibility of increasing production. But if corn, as a vital staple, is missing, it is totally unlikely that the poor will have access to more costly items such as meat, wine or vegetables. The confusion stemming from the ambiguity about foodstuffs is worsened by his fifth argument, that it is industrial production which is now believed to increase faster than population, a classic argument clearly drawn from a widely shared faith, inherited from the Enlightenment, in technical and industrial progress as the source of an unlimited supply of goods. This led quite naturally to his sixth argument, Proudhon shifting now from a purely theoretical to a doctrinal appraisal of Malthus. If some million people could be added and if they were to enjoy a life not overburdened by misery, why should we reject this possibility? This consideration about the happiness of the people was quite naturally complemented by a seventh argument, even more embedded in political philosophy: a more equal distribution of wealth could induce fertility limitation and hence curtail demographic growth. He approved of Duchâtel and of Morogues who related low fertility to small landed property, an argument that was repeatedly asserted by the liberal economists. But the core of the argument, as put forward by Proudhon, is clearly political: the unequal distribution of property is at the root of social evils. We are taken back to Godwin and to the standard radical views on bad governments which Malthus fought.[15]

---

[14] This theory, which originated in the 1950s, was formulated to account for the parallel declines in fertility and mortality which were observed in some countries, notably Malaysia, Singapore, Hong Kong, the argument being that 6 births were needed to provide 2 or 3 adult children to guarantee the parents some insurance against illness, unemployment or other risks, or simply when they are too old to continue to work.

[15] 1st argument (theory of replacement birth): William Godwin, NAF 18261 (July 1844). 2nd argument (short term and long term) : Sismondi, NAF 18621 (July 1844). 3rd argument (a large

To sum up, in 1844, Proudhon simultaneously stood on two contradictory sides, using two sets of no less contradictory arguments. Which of these sparkling bubbles were finally kept and included in his published work? The comparison between the early *Carnets* and books published later reveals three possibilities. In some instances, arguments can be found in the *Carnets*, sometimes only briefly, but they are not taken up later. On the contrary, some published arguments are not traceable in the *Carnets*. Last, published works offer the same material as the *Carnets*, but the general tone and more precisely the degree of expressed anti-malthusianism is quite often different. It has of course not been always possible to account for these discrepancies, but more often than not, a satisfactory explanation can be advanced.

Population Growth

Système des Contradictions économiques starts with the two progressions mentioned in the *Essay on the Principle of Population*. But, unlike many of Malthus' critics, Proudhon did not question the weakness of this concept based solely on the American example, where the principle of population was actually observed: "Malthus, basing himself on a mass of authentic documents, has proved in the first place that population, if it does not meet with any obstacle, such as the lack of means of subsistence, can easily double every 25 years."[16] But he also reproached Malthus for justifying the growth of population in geometrical progression because the United States was a virgin land: "The country was created for the Iroquois and the Hurons, who, before its discovery, were already growing, as we are growing today, faster in terms of offspring than in terms of food, and who, being simple hunters, had been poor for a long time."[17] Although he thought that he was criticising him, he was in fact repeating the very argument advanced by Malthus, who had never denied that the earth's resources were less abundant in a society that depended on hunting for its livelihood than in an agricultural society. Besides, Proudhon did not consider any of the other examples of populations mentioned by Malthus in his *Essay* (e.g. antiquity, Orient, contemporary Europe, etc.). Criticism based on the history of various populations is almost non-existent in his published works. Instead, he used a strictly demographic method, based on hypotheses on marriage, fertility and mortality, and asserts that according to these hypotheses it would take three centuries for the population to double.[18]Sauvy, using the same basic hypothesis as

---

increase in foodstuffs) : Buret, NAF 18261 (July 1844). 4th argument (other foodstuffs) : Sismondi, NAF 18621, (July 1844). 5th argument (industrial production) : Morogues, NAF 18256 (December 1839). 6th argument (demographic increase without misery) : Say, NAF 18258 (early 1840). 7th argument (more equal distribution of riches) : Duchâtel, NAF 18258 (early 1840). Morogues, NAF 18256 (December 1839).

[16] *Contradictions économiques*, II: 316.

[17] Ibid., II: 334.

[18] Ibid., II: 384.

Proudhon, has shown that such a population, far from growing slowly, would rapidly disappear.[19] Proudhon's criticism of the *Essay* on demographic grounds is therefore disappointing.

A partial explanation of these quite contradictory standpoints – being simultaneously fully supportive of Malthus and yet expressing strong reservations – is provided by a comment on Bigot de Morogues, which is stated rather casually, and so to speak *juste en passant.* "I let myself be preoccupied by the means to stop population growth. A perfectly useless search. One sees on the basis of observation and of statistical data that the proportion of poor to the total population is bigger where property is less divided and where industry is more developed (which is the same thing). This ratio will be nil when properties are equal (...). But how can this miracle occur? Through a very simple cause: no one expecting anything except by his own efforts, nor fearing any one, and having nothing to lose and nothing to win, weddings and children will accompany production without needing repressive laws."

Social inequality imposed by capitalism, and its symbol, the unequal division of property, is the key factor which accounts for Proudhon's growing hostility to Malthus. As early as 1844, commenting on Godwin's *On Population*, Malthus is described as "an ardent defender of private property and of inequality". In 1848 when the revolution broke out, Proudhon was obliged to take sides, because his proposal of a credit bank exposed him to heavy fire from the liberal economists, especially when discussing the right to work at the *Assemblée nationale*.[20] It was no surprise that the tone of his pamphlet entitled *Les Malthusiens*, (dated 10 August 1848) was thus much more violent: "Two to four million people will die of poverty and hunger if we do not find the means to make them work. It is surely a great misfortune, the Malthusians tell you, but what can be done? It is better that four million people should die than threaten privilege: it is not for lack of capital that there is no work: at the banquet offered by credit, there is enough room for everybody."[21]

Whereas from 1848 the issue of property and social inequality became more and more central in Proudhon's published works,[22] in the *Carnets*, especially those written between 1840 and 1844, it is much less evident and Proudhon is very ambivalent towards Malthus, sometimes defending him against his critics, sometimes joining those shocked by the allegory of the feast. On this purely demographic level, what he finally published was indeed much less rich than the promising avenues explored in the *Carnets.* However the constant relationship, albeit often only sketchy, which he established between population and economics finally developed in 1846 in the *Système des contradictions économiques* into what he claimed to be a new population law. Commenting on Sismondi in 1844, Proudhon alludes to this quest for the

[19] 1959: 356–358. In fact Proudhon made a mistake while calculating the mortality of different generations contributing to population growth.

[20] Which of course did not prevent him from vigorously attacking the other Socialists.

[21] *Les Malthusiens:* 4.

[22] With the notable exception of *Qu'est-ce que la propriété ?* published in 1840.

Grail in the *Carnets:* "Now, both progressions being at least identical if not opposite to Malthus' formula, there must be a law which synthesizes them (. . .) There must exist a ratio between productivity and population, such that society can be able to limit itself, and to limit its production. What is that ratio? I am completely unaware of it. But it surely exists".[23] Indeed what was at stake was Proudhon's ambition to expose "economic contradictions", one of the most striking being the growth of national wealth despite the poverty of the working classes: work increases and production grows, but poverty becomes worse.

Does Production Really Increase in Geometrical Progression?

Two years later Proudhon was inspired by Adam Smith's famous example of the needle factory. His whole argument was built on his belief in the merits of the division of labour and competition and he tried to show that the increase in wealth was the square of the number of workers.[24] Thanks to competition, the production of wealth took precedence over human reproduction, which meant that the relation established by Malthus between population and the means of subsistence was "economically absurd".[25] As a matter of fact, "two single men working without tools can produce a value equal to 2. If these two poor men change their work pattern and pool their efforts, due to the division of labour and the use of machines and also due to the ensuing competition, their yield will not be 2 but 4, because each of them no longer produces just for himself but also for his companion."[26] He went on lining up numbers with the result that if the number of workers is doubled again, they will produce 16 and still later, the ratio will be 8:64. Malthus's progressions become 1, 2, 4, 8, 16, 32, 64 for population and 1, 4, 16, 64, 256, 1,024, 4,096 for production.[27]

It is by no means self-evident that the physical yield of each worker would be doubled when he combined his efforts with those of another worker: yields do not increase constantly. Further, the benefits of the division of work also depend on two other factors that are indispensable for production, namely raw materials and capital. His argument could however be viewed on a different level: in the long run Proudhon is right. To take a very crude example, it is indisputable that the productivity of a serf in ninth century Europe was infinitely lower than that of an American farmer

[23] Sismondi, NAF 18621 (July 1844).

[24] *Contradictions économiques*, II: 364.

[25] Ibid., II: 330.

[26] Ibid., II: 330.

[27] In addition to his belief in the advantages of the division of labour, we may also mention Fourier's influence in order to understand his insistence on the two progressions. Proudhon considers him to be the only one worthy of being called a modern socialist for having understood "that politics or social economics should be the object of a rigorous science; and that this science is a particular form of Fourier's series." See Cuvillier, *Introduction* à *De la création de l'ordre dans l'humanité*, 21–23, and *Création*. . ., 167, 170.

from the Middle West at the end of the twentieth century. Here again his visionary mind would have produced a brilliant intuition. But since Proudhon's refutation of Malthus is based on a *historicised* criticism and since he is obviously referring to the situation prevailing in France in the 1840s when French society was in the process of industrialisation, one cannot accept this kind of argument. What increases without any doubt with the increase in the number of workers is consumption and if the number of workers increases geometrically, it is because the production of consumer goods also increases geometrically, a fact recognised by Proudhon when he wrote that "It is strictly true to say that if for the last fifty years, France's income has grown fivefold, it is because France consumes five times more."[28] Finally, Malthusian reasoning is reduced to a tautology ex post facto: the *observed* growth of population implies that there was a growth in the production of the means of subsistence, a classical misunderstanding of the Malthusian theory shared by many of his opponents, and again a statement in complete contradiction to the recognition of the role of the principle of population.

Quite convinced that he had established that production increased in geometrical progression, Proudhon thought that he had formulated his own population law that refuted Malthus' law. Did he really? First, it goes almost without saying that his law is by no means a decisive refutation of the progressions as they appeared in the first *Essay* of 1798, since increasing *industrial* production does not eliminate the risk of an absolute scarcity of *foodstuffs*, unless one enters into a wider model, introducing international trade and the import of corn against manufactured goods as Malthus did, but not Proudhon, forgetting his earlier insights of the *Carnets*. Secondly, Malthus himself, as we have seen, shifted from the means of subsistence to the growth of industrial production, while analysing the effective demand. When proposing his model, Proudhon should logically have used it not against the agricultural model of the 1798 *Essay*, but against Malthus' later global model, which stresses the role of industry and of effective demand. If one discusses the functioning of *agricultural* societies, one cannot use arguments relevant to *industrial* societies. It might just be that Proudhon was unaware of Malthus' later editions of the *Essay* and his*Principles of Economics*. Such is not the case, Proudhon being perfectly aware of the controversy between Say and Malthus (the law of markets versus the risk of a general glut). He should therefore have also had in mind Malthus' lengthy argument about modern developed countries and the contribution of industry and international trade to the wealth of England and the Netherlands.

Economics and Population

Proudhon firmly believed in the uses of economics and statistics. His *Carnets* are dotted with numerous demographic, social or macro-economic data such as England's population, statistics regarding charity, production, the price of wheat, the

---

[28] *Contradictions économiques*, II: 335.

volume of its import and export, public debt and daily wages.[29] In 1849, his *Programme révolutionnaire* proclaimed that it was necessary to enact "special laws on public utilities affecting the entire nation." Among these figured education, public works, justice, religious practices, health, the army, the police and statistics "without which the state and society will exist spontaneously and, not being able to understand anything, will move from one pitfall to another and from one disaster to another."[30] His attempts to base his theses on facts or on economic laws can be explained by this dogmatic thinker's desire to be different from his rivals. "Instead of starting like Fourier and Saint-Simon by glorifying flesh, love, passions and sentiments, I would rather start with an economic law as rigorous as numbers."[31] Four topics bear witness to the place occupied by economics, both theoretical and practical, in Proudhon's thinking.

The Demand for Labour

In January 1840, contrasting Say's and Malthus' views on the demand for labour, he ironically observed that Say wondered why and how Malthus could write that landowners and capitalists would acquire a distaste for each others' products, a situation likely to generate a crisis of under-consumption. Malthus stated, as we have seen in Chapter 5, that the effective demand most advantageous for growth was: "the diffusion of luxury therefore among the mass of the people, and not the excess of it in a few, that seems to be most advantageous, both with regard to national wealth and national happiness." Proudhon willingly came to the rescue of Say, but the latter had to pay a price for having his obscure mind illuminated. The clarifying answer to Say came as a backlash clearly favourable to Malthus, but in Proudhon's words, it immediately took a polemical overtone. Why did Malthus come to his conclusions? "because if the rich, who support Say (...), would, once assured of having considerable incomes, consent to gain no more money and to give up their benefits, then property having become stationary in their favour, will cease to exert ravaging effects on the poor class."

Concluding his review of Say and Malthus, Proudhon, as the ultimate referee of the match, is satisfied to assert that neither Say nor Malthus saw that the inequality embedded in property increased production costs for the utmost unhappiness of the poor. "Both economists battled, he writes, in the blind both having some limited understanding, but with neither seeing the beam in his own eye". In a word, once again his obsession with property makes Proudhon short sighted and his final words return us to the register of the invective: "The vices of the nobility, the egoism of

---

29 England's population (III: 14) ; public debt (III: 14) ; price of wheat (IV: 6 ; IV: 57 ; V: 39) ; charity (IV: 139).

30 *Programme révolutionnaire*, 331. Also see *Carnets*, IV: 100.

31 *Carnets*, VI: 30.

proprietors and above all the greed of traders spoiled everything. Property is doomed by its own works. It will never restore itself".[32]

The Right to Work

There is nothing in the *Carnets* on the Right to Work for a purely chronological reason. When the political and social idea of the right to work took shape, Proudhon had already published his major books and was a leading figure of the anti-conservatives. Let us recall briefly the historical context. On 15 February 1848, a decree was issued on Louis Blanc's initiative to guarantee "existence through employment". This resulted in the disastrous episode of the National Workshops set up at Louis Blanc's instigation to reduce unemployment and poverty, the so-called *Organisation du travail*. Victor Considérant insisted that the right to employment should be included in the preamble to the Constitution. But in autumn, by introducing one amendment after another, the Right gradually divested this principle of its significance. On 31 July 1848, Proudhon, who had prepared an impressive speech to defend the right to employment, did not deliver it but Thiers forced him to defend his proposal in the Assembly. At the end of a memorable duel of words with Thiers, he came to be known as the personification of "the Reign of Terror" and won almost unanimous support against him (691 out of 693 votes).[33] He thus lost his credibility for a cause that he was not really interested in. He believed that Louis Blanc's organisation of employment would lead to communism, which he disapproved of totally, not only for ideological reasons,[34] but also on the basis of demo-economic arguments, because he foresaw the possibility of a crisis due to under-consumption "Given the present state of society, and as long as the system of ownership persists, there will always be surplus population, an overabundance of workers and unemployment among one section of the population. This is a result of the essential nature of property and individualistic economics, where each one constantly tries to consume less than he produces, which mathematically results in an overabundance of goods, stagnation and unemployment."[35]

Instead of the right to work, Proudhon wanted to organise an "exchange of property, of the instruments of work and the exchange of goods." He wanted this exchange to be "free, on equal terms and direct, replacing buying and selling (...), to protect independent work more effectively from organised work and property from common ownership".[36] This conclusion follows directly from the classical

[32] See *Carnets*, Say: NAF 18257 et NAF 18258.

[33] See *Carnets*, VI: 311, publisher's footnote No. 4.

[34] "With this regime (referring to public works for providing employment to unemployed persons), far from wiping out the proletariat, you will make them multiply", *Le droit au travail et le droit de propriété*, 421.

[35] Ibid., 440.

[36] Ibid., 455.

economic theory of the stationary condition. "Then population, like commerce and the State, will find its equilibrium and we will be able to witness, without any fear of a cataclysm, the eternal struggle between work and property."[37] To resolve the problem of the opposition between work and property, it was necessary to give up Louis Blanc's *Organisation du travail*, and to implement "mutualism". Since everybody would be a worker and an owner, corporatism would be replaced by a system of mutual guarantees, which he proposed to include in Article 13 of the preamble to the Constitution.[38] This proposal reveals a fundamental dimension of Proudhon's thinking, the desire to develop new forms of association ("mutual benefit", "mutualism", "federation"), meant to be totally free from control, either by the state or any other institution. Ansart has shown how Proudhon was influenced by the *canuts*, those silk-weavers of Lyon, whom he certainly knew well when he lived in Lyon. They were a perfect example of mutualism and their revolt in 1832 corresponded to the forms of political expression that Proudhon wanted to see in the workers' struggle against capitalism.[39] In more general terms, federalism, his great idea for the world to come, would be the key to the balance between the unity of society as a whole and the diversity of specific groups, which implies that federalism must be both economic and political. "All my ideas on economics formed during the last twenty-five years can be summarised in three words: industrial and agricultural federation. All my political views can be reduced to a similar formula: political federation or decentralisation."[40]

[37] *Le droit au travail et le droit de propriété*, 455–457. Regarding the reference to the Exchange Bank and interest-free credit: 433.

[38] Regarding the Exchange Bank, see Oualid, 1920: 138–155; Gide and Rist, 1926: 359–371.

[39] While he refused to accept the "peasant model" and "capitalistic structures, there was a "homologous relationship between the fundamental evidence offered by Proudhon and the mental universe of these worker-managers, a typical example of whom is the head of the Lyon workshop, a craftsman and an independent salaried worker" Ansart, 1970: 188. For these different topics, see: 59–66, 45–51, 141–182.

[40] "Political economy is a science, which starts with simple principles leading to wonderful consequences (. . .). The greatest of these principles is the principle of mutual benefit"*Carnets*, VI: 5. And later, "Economists, self-sufficient beings, without entrails, devoid of philanthropy, toadies of capital and power; parasites, scroungers living off the bourgeoisie (sic) (. . .). Political economy is actually the substance of philosophy. These principles should have led to peaceful reforms and to the transformation of the bourgeoisie and the proletariat", *Carnets*, VIII: 19. Let us stress that his political federalism was visionary: at the national level, he proposes to avoid the all-powerful centralised state through the creation of twelve large autonomous "provincial regions that will protect one another." At the international level, the future institutional form of Europe would be similar. Quoted by Bancal (s.d.: 139: regional federalism) and Gurvitch, 1965: 55–56. "Europe will still be too big for a single confederation; she can only form a confederation of several confederations." Also see Leroy, 1950: 290- 295.

Emigration, Colonisation and Economic Power

Following several earlier allusions in the *Carnets*, Proudhon took note in October 1847 of the terrible poverty that ravaged Ireland during the potato famine. He nevertheless persisted in his Malthusian thinking: "Insisting even more," as he wrote in his *Carnets*, "on the uselessness of emigration."[41] But unlike some of his contemporaries, he clearly saw the link between colonisation and economic power, especially because his was fully aware of England's strength. "Due to its trade and industry, England has enslaved India, China and Portugal and is devouring them, and it is now preparing to burst into the whole of Europe. Great Britain's enormous strength can be felt everywhere".[42] Contrary to the opinion expressed by the newspaper *National*, he was happy about the progress of colonisation in Algeria. "In 30 years there will be a million French people on African soil: everywhere Arabs, Kabilians and Moroccans will submit [to French authority]; with the spread of trading posts, Europe will gradually invade Africa with its business, capital, industrial enterprises and, whenever necessary, through war and conquest. Sooner or later, we will have a treaty with Egypt, our neighbour; it is necessary to drive away the English one day from the Mediterranean, despite Gibraltar, Malta and Cephalonia. The English have no business to be there. (...). Let them go to Australia."[43] Observing in 1864 how sparsely Algeria was populated in spite of its excellent lands, he held the Second Empire's militaristic and centralising policy responsible for the lack of development in the colony, as had happened in Canada, Louisiana and Santo Domingo.[44] On this point, he agreed with the diagnosis of the liberal economists, who recognised the need for an effective colonial policy during the second decade of the Second Empire and disapproved of the steps taken in Algeria.[45]

Industrialisation and Free Trade

The liberal economists developed a new argument regarding Malthusian theory consistent with the industrialization of France, namely that mass well-being induced by a large access to manufactured goods automatically led to a decline in fertility.[46] This implied a major doctrinal shift, according to which the prudential restraint recommended by the neo-Malthusians seemed unnecessary. Proudhon, being a keen

---

41 *Carnets*, IV: 1.

42 *Carnets*, IV: 88.

43 *Carnets*, V: 48. Against *National*, see *Avertissement aux propriétaires*: 237–239.

44 *Capacité politique...* : 306–308.

45 Particularly Paul Leroy-Beaulieu. This refers to the policy of *cantonnement*, limiting the space available to the Arab tribes, which in reality amounted to the pure and simple expropriation of their lands.

46 Regarding England, see Eversley, 1959, particularly Chapters 4, 5, 8 and 9.

observer of his times, could easily have adopted this line of thought. He actually alluded to this process in a few lines of the *Carnets* written in 1841, but he did not go further than this insight.

Commenting on Rossi's *Cours d'économie politique*, who asserted, in the pure Malthusian doctrinal tradition that reducing social inequality would reduce foresight and thus induce disastrous demographic growth, Proudhon answered that fear of a decline in social standing prevented too high fertility among the wealthy. Then we are told that Rossi "did not care about organizing equality. Had he done so, he would have seen that the same obstacles apply to the poor: minimum legal age at marriage and the desire to obtain for one's children the possibility of rapidly establishing them as a new household".[47] Clearly enough, what shocked Proudhon was the underlying idea that what was good for the bourgeoisie could not apply to the poor, simply because social factors were not recognized. The same argument took a sharper tone, as usual, in his *Système des contradictions économiques*. Against Charles Dunoyer, who deplored that the "passion for well-being", a "very natural sentiment" should be absent among the lower classes, Proudhon retorted, "Since this absence of desire is itself a consequence of poverty, it follows that poverty and apathy are both the cause and the effect and that the proletariat is caught in a circle."[48]

In his last book, *De la Capacité politique des classes ouvrières*, published after his death by the executor of his will, Gustave Chaudey, Proudhon clearly perceived that the development of the railways had led to the enrichment of the rural areas (he mentioned in particular the departments of Gard, Jura, Doubs and Hérault), which were able to market their produce, especially since free trade had given them access to the international market.[49] But he also denounced the coexistence of political centralisation and imperial absolutism with the anarchy of free trade, which both contributed to establish the supremacy of the bourgeoisie[50] Like Marx, he believed in the proletarianisation of the middle-class for although the principle of equality had been established by the revolution in 1789, developments since 1840 had strengthened capitalistic and industrial feudalism, while taxes and free trade had contributed to the decline of the middle-class.[51] To defend this idea, Proudhon developed a remarkable demo-economic line of reasoning, which was a true estimate of what is today termed the carrying capacity of France which he had sketched much earlier in 1839, while reading Say, especially in a paragraph entitled "What population can France feed?" where he had based himself on Young's figures

---

[47] Rossi, NAF, 18259 (October 1841).

[48] *Contradictions économiques*, I: 162.

[49] *Capacité politique...* : 69. In 1863, he quoted figures relating to foreign trade to argue with one of the leading protectionists, the industrialist Pouyer-Quertier, about the results of the 1860 free-trade treaty with England.

[50] *Capacité politique...*: 224–225. Free trade exposed "the immorality of the bourgeoisie", who denounced protectionism favoured by its adversaries and wanted "to have a favourable balance." Ibid.: 229.

[51] *Capacité politique...*, 231. Regarding this point, see Gurvitch, 1965: 61–66 and Ansart, 1967: 82–86.

collected during his tour of France in 1789.[52] On the basis of figures published by the *Statistique Agricole de la France*, he assessed how many people the country was capable of feeding. France had an area of 54 million of which 43.4 million produced food crops. He estimated that a peasant family of 4 or 5 members needed 4.92 hectares of arable land in the form of pastures, vineyards, meadows, fields producing diverse crops, and use of forests and moors to make a living. On the basis of these estimates about 9 million families or 40 million persons could live in France. After calculating that a family having 4 hectares of land could set aside a third of its agricultural income for taxes and for buying non-agricultural goods, he came to the logical conclusion that it was possible to increase the rural population by one third or 13.5 million to cover "the industrial population, government officials, army, etc." France could thus afford to have a population of 53.5 million, while its population peaked at 37.5 million. The reason for this low population was "capitalistic, mercantile, industrial and property-holding feudalism, which has the total freedom to advance at the cost of the middle and working classes and which is presently trying to spread its influence all over Europe and throughout the world through free trade."[53] These lines can indeed be read as his final polemic against the Second Empire. But this analysis, which established a link between micro- and macro-economic demographic data, proposed a *negative political* diagnosis of the development of capitalism. Had Proudhon, like Marx, developed a theory of capitalistic accumulation, the link between quantitative data and the general accusation on which he based his conclusion would have been better established and these lines would have constituted a real demo-economic demonstration of the damaging effects of free trade in a society with widespread economic inequality. Unfortunately, he limited himself to general observations: "due to the imperfection of the social organism, practice proves that wherever competition has spread, there are as many poor people as there are newly rich."[54] In spite if these weaknesses, this denunciation is interesting as an alternative to the complacency of the French liberal economists, who were happy with the introduction of free trade which made goods cheap by reducing import duties. In keeping with the liberal ideology, importance was given to the consumer who was supposed to embody the general interest, and as for the demographic consequences of free trade and industrialisation, the drop in the birth rate in France was regarded as a sociocultural phenomenon produced by a rise in the standard of living.

Whether we consider Proudhon as a demographer or as an economist, we encounter evident limitations to his thinking on both counts, despite acute, if not visionary insights. But what about his social criticism based on his economic analysis?

---

[52] Say, NAF 18258 (s.d., 6 janvier 1840?).

[53] *Capacité politique*...: 364–365.

[54] *Contradictions économiques*, II: 332.

Moral Philosophy and Social Criticism

The first four chapters of *Système des contradictions économiques ou philosophie de la misère*, respectively devoted to the division of labour, machines, competition and monopoly contain pages that have lost nothing of their denunciatory fervour. His writings show him to be a remarkable sociologist of working class conditions, who had read the reports of the major social studies on poverty conducted by Eugène Buret, Théodore Fix, perhaps also Louis Villermé, and certainly Jérôme-Adolphe Blanqui, brother of the revolutionary Louis Auguste Blanqui, as well as the Social Catholics (Bigot de Morogues and Duchatel). Although Proudhon's sociological views lie beyond the scope of this study, his social criticism and moral philosophy are worthy of our attention insofar as they are behind the relation he established between population and issues such as the division of labour, mechanisation and competition.

Philosophy and Poverty

It was not possible to have an ideal situation where wealth grew faster than population because of certain "flaws in the organisation of labour" inherent in the "ownership system". In fact Proudhon firmly distinguished advances arising from the "basic elements of science" from those occurring "in actual practice."[55] He acknowledged that both in France and in England poverty grew faster than population, as demonstrated by the increase in the number of illegitimate children, crimes and offences. He was struck, like some of his contemporaries, by the difference in mortality rates between the rich and poor districts of Paris and between different professions in Mulhouse. Finally, like Reybaud or Villermé, he underlined the contrast between the increase in the "average life span" and the poverty of the working classes.[56]

The flaws in the organisation of labour lay above all in "the division and separation of industries" as well as in the use of machinery which had created a gap between masters and employees, capitalists and workers. Because of these divisions, work was even more alienating: "the worker (...) loses his human qualities, his freedom and is reduced to a tool (...). Already heralded by the fragmentation of landholdings, poverty has officially come into the world."[57] He was right to note that by eliminating cottage industries, mechanisation played a decisive role in the pauperisation of families[58]. It made work tedious and created a feeling of psychological depression because, due to the low wages, it was well nigh impossible to resist the temptations created by the abundance of goods produced by these same industries.[59] Contrary to Malthus and the economists, "It is neither nature nor providence

---

[55] *Contradictions économiques*, II: 326, 339.

[56] Ibid., I: 190–191 ; II : 337–338. See Chapter 6.

[57] Ibid., I: 329.

[58] Ibid., I: 194.

[59] Ibid., II: 328. Also see *Création de l'ordre dans l'humanité*: 333.

that is at fault, it is the economic routine that lacks balance".[60] In other words, he reproached them for reducing the problem to its biological dimension without questioning the existing social order. He saw through the trickery and was infuriated by it, and in 1848, in the midst of the revolution, his criticism of the upper classes became extremely virulent: "The press, the government, the Church, literature, the economists, the large landowners, everybody in France has become Malthusian."[61] Ten years later, a similar tirade appeared in *La justice dans la révolution et dans l'église*, only this time it was aimed at the ideological nature of economics. "What in God's name has this Christian and Malthusian economics, whose philanthropic flag is carried by the Church and which can be defined as a crusade against work and Justice, been teaching us through the centuries about issues such as labour, charity, pauperism, begging, etc.?"[62] As a matter of fact, Duroselle has shown how, within social Catholicism, the democratic tendency ceded its place to counter-revolution.[63]

Progress and Providence

In *Philosophie du Progrès* a long footnote quotes in a disorderly manner and with many inaccuracies, the thinkers who delved into the idea of Progress: Plato, Aristotle, Cicero, Pascal, Bossuet, Lessing, Saint-Simon, Comte, Leroux, Buchez, Louis Blanc and Proudhon himself defined progress as "the physical, moral and intellectual improvement of the largest and the poorest class", the mission of philosophy being to contribute to the solution of social problems.[64] Proudhon felt that unlike philosophy, religion, which was "hostile to progress", was synonymous with immobilism.[65] He placed this progress in a theory of human evolution borrowed from Auguste Comte, giving new names to the various stages: thus the theological state is "religion" according to Proudhon, while the metaphysical state is "philosophy" and Comte's positive philosophy becomes "metaphysics". So, instead of progressing towards "wealth and virtue", society witnessed the development of "poverty and crime" and once again Proudhon opposed Malthus: "The Malthusian theory of the productivity of capital, though justifiable as a mercantile policy, becomes (...) if one tries to extend it and make it a social law, incompatible with (...) social life itself."

[60] Ibid: 328. And going against Malthus once again, Proudhon concluded that it was not the excess of men that caused poverty but the social organisation (Ibid.: 329).

[61] *Les Malthusiens*: 2. *Les Malthusiens* was initially an article that appeared in *Le Peuple* on 10 August 1848.

[62] *De la justice dans la révolution et dans l'église*, II : 263. In 1844, about an article by T. Fix, the *Carnets* attacked the English economists as a whole: "they all worked to the oppression of the poor. Arthur Young through his agricultural doctrine, Ricardo with his theory of rent, Malthus through his ideas on population" (Ms. 2844, Bibliothèque Municipale de Besançon).

[63] Duroselle, 1951: 650–710.

[64] *Philosophie du Progrès,*: 46–47, footnote 2. See on p. 47 the remarks of the editors, Puech and Ryssen, after Proudhon's note. Proudhon's quotation: 49.

[65] *Création de l'ordre dans l'humanité*: 37, 45.

The argument is explained in *Système des contradictions économiques*: "Malthus' mistake, or to be more fair, the mistake of political economy (...), is to declare a transitory condition as a permanent state, namely the distinction made by society between patriarchy and the proletariat".[66]

According to Proudhon's moral code, man fulfilled himself through his work, and love and family were the most appropriate and the most powerful incentives to make him work.[67] It was Providence, Proudhon wrote, that ordered that it should be thus, so how could it contradict itself? "What! Man alone of all the animals has been made a worker by the most glorious distinction; Providence has commanded him to possess the earth and organise humanity into families; happiness has been given to him for exercising this dual function of work and love; that is how he was meant to increase his energy constantly, multiply his means, develop his industrial fertility (...); and when the time comes to fulfil the magnificent promises, Providence, who never lies, will transform itself suddenly into a hideous disappointment!"[68] Proudhon refused to accept this "utilitarian materialism".[69] According to him, killing or preventing birth, for that was what Malthus' theory amounted to, was the "penal code of political economy"[70], because in this system, death was responsible for restoring the balance between population and production. By emphasising the lethal role of Providence in the Malthusian system, Proudhon was once again in a precarious position: the pessimism that he denounced in Malthus' vision of Providence was only characteristic of the first edition of Malthus' *Essay* (1798), whereas Malthus developed later a much more complex model of growth, which he believed possible in view of the spread of "prudent restraint" he had observed in England and in Europe. But there is something more serious. Proudhon contradicts himself. In his *Système des contradictions économiques*, he was indignant because foremost among the obstacles to population "in a society based on ownership and in Malthus, its spokesman, figure famine, plague and war, acting as executioners for property owners."[71] However, *La guerre et la paix* is a true apology for war that he declared a "divine act", "a religious revelation", "a revelation of justice", "the revelation of the ideal", and whose "primary cause" he described as follows: "A state, whose population is increasing and which is being hounded by poverty, must increase its resources, extend its territory, acquire colonies, etc. All this must first be conquered."[72] Finally, Proudhon followed a logic that was fully in accordance with Malthus' first *Essay*, because he admitted that the problem posed by a surplus

---

[66] Ibid.: 75–76. *Contradictions économiques*, I: 84–85.

[67] *De la justice dans la révolution et dans l'église:* the right to work implies "the dignity of man or citizen (...) access to political sovereignty (...) a more just economic balance (...) a better education" (II: 267).

[68] *Contradictions économiques*, II: 319.

[69] The expression was coined by de Lubac (1945: 204).

[70] *Contradictions économiques*, II: 345.

[71] *Contradictions économiques*, II: 346.

[72] *La guerre et la paix*: 381.

population had to be solved by its violent destruction if the means of subsistence were insufficient.

The Proudhonian Model

Against Fertility Control

Proudhon, who believed that it was possible to reach an "equilibrium of population" that "science must discover"[73], tried to demonstrate the existence of an automatic and successful process of controlling demographic growth, directly linked to work. But this made it necessary first to reject all forms of fertility control independent from work. He therefore embarked on a criticism of the different theories of his time, which he refuted one by one: inducing sterility "by fattening", "breast-feeding for three years", the use of abortion and the periodic abstention from sexual relations by couples during the risk period.[74] Behind the diversity of arguments one element is however constant in Proudhon's search for a natural and automatic system: an uncompromising refusal of all artificial means of reducing fertility and all practices that he believes will debase humans. This, in turn, bring us to one of the most central components of Proudhon's thinking, his hostility to sexuality, very clearly expressed in an unpublished letter to Garnier: "I consider our current lascivious behaviour as totally unnatural and all this display of tenderness, these passionate descriptions of women, which fill our modern writings, seem to me the result of a disordered excitement rather than the symptom of a legitimate change". Fourierism was particularly vehemently denounced for its immorality: "Fourierists lay store by their system of fattening women to prevent unwanted fertility. I know of nothing more ignoble, more degrading for humans than this idea. Who can deny that corpulence does not lead to sterility in some cases? (...) But it is absurd to take Fourier's unscientific theory literally. The real way to control population is through Work and Love, that is to say Chastity. The Phalansterians praise sensualism to the skies. According to them, having an orgasm is all that matters for humans. You are disgusting! That is all that I can say." And he did not stop reproaching the Fourierists for their immoral practice of sharing their women.[75]

As for Malthus and the Malthusians he objected to moral restraint as well as to prudential restraint. He reproached Malthus for believing that moral restraint can prevent the growth of population: "Postponing marriage till the age of thirty or forty

[73] *Contradictions économiques*, II: 319. He announced it in a very enigmatic manner in *Qu'est-ce que la propriété ?*: 284–285.

[74] Ibid.: Fourier, II: 351–352 ; Dr. Gros, II: 353–355 (also see *Carnets*, IV: 158) ; Charles Loudon, II: 356–359. His critics were developed in *Qu'est-ce que la propriété ?*: 279–285.

[75] letter to Garnier: XXXXXX; also *Carnets*, II, 86. Regarding his moral reprobation of the Fourierist sharing of women: *Carnets*, VII, III: 7; IV: 49–50; VII: 69, etc. Also see *Contradictions économiques,* I: 275–292 and II: 352–353.

is what Malthus (. . .) imagined would be most practical (. . .) and most moral to prevent the uncontrolled growth of population."[76] This solution is a "constraint" because even as Nature tempted man to procreate, society forbad him to do so. There could not be a stable balance because it was based on a contradiction. Besides, this solution "amounts to a lack of trust in nature" and he exclaimed, "What kind of a theory is this that takes for granted the need to correct the works of God through man's prudence!"[77] All said and done, it was "impracticable" and "ineffectual". Proudhon wrote in all seriousness that the theory was impracticable because it advocated the marriage of "old spinsters and lechers" while discouraging young persons from marrying. It was ineffectual because "since the immediate cause of poverty is not, as it is generally believed, an excess of population, but the impositions of monopoly, poverty is bound to occur in a system like ours."[78] A little further Proudhon reproaches Malthus for turning marriage into a "privilege reserved for the rich." In a comment on Droz in the early *Carnets*, he had expressed his mistrust: "One does not dare say that for the workers marriage must be restricted. One begins with the advice to be prudent and it will end up in an interdiction to marry. Why should the worker be compelled to virtues from which the rich would be exempt?" Concerning prudential restraint, answering Destutt de Tracy's assertion that "The interest of people is, to all intents and purposes, to diminish the consequences of their fertility", he became quite furious: "Destutt de Tracy not having found necessary to tell which are these remedies against fertility I am going to quote some of them: masturbation, onanism, pederasty, tribadic love, polyandry, prostitution, castration, seclusion, abortion, infanticide".[79] No less than that. Beyond the violence of the tone, the important point about these lines is that they reveal the necessity, when dealing with Proudhon, to take into account all possible registers of arguments, his criticism addressing both the individual and the social dimensions, the moral as well as the economic rationales. Let us, for a while, return to economics.

Fertility and Work

The path being cleared, Proudhon could put forward a solution to the control of fertility directly linked to work. He began with one of the contradictions of economics. By not taking any action against fertility, excess population would rapidly create a strong demand that production would not be in a position to satisfy. But if population were reduced, the number of producers would also go down. Proudhon resolved the contradiction from a perspective that Marx would have described as "petit bourgeois", in any case embedded in the morality of individuals. In the first place, the labour situation of the workers becomes worse every day, and it is so

76 *Contradictions économiques*, II: 347.

77 Ibid., II: 348.

78 Ibid., II: 349.

79 Droz, NAF 18256 (not dated). Du Tracy, ibid.

because such is the functioning of the economic system.[80] The *Carnets* provide a crisp and concise answer: "Man must work harder; up to 18 hours a day, regularly and throughout his life. Because needs grow constantly and faster than the means of satisfying them."[81] But how can this need to work influence population and reduce it by a natural mechanism? There is an original idea here that is half way between sociology and physiology. "The principle for controlling population is WORK", because a decrease in the reproductive strength naturally leads to industrial development for humans.[82] Nature provides numerous examples of this principle: among the bees, only the queen who does not work indulges in sexual activity; inversely, horses in a stud farm do not work. As for Mirabeau, he died in spite of his strong constitution "because he tried to combine sexual prowess with oratorical success."[83]

This socio-physiological concept does not merit more than a brief mention. However, it corresponds to beliefs that were prevalent in the latter half of the nineteenth century. What is quite surprising is that Proudhon did not take into account the importance socio-economic factors. As we have seen, when talking about the production of wealth, he made a careful distinction between what results from "the basic elements of science" and what is inherent in the "ownership system". Why did he not make a similar distinction in the case of human reproduction or fertility? To explain this shift in his argumentation, it is necessary to go back to his ideology. While emphasising the existence of an economic contradiction between production and consumption without pursuing the dialectics to its end, Proudhon found himself compelled to propose a biological interpretation of fertility, which was not in anyway incompatible with an escape into morality, in accordance with the traditional distinction between man's animal and spiritual dimensions. Man could escape his biological or – in Proudhon's terminology – animal compulsions, and fertility in particular, only because of his moral resources. Against Malthusian pessimism, Proudhon proclaimed his faith in man. This escape into morality is quite evident in the way he avoided any socio-economic analysis and claimed that marriage was the best guarantee that population would not be excessive. Marriage idealised love, it transformed it and made it "incorporeal". "Marriage is the tomb, that is to say the EMANCIPATION of love (...) love loses its indecent and obscene attributes."[84] Consequently, the "accepted standards of behaviour" and morality gained the upper hand and Proudhon was convinced that he had successfully suggested a solution to the population problem that was automatic but not restrictive, dignified and not degrading: "To defeat Malthus and to balance everything, all that you have to give men is work, honour, health, intelligence and love; there is no need for restrictive laws, everything will then happen on its own."[85]

---

80 Ibid., II: 361–371.

81 *Carnets*, II: 40–41.

82 *Contradictions économiques*, II: 364–371. Also see*Carnets*, I: 86.

83 *Contradictions économiques,* II: 372.

84 *Contradictions économiques,* II: 376–377.

85 *Carnets*, III: 11–12.

Malthusian Recommendations

Proudhon's morality was based on the virtues of individual work, marriage and family, it was essentially a petty bourgeois and individualistic concept in view of which his "belonging to the socialistic protest movement", as he claimed, did not have much to do. For example, in October 1847, he was angry that Plato and the socialists should "rob the parents of their child while it is still in the cradle."[86] By resorting to morality, Proudhon not only set himself up in opposition to Malthusian pessimism, but also proposed a population policy based on the age at marriage. The chapter on population in *Système des contradictions économiques* ends by dividing human life into five periods: childhood, adolescence, youth, virility or the reproductive period and maturity or old age. "During the first period, a man loves a woman as his mother, in the second as his sister, in the third as his mistress, in the fourth as his wife and in the fifth and last period as his daughter."[87] Such a life cycle rested upon very traditional ideas about women: "their true dignity is in household work", "there is a strong antipathy between the family and gender equality". Proudhon detested George Sand, who was the very embodiment of gender equality.[88] In *Qu'est-ce que la propriété ?* he went to the very extreme: "the difference between genders creates between them (the man and the woman) a separation of the same kind that the difference in races creates between animals. Also, far from praising what we now call women's emancipation, I would be more inclined, were it necessary to go so far, to seclude women."[89]

It is essential to remember these moral convictions in order to understand the doctrinal recommendations that Proudhon arrived at regarding population. Since there were periods when a worker is active and productive, Proudhon felt that there was a well-defined period of fertility in a couple's life. It began at the age of 21 in the case of women and 28 in the case of men and it lasted for 10–15 years. After that, sexual relations were immoral and repugnant, even between married couples. "Towards the age of forty, the changes that take place [in a man] make him give up love (. . .) Man loses his rights as a husband. His wife should then be treated as sacred! They should look upon each other from a purely spiritual angle."[90] And Proudhon concluded that according to these principles marriage should take place at the age of 21 for women and 28 for men.[91] His conclusions thus appear to be very similar to those of Malthus, after having criticised him violently. And his failure to

[86] *Carnets*, VI: 31.

[87] *Contradictions économiques*, II: 379.

[88] *Carnets*, III: 47–48, 51–53; IV: 9; IV: 74–77; VII: 134. Regarding George Sand (III: 7). Or again: "The most shameful things indicate inferiority. During copulation, the man is active and the woman is passive", (*Carnets* VII: 134).

[89] 314, footnote.

[90] *Contradictions économiques*, II: 353.

[91] Ibid., II: 384.

form an original population doctrine takes us back to the limitations of Proudhon's ideology.

The Limitations of Proudhon's Ideology

It is not possible to study the ideas on population of a writer like Proudhon from the point of view of his theoretical contribution. So let us first eliminate a reason that seems valid but is really wrong. Since Proudhon, though proud of his rational thinking, was deeply involved in the political struggle, the price he had to pay for this involvement would have been scientific incoherence as an inevitable result of his ideological outlook. All the major thinkers of the past had enriched and sustained their efforts at theorising by putting these principles into practice and it is necessary to look for clues in their ideologies to understand the most abstract constructions that are apparently unrelated to the context. If Proudhon did not succeed in advancing either a doctrine or a population theory consistent with his socio-political ideology, it was because of his inability to go beyond his own internal contradictions.[92] His doctrinal contribution is more interesting: being an effective polemist, he brings out the central point of the commonly accepted version of the Malthusian theory, explaining human behaviour from the biological viewpoint and giving a free hand to institutions; but he does it essentially as a polemist. As for his demographic doctrine, a double contribution had been expected. First, as a keen observer of the progress of industrialisation, Proudhon like the French economists of his time, could have attacked Malthus by drawing attention to the effects of the rise in the standard of living and the spread of prosperity on fertility during the Second Empire. But Proudhon does not broach this aspect in his analysis because of his own ideology. Secondly, as a left-leaning ideologue, he could have opposed to the Malthusian system a different view of the relation between population and production and formulated an original demographic doctrine and policy. He thought of Malthus as the incarnation of the counter-revolution and looked upon the author of the *Essay* as the defender of the upper classes and the established order. Unfortunately, Proudhon is a typical anti-Malthusian who is unable to avoid the traps of Malthusian logic and ends up by developing arguments worthy of Malthus. The reason for this failure lies in the narrow individualistic concept of happiness and morality, which leads him to pose the question of fertility control in Malthusian terms at the level of the demo-economic balance *of the family*, whereas a *macro*-analysis would have led to a new approach, which is what Marx did by questioning the social order from a revolutionary viewpoint.

However, specialists such as Gurvitch and Ansart point out the numerous similarities between Proudhon and Marx, the two figures who dominated the leftist ideology during the nineteenth century. They remarked that Marx's biting criticism

[92] In *Misère de la philosophie* Marx makes a cruel remark: "he claims to be the synthesis, (but) he is only a composite error".

of Proudhon is undoubtedly due to the similarity of their ideas. They had the same adversaries: economics and its individualistic axioms, positivist sociology and organicism. They wanted to build a total science – Proudhon a "social science" and Marx a "science of history". In both cases their sociological analysis is equally penetrating, though it is more intuitive in Proudhon's case and more structured in Marx's case. They share the same epistemological approach "it is a matter of showing that dialectics is not just an intellectual method but that the social movement is dialectic, that is to say it is in perpetual motion and riddled with contradictions which lead to changes."[93] They also have the same idea about the social role of theory which should precede political action and make it rational. This explains why the question of ownership is at the core of their demonstration of the mechanism of capitalistic appropriation. And finally, they chose the same revolutionary option, though it happened rather late in the case of Proudhon, who, for a long time, believed that an alliance between the proletariat and the "middle classes" was possible. But the major difference between Marx and Proudhon was the latter's belief in the value of technical skills and "original practices" among workers and hence his aversion to strikes, which he believed were an inherent part of the capitalist system, even though he denounced their misuse. He had more faith in emancipation through the invention of new types of organisation and solidarity, in other words mutual benefit and industrial federalism. If one follows Ansart's and Leroy's arguments on this point, it is easier to understand why Proudhon treated work as sacred, a conviction that undoubtedly had its roots in his plebeian origin.[94]

The Misuse of Metaphysics

Proudhon criticised Malthus on several counts: social observation, demographic theory, economic theory and his reduction of population-related facts to biology. But he could not avoid the Malthusian trap of double progression. There are three possible reasons.

The first one is the influence of classical economics on his thinking. Let us dwell for a moment on Proudhon's belief in the law of the "balance of population". He was convinced that population could not be separated from the means of subsistence and looked upon the two terms "as a new entity formed by this union". That is why he continued to look at combinations of the two series different from those mentioned by Malthus ("Wealth grows as the square of the number of workers"). And almost every time he mentions a figure in his *Carnet*, he immediately sets about comparing

---

[93] Ansart, 1967: 193.

[94] Leroy (1950: 507, 508) puts forward a penetrating formula: "The France of peasants and craftsmen, the France of the lower middle-class, of people leaving on their savings, thrifty and hardworking, found its ideologue in Proudhon: Proudhon, the son of rural artisans, thought like the son of artisans, raised in the backward suburbs of a small and mediocre town... He was passionate about liberty, he liked things to be done well and he linked public future and happiness with the strong humble virtues of the peasant and craftsman."

the two terms as in the following calculation: "Making the earth yield all that it is capable of raising work to its maximum and population to its maximum. The present income of France is 8 billion. If the maximum could be quintupled or the capital became 40 billion, the maximum population could be 70 million."[95] Proudhon is quite satisfied with establishing a parallel and does not go any further. So it is not surprising that Marx's criticism in *Philosophie de la misère* makes no reference to Proudhon's population theory or doctrine, which he dismisses in one word as "ravings".[96]

The second reason lies in the manner in which he denounced Malthus. When in 1848, in a fit of extreme anger, he indiscreetly denounced the Church, the government, etc. in *Les Malthusiens*, he was in fact rejecting the apology of the banquet. But this meant that he was arguing *within* the Malthusian logic, without trying to dismantle it first, while Marx, as we shall see later, instead of launching a frontal attack on the geometrical progression, demonstrated, on the basis of historical evidence, the necessity of primitive accumulation in the capitalist system. When separated from its demographic context and re-evaluated as an economic theory, the Malthusian construction obviously ceases to be an unavoidable trap. One point that is very clear, as regards the significance of Proudhon's and Marx's criticism, is the concept of labour. In Proudhon's case, it has an essentially moral and metaphysical dimension, whereas Marx does not spend much time denouncing the exploitation of the working classes per se, instead he conceptualises it, creating the concept of the industrial reserve army. We are thus far from the narrow demographic issues and from the protests raised by Proudhon.

The third reason for Proudhon's failure is the importance he gives to metaphysics. Certainly, as Pirou put it, his great treatise on social and political economy, *Système des contradictions économiques*, "poses the problem of the relationship between economics and socialism in a new form, imbued with relativism and historicism."[97] The reader of *Système des contradictions économiques* is somewhat puzzled when he is introduced to economics in a lengthy prologue running into thirty-two pages whose central idea is the hypothesis of God: "I need the hypothesis of God to establish the authority of social sciences (. . .). Similarly, social philosophy does not recognise a priori that humanity can delude itself or be deceived by its actions: without that, what would happen to the authority of humankind, that is to say the authority of reason, which is essentially synonymous with the sovereignty of the people? (. . .). The preamble of any political constitution, in search of sanction and a principle, is necessarily this: *There is one God* [in italics in the original text], which

95 *Carnets*, IV: 173. Or again: "always more men than wealth: that is the eternal truth", *Carnets*, II: 120.

96 "This brief observation will give the reader a correct idea of Mr. Proudhon's ravings on the police, on taxes, on the balance of trade, on credit, communism and population." (466).

97 Pirou, 1920: 180.

means that society is governed with purpose, premeditation and intelligence."[98] Thus emerges the quasi Voltairian concept of the Great Clockmaker reinforced by the parallel with astronomy on the same page. Even better is the eighth chapter, after the one on taxes and before the one dealing with the balance of trade, entitled *De la responsabilité de l'homme et de Dieu sous la loi de contradiction, ou solution du problème de la providence* (About the Responsibility of Man and God under the Law of Contradiction or the Solution to the Problem of Providence). We find that Proudhon is very much at ease in the role of Prometheus revolting against Zeus: "The first duty of an intelligent and free man is to constantly drive out the idea of God from his mind and conscience. Because God, if he exists, is essentially hostile to our nature and we do not in any way come under his authority. We have discovered knowledge despite him, we have found well-being in spite of him: each of our advances is a victory in which we crush Divinity."[99] If it is accepted that this metaphysical dimension of economics is at the heart of Proudhon's thinking,[100] it is easy to understand that man's work, which "continues the work of God",[101] seems to him to be almost redemptive and the basis of a law on the balance of population. It is therefore necessary to view his narrow moral ideas about sexuality, women and the family in this perspective. They can certainly be considered as petty bourgeois, but that would mean depriving them of their deeper meaning. If this metaphysical dimension is accepted, it is easier to explain why Proudhon was unable to escape the Malthusian trap. Once his recommendations regarding abstinence are interpreted *objectively* and separated from their metaphysical background and somehow considered by themselves, it becomes clear that they are not essentially different from the precepts of Malthus, the Anglican pastor. The judgement passed on Proudhon by Gustave du Puynode, an orthodox Malthusian, is merciless in this respect: "The most orthodox economist would sign with both hands (...) the last pages of Mr. Proudhon's writing on population."[102] There is a more pernicious element in this fragile balance between scientific construction and metaphysical perspectives. In Proudhon's eyes, his own law has the same strength as Malthus' law because of its coherence due to his certainty about God. Totally ignoring the religious dimension of Malthus' work, he opposes his own system to that of Malthus with the firm conviction of his own superiority because, unlike other economists, he does not separate economics from its metaphysical foundation. But so long as Malthus' two progressions benefit from a credibility based on facts (growth of population in the United States and decreasing yields), how is it possible to believe Proudhon when he proclaims that production can increase in geometrical progression? Hence the superiority of Malthus, who succeeded in reconciling socio-demographic observations, economic modelling and divine commands.

---

[98] *Contradictions économiques,* I: 52. In the words of Ansart (1970: 208) work is "the active force behind social life and history."

[99] Ibid., I: 382

[100] He wrote to Grün in December 1844, "political economy is metaphysics in action."

[101] Ibid., I: 66.

[102] *Journal des Economistes*, 1848, T. 25: 155.

Let us revert to the brief intellectual portrait drawn in the first pages of this chapter. The following conclusion may be drawn from Proudhon's failure: because he had a spontaneous and immediate knowledge of the society in which he grew up, this visionary thinker was a good observer of his times. But when confronted with the narrow logic of the applied statistics that constitute demography, the visionary was reduced to a state of helplessness.

Chapter 5
Capitalism and Population: Marx and Engels Against Malthus

An Ambivalent Hostility

The violence of the attacks on Malthus by Marx and Engels and the virulence of their criticism cannot but strike the reader of *Capital* and especially the *Theories of Surplus Value*, although they are not overtly political or polemical works (like *The Communist Party Manifesto, The Eighteenth Brumaire Of Louis Bonaparte, The Class Struggle in France* or *The Poverty of Philosophy*). The criticism is directed towards the law of population, which is the very core of Malthus's thinking and the main complaint against him is the accusation of plagiarizing from James Stewart, Benjamin Franklin, Walace and Townsend.[1] Further, had Marx and Engels confined themselves to refuting the demographic aspects of Malthus's thinking, their persistence in this matter could be explained quite easily for he was held intellectually responsible for the 1834 Poor laws reform abolishing all assistance at the parish level. But the truth is far more complex: Marx had taken care to acquaint himself with Malthus's work in the field of economics and his attitude was much more ambivalent. He scornfully rejected his theory of value calling it "a very model of intellectual imbecility", but also gave him credit for his decisive inputs as compared to Ricardo.[2] He respected Ricardo intellectually, but he accused Malthus of servilely defending the interests of the landed aristocracy. It therefore follows that there must be something fundamental in Malthus's writings that drives Marx to refute him so persistently. Explaining Marx's ambivalence towards Malthus is the primary aim of this chapter.

Marx's and Engel's principal thoughts on population are to be found in *The Condition of the Working Class in England in 1844* (published by Engels in 1845), *Capital* (1867) and the *Theories of Surplus Value*, written between 1861 and 1863, but published by Kautsky in 1905 after Marx's death.[3] Like Malthus, Marx too can be interpreted at two levels. *Capital* is essentially a treatise on economic theory

---

[1] *Capital*: I, footnotes 26: 633; 5: 675: 37: 677; *Theories*, Vol. VI: 42, 94 and Vol. IV: 6.

[2] *Theories*..., Vol. VI: 38, and his "peculiar considerations" Vol.VI: 60.

[3] Translated into French under the title *Histoire des doctrines économiques*. Only Book I of *Capital* was published during Marx's lifetime. The manuscripts of what would become Books II and III

Y. Charbit, *Economic, Social and Demographic Thought in the XIXth Century*, DOI 10.1007/978-1-4020-9960-1_5, and claimed as such, population being one of the three main variables in his analysis together with land and capital. However, jointly with Engels, Marx made a significant contribution as a sociologist as his theoretical claims are supported by very precise examples taken from English life in the mid-nineteenth century. He constantly tried to prove what he proposed at the theoretical level, just as Malthus had done before him, to demonstrate the universality of his population principle. The second aim of this chapter is to establish a link between the economic and demographic aspects of Marx's writings and we shall therefore approach them from a theoretical as well as empirical viewpoint. Marx is very precise in conceptualising and analysing the principal demographic variables but, unlike his contemporaries, he is more interested in mortality and the various forms of mobility than in fertility. Why should it be so when other writers of his time, undoubtedly fascinated by the implacable logic of Malthus's *Essay on the Principle of Population*, were eager to either refute him or support him on the vital point of fertility while ignoring the other variables?

We intend to show that the answers to these two questions, viz. Marx's ambivalence towards Malthus and the nature of his views on population, are actually directly linked with two fundamental theoretical elements of *Capital*, viz. accumulation and surplus value, referring to his main interest which is the prediction of the collapse of capitalism. When analysing Malthus's thinking, it was necessary to start with demography and then go on to economics, following the chronological order of his writings. It must be remembered that *the Essay on the Principle of Population* was published in 1798 and the subsequent editions were profoundly revised before the publication of the *Principles of Economics* in 1820. In the case of Marx and Engels, it is necessary to move in the opposite direction because demographic theory can only be understood on the basis of economic theory. As a matter of fact, though they refer to Malthus and population much before the publication of Book I of *Capital* in 1867,[4] their ideas do not have the strict coherence that they gained from 1867 onwards. In fact, when they denounced the Poor Laws or the crises induced by capitalism, it is evident that they were still trying to sort out their ideas until the final epistemological change occurred in 1845. It is necessary to start afresh from basic economic concepts and once the theoretical base is established, the law on population logically fits into the structure, both theoretically and empirically. Let us finally point out that this chapter confines itself to Marx and

---

were published by Engels in 1885 and 1894 and the draft of Book IV (Theories of Surplus Value) was published by Kautsky in 1905.

[4] A careful reader can discern references to Malthus and to population in general in articles published in 1848–1849 in the *Neue Reinische Zeitung*, but they are not expressed in the form of a theory. For example, the journal *Die Constitution* contains a "fairly long" report on a lecture by Dr. Marx in Vienna on 2 September 1848, at the first meeting of the First Workers' Union. It says, "The speaker also talks of the remedies used and their inadequacy, as for example Malthus's theory of overpopulation." Vol. III: 475. Also see issue No. 60, 30 July 1848, regarding a mobile scale of duty on cereals, proposed by Hansemann-Pinto, which reminds Marx of Malthus's double progression (Vol. I: 330).

Engels and their criticism of Malthus. It does not deal with either Darwin, whom Marx and Engels rightly considered Malthus's heir, or with later anti-Malthusian doctrines formulated by Marxists and orthodox Communists, except for brief allusions when they are necessary to understand Marx (e.g. Rosa Luxembourg and Lenin).[5]

It is surprising indeed that there should be so few in-depth studies, or at least studies easily available in English or French, dealing with the thoughts of Marx and Engels on population. Among the French sociologists, for example, Raymond Aron peremptorily declares that Marx "is first and foremost a sociologist and economist of the capitalist regime." Referring to the demonstration of pauperisation, he dismisses it in one line as "a socio-demographic mechanism based on an unemployed reserve army of workers" and does not return to the subject again. Similarly, in *Homo Æqualis* Louis Dumont notes that Marx's conclusions and results regarding "the exuberant production of socio-historical analyses" are "very unevenly integrated in his general theory", but when he quotes Malthus in the same chapter, he compares him with Ricardo and not with Marx.[6] As it could be expected, the most meaningful writings are those of economists and demographers. As regards specialists of economic theory, the main contributions have come from Sidney H. Coontz, who focuses on the concept of the demand for work, and Ronald Meek, whose indispensable work brings together the main writings of Engels and Marx, preceded by a long introduction.[7] Among the early XXth century specialists, René Gonnard devotes barely two pages to Marx. He rapidly presents the two laws of population put forth by Marx and Malthus and concludes with the astonishing statement, "It is curious to note that Malthus was, however, a precursor of Marx, due to his general attempt to explain economic development from the viewpoint of historical materialism."[8] As for Charles Gide and Charles Rist, they do not say a word about what Marx has to say regarding Malthus or even his theory of value. Joseph Schumpeter briefly mentions Marx's and Malthus's laws on population in the preface and refuses to get involved in any argument about them. Recent publications by specialists of the history of economic theory have a limited approach and even tend to be evasive on

[5] The assessment by Berelovitch in *Malthus hier et aujourd'hui*, suggests that in Russia Marx is essentially cited by nineteenth century communists (pp. 405–415); the twentieth century point of view is confirmed by Behar quoting Spirkine, Yakhot, Gleserman, Koursanov, Urlanis, Valentey and Guzevaty (1976: 9–12, 21). Regarding Marxist thinkers, see Gani (1979) on Laffargue and Guesde; Meublat (1975) and Behar (1974) on Otto Bauer, Rosa Luxemburg, Antonio Gramsci and Paul Sweezy. Articles by McQuillan (1982) and Brackett (1968) are more thorough than those by Mertens (1962) and Sauvy (1966). One of the popular works by Alfred Sauvy with the enticing title (*Malthus et les deux Marx, De Malthus à Mao-Tsé-Toung*) does not deal with the subject in depth.

[6] Raymond Aron: *Les étapes de la pensée sociologique*: 144, and again 145, 158, 177; on the socio-demographic mechanism of the unemployed army of workers: 170. Louis Dumont, *Homo* Æqualis: 204–205.

[7] *L'épouvantail malthusien*, by Jean Fréville, which can be considered as another example of orthodox Marxism, is outdated and, in the final analysis, also quite superficial.

[8] 1923: 324.

this subject which is nevertheless so vast (Heilbroner, 2001). Finally, even a systematic survey (1969–2004) of the *History of Political Economy*, considered to be a reference journal on the history of economic thought, proves to be disappointing. There are relatively few articles on Marx and hardly any mention (even indirect) of the law of population through references to the organic composition of capital.[9] The debate in the *American Economic Review* starting in 1983 between Baumol, Hollander and Ramirez is more meaningful even though it is rather confused. It was continued in 1988, 1991 and 1995 in the *History of Political Economy* by Cottrell, Darity, Green and Brewer. Essentially, these writers differ on one point: whether Marx succeeded in demonstrating that the growth of the industrial reserve army and, consequently, the growth of wages are independent of population growth. In other words, if population is assumed to be an exogenous and uncontrollable variable, Marx failed to refute Malthus's theory. On the other hand, Marx and Malthus have seldom been read in the light of present-day environmentalist concerns. Michael Perelmann has devoted significant and convincing studies to the position of Marx and Malthus on the subject of rarity while a recent issue of the journal *Organization and Environment* is questionable, if not ludicrous.[10]

What about demographers? E.P. Hutchinson (1967), Johanes Overbeek (1974), John R. Weeks (1992), William Petersen (1988), who say little about Marx, are almost silent about the antagonism between Marx and Malthus or pass very swiftly over it. Only Cem Behar (1974, 1976) delves deep into the Marxist theory of population; but, on the other hand, he hardly touches on Malthus. A systematic survey of the five main journals since they were started, viz. *Demography* (1964), *Genus* (1942), *Population* (1945), *Population Studies* (1950), *Population and Development Review* (1985), yields a poor harvest. *Malthus hier et aujourd'hui*, a collective work touching upon a wide variety of disciplines, which was the result of an international seminar in 1981, gives an idea of the present state of thinking on the subject. In her review of the papers presented during the session on "Malthus and Socialism", Michelle Perrot restricts herself to only two paragraphs on Marx. And in the session on "Malthus the Economist", no paper deals seriously with the relationship between the ideas of Marx and Malthus.[11] Referring to an

[9] The "mini-symposium" on Marx in 1995, which brought together ten authors, mentioned population in two places: 3 pages in an article on "Wages and the Value of Labour-Power" and sixteen lines by Foley on pauperisation, to affirm without argument that Marx "simply would not admit the possibility that capitalist industrialization would raise workers' standards of living as in fact it did" (Foley, 1995: 163).

[10] The first, published in a brief presentation of Marxist theory, treats it as though it were a logical development of the latter and does not hesitate to surreptitiously slip in the sentence, "in the capitalist system, men should adapt themselves to the environment which results from the tendency of capitalism to create widespread unemployment" (Wiltgen, 1998: 453). The other article gives the same importance to the devastation of land denounced by Marx and to the forced exodus of men due to relative overpopulation, which is, to say the least, disproportionate (Gimenez, 1998: 463).

[11] *Malthus Past and Present*... (1983: 261–262). Jacques Wolff devotes 21 lines to this topic which include a comparison between Marx and Keynes (1983: 68). But Martin Bronfenbrenner, Guy Caire and Jean Cartelier (all in the 1984 French edition of that book) are silent on the subject

unpublished paper by Raimondo Castagno Azevedo, Michelle Perrot says without taking sides, "knowing whether Marx had actually read Malthus" is subject to debate.[12]

Last, the appendix to this chapter discusses the purely philosophical reading of Marx, which has been proposed by the Althusserian school, which had the great merit to raise the problem of the epistemological status of the population, but excludes all the other levels of interpretation. It will be shown that this narrow line generates inner epistemological contradictions.

The Poverty of the Working Classes and the Poor Laws

Engels wrote one after the other, *Outlines of a Critique of Political Economy*, an article published in the short-lived *Deutsch-Franzosische Jahrbücher* (only one issue of which appeared in February 1844) and a book, *The Condition of the Working Class in England in 1844*, which continues to serve as a frame of reference for writers on English capitalism. He was well placed to do this as he was born in a family belonging to the German industrial bourgeoisie and was well aware of the realities of the business world even as he frequented radical circles, and especially because he had been living since 1842 in Manchester, the capital of the cotton trade, where he conducted a genuine social survey.[13] His analysis of the functioning of the labour market, which opened the way to the concept of relative overpopulation, regarding which Marx would theorise in *Capital*, is simultaneously micro- and macroeconomic. He pointed out that following the deterioration of working conditions, workers married early and increased their fertility so that they could earn faster from the extra income brought in by their wives and children. Engels thus combined Malthus's population theory with Adam Smith's analysis to show that the workers' behaviour was directly governed by the ruthless competition they had to face to obtain employment. At the macroeconomic level, he explained how, thanks to the flexibility of capitalism and to what Rosa Luxemburg and Lenin would turn into a theory based on the concept of imperialism, the demand for work went up, as a result of which the population of the British Empire continued to grow instead of decreasing. He finally concluded his analysis of this ruthless competition by emphasising the need for an "unemployed reserve army of workers" and the

---

of Marx. According to Michel Herland, "Marx sought to ridicule Malthus the theoretician because he saw in him a political enemy." (1984: 293). As for A.W. Coats, he says that Marx is particularly brutal when he describes Malthus as a 'plagiarist', a 'professionnal sycophant' and an 'ideologue of the landed aristocracy' (1984: 310); only Etienne Van de Walle questions the reason for this hostility (1984: 425), but he does not provide an answer.

[12] Perrot: ibid.: 261. Going by a chapter written by this writer in a collective work published in 1977, this is hardly what he says: Marx had well and truly read Malthus, but, due to lack of time, he never applied himself to an exhaustive rebuttal. And as this chapter will show, there is no doubt on this point.

[13] Regarding the quality of the research done by Engels, it is interesting to read Eric Hobsbawm's preface to *The Situation* . . .: 7–23.

so-called "surplus population" of England. Then he went on to denounce the "social policy" formulated in 1833 following the amendment of the Poor Law of 1601, firmly establishing a link between Malthus's theory and "surplus population". He declared, "The most open declaration of war of the bourgeoisie upon the proletariat is Malthus's Law of Population and the new Poor Law framed in accordance with it." He challenged conservative opinion according to which there was no point in continuing aid (e.g. the *Speenhamland System*, which decreed in 1795 that the relief given to parishes should be proportionate to the number of children and the price of bread), on the pretext that it would spur the growth of this surplus population by encouraging "improvident marriages" and a higher fertility. But when he wrote that this aided population puts a strain on the wages of employed workers, it must be noted that he subscribed to the classical theory of a wage fund. The break with classical economics would occur later under the influence of Marx. Finally, he believed that those who amended the Poor Law did not dare to apply Malthus's theory in its entirety as the allegory of the banquet implied that the man who was incapable of satisfying his needs was surplus on earth and condemned to die of hunger. "Good," said they, "we grant you poor a right to exist, but only to exist; the right to multiply you have not, nor the right to exist as befits human beings. You are a pest, and if we cannot get rid of you as we do of other pests, you shall feel, at least, that you are a pest, and you shall be at least held in check, kept from bringing into the world other 'surplus'." Workhouses were invented and their regulations conceived "so as to frighten away everyone who has the slightest prospect of life without that form of public charity".[14]

This condemnation was based on the conventional interpretation of Malthus, viz. regulating surplus population through mortality, and denouncing the allegory of the banquet, which justified the absence of any questioning of social inequalities. It thus ignored other aspects of Malthus's thinking and amounted to an instinctive rejection of the Malthusian doctrine, so characteristic of radical English reformers (like William Godwin or William Cobbett) and French socialists all through the nineteenth century. In 1845, Engels' thinking represented the optimism inspired by the Enlightenment for another reason. The other way to refute Malthus was to reject his contention that the means of subsistence are insufficient. On the basis of Archibald Alison's *The Principles of Population in Connection with Human Happiness*, published in 1840, Engels held that "the 'overpopulated' Great Britain could be so developed in the course of ten years to produce sufficient corn for six times its present population. Capital increases daily; labour power grows together with population; and science masters natural forces for mankind to a greater extent every day." This is so because scientific progress is as limitless and rapid as the growth of population and he gave the example of agriculture's debt to chemistry and particularly to Humphry Davis and Justus Liebig. How can it be it possible to talk of overpopulation while "the valley of the Mississippi alone contains enough waste land to accommodate the whole population of Europe, while altogether only one third of the earth can be described as cultivated and while the productivity of this

[14] *The Situation...*: 348.

third could be increased six fold and more merely by applying improvements that are already known"? Finally, in 1844, he believed that he could still resolve, thanks to science and education, the contradiction raised by Malthus, "With the fusion of those interests which now conflict with one another, there will disappear the antithesis between surplus population in one place and surplus wealth in another."[15] This shows to what extent Engels' thinking was still very idealistic. Such is the essence of the anti-Malthusian arguments put forth by Engels. What does Marx have to say?

During the summer of 1844, an article by Arnold Ruge titled "The King of Prussia and Social Reform" appeared in *Vorwärts*, a magazine published by a group of German revolutionaries exiled in Paris. On 7 and 14 August 1844, Marx published in the same magazine a critical review of this article as a rebuttal of the belief that the problem of chronic poverty in Prussia was caused above all by the shortcomings of the administration and the lack of philanthropic action. Marx had closely followed the developments in England and refused to pay attention to the differences between the Whigs and the Tories. The former held that the principal cause of poverty was the existence of large landed estates and the ban on the import of wheat. According to the Tories, who defended the landed aristocracy, the real cause was liberalism and ruthless competition unleashed by industrial capitalism. Both the political parties blamed each other's political conduct, but neither saw the causes of pauperism in "politics in general" and "neither of the two parties ever dreamt of a reform of society".[16] So England, he continued, is the only country characterised by a large-scale "*political* action against pauperism" that attributes the acute nature of present-day poverty to the Poor Law and hence to shortcomings in the management of poverty. But the comparison with Prussia stops there. In England, this national epidemic was attributed to the worker's lack of education, which reduced him to poverty and drove him to revolt, which might – and here Marx quotes Eugène Buret – "affect the prosperity of manufactures and trade (...) and diminish the stability of political and social institutions."[17] Marx wondered why the English bourgeoisie, which had dealt with poverty *politically*, had gone astray to the point of "misunderstanding the general significance of universal need" and distress whose general importance had been accentuated "partly through its periodical recurrence in time, partly through its extension in space, and partly through the failure of all attempts to remedy it." Thus he came back to Malthus, pointing out that in England, unlike Prussia, "Pauperism is looked upon as an eternal law of nature, according to the theory of Malthus." So the English Parliament combined this theory with the opinion that "pauperism is *poverty*

---

[15] Quotations: *Esquisse...*: 50, 58, 61–62.

[16] *Gloses...*: 402. On Marx 's views on natural resources, see Pearlman, 1985.

[17] Interesting notes can be found in Althusser (1996, 72–74) on the difference between England and Prussia as well as on Prussia's "historical incapability of bringing about national unity and a bourgeois revolution". This was the cause of "ideological overdevelopment" of which Hegel is a prime example, while the reading of theoretical works by French and English writers together with purely historical works prepared Marx for his break with Hegelian idealism.

which the workers have brought on themselves, and that it should therefore be regarded not as a calamity to be prevented but rather as a crime to be suppressed and punished."[18] Marx thus complements Engels when it comes analysis of the reform of the Poor Laws. Even though both of them firmly link it with the Malthusian theory, Marx goes further than Engels by exposing the limitations of bourgeois ideology owing to the "inability," writes Meeks, "to understand the problem of its uncritical acceptance of Malthus's explanation in terms of an 'eternal law of nature'."[19]

The Epistemological Break of 1845 and Population

In 1965, Louis Althusser pointed out that the young Marx, who wrote *The German Ideology* broke away from his Hegelian idealism in 1845 to write his major works showing proof of maturity like *Capital* (1867) and the theories of surplus value, written between 1861–63 but published after his death by Engels and Kautsky.[20] In 1969, in the foreword (*Avertissement aux lecteurs*) to a new edition of *Capital*, Althusser qualifies his judgement. The preface written in 1859 to *A Contribution to the Critique of Political Economy* is still profoundly Hegelian and evolutionist because, even though "something decisive started in 1845, Marx still had to put in a lot of work before he could translate into truly new concepts the revolution accomplished with Hegel's ideas."[21] We will come back later to Althusser's arguments and to the total absence of any mention of population in his book *Lire le Capital* which is surprising because if there is one point on which Marx takes a definite position against Hegel, it is the conceptualisation and theorisation of population.

Applying the Method of Political Economy to Population

After writing *A Contribution to the Critique of Political Economy*, Marx denounced the reification of population by economists. It is significant that the section titled "The method of political economy" begins with the example of population, as if Marx believed that it was the best example for denouncing the claim that this bourgeois science was capable of separating facts from their social base. "When examining a given country the economists begin with its population, the division of the population into classes, its distribution between town and country. They carry on with hydrography, the different branches of production, export and import, annual

[18] Ibid.: 403–405. Also see p. 408. According to Eugène Buret, Marx quotes an anonymous pamphlet by "Dr Kay". E. Buret took this extract from the 11th edition of Kay's pamphlet (who was later found to be Sir J-D Kay-Shuttleworth) published in 1839. Buret's book, *De la misère des classes laborieuses en Angleterre et en France*, appeared in 1840.

[19] *Op.cit.*: 53.

[20] *Lire le Capital*, particularly 345–362.

[21] Althusser, *Avertissement...*: 21.

production and consumption, prices, etc (...). Population is an abstraction if, for instance, one disregards the classes of which it is composed. These classes in turn remain empty terms if one does not know the factors on which they depend, e.g., wage-labour, capital, and so on. It would seem to be the proper thing to start with the real and concrete elements, with the actual preconditions, e.g., to start in the sphere of economy with population, which forms the basis and the subject of the whole social process of production. Closer consideration shows, however, that this is wrong. It is a sham that results in a chaotic interpretation of everything, for one would arrive analytically at increasingly simple concepts; from imaginary concrete terms one would move to more and more tenuous abstractions until one reached the most simple definitions." The right method, on the contrary, would be to "make the journey again in the opposite direction until one arrived once more at the concept of population, which this time is not a vague notion of a whole, but a totality comprising many determinations and relations". Having denounced this pseudo-scientific method, he goes on to attack the basics of false science. "The first course is the historical one taken by political economy at its inception (...). The first procedure attenuates meaningful images to abstract definitions, the second leads from abstract definitions by way of reasoning to the reproduction of the concrete situation. Hegel accordingly conceived the illusory idea that the real world is the result of thinking which causes its own synthesis, its own deepening and its own movement; whereas the method of advancing from the abstract to the concrete is simply the way in which thinking assimilates the concrete and reproduces it as a concrete mental category."

Why did Marx choose population as an example? On this point, it may be a good idea to side with Althusser in the controversy that opposed him in 1963 to Garaudy and Mury. Marx was bent on "overturning" Hegelian dialectic and his *Introduction to the Critique of Political Economy*, written in 1859, is "a methodological text of the first order" where the word overturning does not appear, but which "speaks of its reality: namely; what are the conditions for a valid scientific use of the concepts of political economy. It is enough to think about this use to draw from it the fundamental elements of dialectics."[22] From Althusser's point of view, population is actually the object of a double movement: idealisation into categories of figures that we would call individual socio-demographic data and then the substantiation of these categories, irrespective of their participation in the dialectic balance of power. Thus, when one talks of a rural exodus and of push and pull factors, the deeper meaning is lost, because leaving the countryside after being expropriated is not the same as voluntary migration. And if the need for this theoretical break with Hegelian idealism is illustrated in Marx's case by the example of population, it is not an accident. It is, as we shall see, the prerequisite that allows Marx to move to the analysis of primitive accumulation, which in its turn gives a theoretical perspective to population movements before the industrial revolution. The crises of capitalism

[22] Althusser, *Pour Marx*: 184. The expression is found in the afterword of the second edition of *Capital*.

show how Marx gave himself the means of cutting himself off from idealism, which is naïve, being more often than not trapped by the observation of reality. This is seen in the changes that occurred in relation to Engels' analyses.

From Engels to Marx: Analysing the Crises of Capitalism

In *The Condition of the Working Class in England in 1844*, Engels defines the overpopulation of England as an "unemployed reserve army of workers." But in *Capital*, Marx uses the concept of an "industrial reserve army". The change of adjective with *industrial* replacing *unemployed* is not without significance as it refers to a totally different conceptualisation. When Engels talks of unemployed workers, he does so in a passage describing the nature of commercial and ruthless competition which emphasises the key role played by the capitalist.[23] The latter performs his function in an environment over which he has little control and although he knows the quantity of a particular product bought in the course of a year in the markets of various countries, he does not know anything about the market demand for the product, the stocks available or the volume exported by his competitors, which he can assess only roughly on the basis of price fluctuation. And since all company heads are in the same position, the slightest favourable sign in a foreign market causes a spurt in exports leading to the saturation of the market. As soon as the sales lose momentum, production stops and there is less work for workers employed in that branch of industry. So, with the advance of capitalism, markets become so unstable that the crisis affecting a particular market is not limited to it alone; all sectoral crises end up as a chronic crisis affecting all markets (domestic as well as foreign) and all branches of industry. Small enterprises cannot survive such situations and go bankrupt.

The rest of the argument takes us to the socio-demographic consequences of such crises caused by overproduction: "wages fall by reason of the competition of the unemployed, the diminution of working-time and the lack of profitable sales; want becomes universal among the workers, the small savings which individuals may have made are rapidly consumed, the philanthropic institutions are overburdened, the poor-rates are doubled, trebled, and still insufficient, the number of the starving increases, and the whole multitude of 'surplus' population presses in terrific numbers into the foreground. This continues for a time; the 'surplus' exists as best they may or perish." The return to prosperity is unfortunately accompanied by fresh speculative action whose intensity is explained by the need to ensure an immediate return on capital. Engels believes that economic cycles last on an average for five to six years and concludes that, "English manufactures must have at all times, save the brief periods of highest prosperity, an unemployed reserve army of workers, in

[23] *Op.cit.*: 126–127. We have at times modified the quotations taken from the French translation and quoted the original English words as given in Meek, when they appeared to be more exact (*op.cit.*: 76–79).

order to be able to produce the mass of goods required by the market in the liveliest months." To maintain this army in times of prosperity, the less active branches of industry provide the required labour, agriculture too contributes to the work force and women and children are put to work.

This analysis is directly related to the analysis of the labour market, even if it lays stress on the paroxysm caused by competition resulting in the creation of a reserve army whose strength goes up in the short term due to the workers' mobility. Engels is quite clear and mentions the need to employ women and children and the rural exodus in the case of agriculture. But quite logically he does not foresee any mechanism for increasing labour supply apart from early marriage and high fertility because he describes short economic cycles, whereas it takes time for birth cohorts to take their place in the labour market, as Malthus observed earlier. The demand for labour was crucial for Malthus and the entire classical school, adjustments being made by hiring or dismissing surplus labour. It is therefore easy to see the need for a reserve army of *unemployed* workers. Engels was also limited by his reading of Malthus's first *Essay* on another point, viz. regulation of population according to the means of subsistence. "Malthus, who carried the foregoing proposition of Adam Smith farther,[24] was also right, in his way, in asserting that there are always more people at hand than can be maintained from the available means of subsistence. Surplus population is engendered rather by the competition of the workers among themselves, which forces each separate worker to labour as much each day as his strength can possibly admit."[25] We may therefore conclude that in 1844 Engels was still caught in the trap of Malthusian logic.

In *Capital*, especially in Chapter 25, the analysis of the crises caused by capitalism reveals a radical change of perspective. Marx was not interested in economic movements but in structural changes, while Engels, focused on cyclical crises. It is tempting to interpret this difference by opposing empiricism to theoretical construction with Engels playing the role of an observer and describing the true situation of workers in England in the 1840s. However, this interpretation is not quite satisfactory because throughout Book I of *Capital* there are numerous and particularly well documented pages, which are remarkable examples of sociology of labour. Marx, when analysing the need to employ of women and children, to extend working hours and increase the intensity of work, relies on a mass of concrete data. In addition to Engels' book, he uses, particularly in Chapters 10, 15 and 25 of Book I of *Capital*,

---

[24] In the chapter on wages for work, Adam Smith writes, "If this demand increases continuously, the remuneration for work will necessarily encourage marriage and the multiplication of workers in such a manner that it will enable them to satisfy this constantly growing demand of a constantly growing population. (...) the demand for men, like the demand for any other good, which necessarily regulates its production. It will make it grow faster when it grows too slowly and it will stop when it grows too fast." (*The Wealth of Nations*, Book 1, Chapter 8, p. 183). Regarding the demand for readers may consult Coontz, 1961.

[25] *Op. cit.*: 124.

material from *Reports of Inspectors of Factories,*[26] *Reports on Public Health,*[27] *Reports of the Children Employment Commission*[28] and various specific surveys and accounts available from time to time.[29] Thus it is not possible to use the argument of Engels' empiricism due to the very nature of his subject, which was the description of the social situation in 1844. Besides, when he describes economic crises, Marx is more concerned about their social implication, e.g. malnutrition following the cotton crisis of 1862 or mortality following the starvation of the poor in London in 1866–1867.[30] However, his thinking on economic crises is based on a perspective that is very different from Engels'. The speculator, who is a central figure in Engels' writings, is hardly mentioned and no specifically speculative action is actually censured.[31]

When Marx makes a careful inventory of crises over a long stretch of time (1770–1866) with particular reference to the cotton trade, which illustrates capitalist mode of production in its purest form, his objective is very clear: counting the years of crisis to prove that they continuously increased as compared to periods of prosperity and that this is an inevitable consequence of greater international competition and therefore closely related to the functioning of capitalism. "We find then, in the first 45 years of the English cotton trade, from 1770 to 1815, only 5 years of crisis and stagnation."[32] To support our interpretation, the penultimate chapter of Book I[33] and indeed the final section of Book I devoted to primitive accumulation acquire a historical depth that the previous sections do not have. "The economic structure of capitalistic society has grown out of the economic structure of feudal society".[34] Marx proposes to his readers a synthetic overview based on "The expropriation of the agricultural population from the land" since the last third of the fifteenth century, which was a period of great discoveries, of mercantilism and of the enclosures movement (Chapters 27–29), which logically led him to the "Genesis of the industrial capitalist" (Chapters 30 and 31). In Chapter 32, which is very short (just two and a half pages), he turns his attention to the future. The "Historical tendency

[26] Reports dated 31 October 1855, 31 October 1856, 10 June 1857, 31 October 1858, 30 April 1860, 31 October 1861, 31 October 1862, 30 April 1863, 31 October 1865 and 31 October 1866.

[27] *Sixth Report on Public Health*, London, 1864. He also quotes the 1863 and 1866 reports.

[28] Especially the 1863, 1864 and 1866 reports. Also see the analysis of the labour law governing mines (*Factory Acts* of 1833, 1844 and 1847) in Chapter 15 of *Capital* (355–362) and the duration of work (Chapter 10 *Capital*: 208–221).

[29] *Report by Dr Julian Hunt on the excessive mortality of infants in some rural districts of England*, speech by Lord Ashley on the ten-hour law in the House of Commons in 1844; Alexander Redgrave, *Journal of the Society of Arts*, 5 January 1872; statement of Mr. Ferrand in the House of Commons on 27 April 1863.

[30] Crisis of 1862: 497–482. Crisis of 1866: 490 and footnote 84: 680.

[31] Except for the crisis of 1866 (*Capital*, I: 490).

[32] *Capital*, I: 325–326. Quotation p. 329.

[33] Chapter 32 "Historical Tendency of Capital Accumulation".

[34] *Capital*, I: 528 (Chapter 26).

of capitalistic accumulation", which is barely outlined in contrast with the long developments on the accumulation in England in the middle of the nineteenth century, assumes a prophetic character, which explains the meticulous counting of the years of crisis between 1770 and 1866. Marx refers to "the immanent laws of capitalistic production itself, which generates the concentration of capital" and he ends up predicting the system's inevitable collapse. "Along with the constantly diminishing number of the magnates of capital, who usurp and monopolise all advantages of this process of transformation, grows the mass of misery, oppression, slavery, degradation, exploitation; but with this too grows the revolt of the working-class, a class always increasing in numbers, and disciplined, united, organised by the very mechanism of the process of capitalist production itself". Why and how, Marx does not tell us, but all through the preceding chapters, he has been taking note of the strikes and the movements of resistance to the most glaring instances of capitalistic exploitation. He concludes by saying, "The monopoly of capital becomes a fetter upon the mode of production, which has sprung up and flourished along with, and under it. Centralisation of the means of production and socialisation of labour at last reach a point where they become incompatible with their capitalist integument. This integument is burst asunder. The knell of capitalist private property sounds".[35]

Thus the conditions that produced the epistemological break with the writings of 1844 are brought together. His rejection of the concept of the "unemployed reserve army of workers" in favour of the concept of an "industrial reserve army" cannot be separated from a double movement consisting of a passage from short-term cyclical crises to long-term structural changes and rejecting the belief in the crucial role of actors like the capitalist and the speculative financier in favour of a picture showing entrepreneurs subjected to an inevitable process of accumulation, in other words a passage from a micro-economic analysis of the firm to a macro-economic analysis of development. In the same way, Jacques Rancière writing about the *Manuscripts* of 1844 says that "the importance given to competition in the *Manuscripts* – and even more in Engels' writings – reveals the still ideological nature of their criticism of political economy, and the confusion between what Marx will distinguish as the real and the apparent movement in *Capital*."[36] Let us return to Engels for a moment to get an idea of the distance covered. On 29 March 1865, Engels wrote to F. Lange about his book on the subject of workers, "You ask yourself how increase of population and increase in the means of subsistence are to be brought into harmony; but except for one sentence in the preface I find no attempt to solve the question. We start from the premise that the same forces which have created modern bourgeois society – the steam engine, modern machinery, mass colonization, railways, steamships, world trade – and which are now already, through permanent trade crises, working towards its ruin and ultimate destruction, these same means of production and exchange will also suffice to reverse the relation in a short time, and to raise the productive power of each individual so much that he can produce

[35] *Capital*, I: 566–567.

[36] *Lire le Capital*: 105. Also see 104, on the personality of a capitalist; 105, on competition; 154–159 on the capitalist's subjective attitude.

enough for the consumption of two, three, four, five or six individuals."[37] Engels, in accordance with what would later be termed as Marxist orthodoxy, implicitly refers to the contradictions of capitalistic accumulation and the break with the utopian views of 1844 is complete.

Proudhon could not escape the trap of Malthusian logic. Marx, on the contrary, succeeded in doing so but at the cost of theoretical work done much before the formulation of the law of population, whereas he would inevitably have fallen into the trap had he referred to the concept of the labour market and the adjustment between supply and demand. The epistemological break was therefore indispensable to escape the Malthusian trap and Marx was able to refute the Malthus's population theory, widely accepted by his contemporaries as a universal law, only by demonstrating that it was inseparable from the working of capitalism and by linking it firmly with social classes, the theory of surplus value and the process of widespread accumulation. This is the subject of the following pages.

The Accumulation of Capital and Its Organic Composition

The *Theories of Surplus Value*, written between 1861 and 1863, marks a crucial turning point in the formulation of Marx's population theory. What is remarkable is that, contrary to the article that appeared in *Vorwärts* in 1844, the argument lies entirely and *solely* in the domain of economic theory without any reference to social policy or to the analysis of the bourgeois ideology. Marx begins with the accumulation of capital and emphasises the decisive progress made by John Barton[38] in 1817 as compared to Smith and Malthus. Even though the latter were well aware that the demand for labour governs population and Malthus had correctly understood that the risk of overpopulation was a consequence of the accumulation and reproduction of capital at a pace slower than that of population, Barton was the first to emphasise that "the different organic constituencies of capital do not increase at the same rate when capital is accumulated", as the part which resolves itself into wages diminishes while the fixed capital increases, and this is more marked in industrialised countries than elsewhere.[39] Ricardo, Marx continues, abandons in the third edition of his *Principles of Political Economy* Smith's approach in favour of Barton's and – an "important" point according to Marx – Ricardo goes even further to assert that the machine itself causes a "redundancy of population", thus creating overpopulation.[40]

---

[37] affirms the same thing in a letter written to Kautsky on 1st February 1881. *Letters...*: 299.

[38] *Observations of the Circumstances which Influence the Condition of the Labouring Classes of Society*, London, 1817.

[39] *Theories...*, Vol.V: 167. Taken up in Chapter 15 of *Capital* (I: 325).

[40] *Theories...*, Vol. V: 167–168. We have borrowed Meek's translation (1971: 83), which is much better than Molitor's (who misinterprets the word "price" on p. 168).

What is important is that "the whole absurd 'theory of population' was overturned by this and also in particular the empty assertion of the vulgar economists to the effect that the workers must strive to keep their rate of reproduction below that of the accumulation of capital. It follows on the contrary from the arguments of Barton and Ricardo that such a restriction on the reproduction of the working population, because of the decrease in the supply of labour and the consequent rise in its price, would only speed up the employment of machinery, the transformation of circulating capital into fixed capital, and would therefore artificially create a surplus population, a surplus which is usually caused not by a lack of subsistence, but by a lack of means of employment of the workers, a lack of demand for labour."[41] Marx, in line with the classical economists, holds that demographic growth is induced by economic growth, but he breaks new ground by demonstrating that any autonomous movement of demographic growth necessarily reintegrates itself in the accumulation process. If so, it was not possible to foresee any significant effect on the demographic growth due to the population principle itself. Marx thus solved the problem confronting Malthus, viz. how to integrate the population principle in the mechanism of adjusting the supply and demand for labour. Malthus the demographer, who had always assumed that this exogenous *demographic* variable would come into action *ex ante*, had to somehow *import* it in his *economic* model of the analysis of the market for products and work in the agricultural sector.[42]

Marx took this up as his central idea and improved upon it many times in Chapter 25 of Book I of *Capital.*[43] In the absence of any change in the organic composition of capital (the division between constant capital and variable capital remaining the same), the demand for work increases directly due to an increase in the total mass of capital. This leads to a regular rise in wages because a part of the surplus value is annually integrated into the fixed capital.[44] For the reason mentioned in the *Theories of Surplus Value*, the objection that immediately comes to mind, namely a faster growth of population, cannot be raised in that case; the demographic characteristics of the working class, and particularly its fertility and mortality levels, do not change anything in the accumulation process.[45] And he

---

41 *Theories...*, Vol. V: 167–168.

42 As with all classical economists, the Malthusian concept of dynamics – at least in the first *Essay*, but not in the later works – is reduced to an analysis of the fluctuations around a point of equilibrium in two distinct markets: the labour market and the agricultural produce market. (see Chapter 2, the second Malthusian model).

43 In particular: 444–445, from where the following quotations have been taken.

44 Any new avenue for production giving rise to the additional accumulation of capital, "since in each year more labourers are employed sooner or later a point must be reached at which the requirements of accumulation begin to surpass the customary supply of labour, and therefore a rise of wages must take place. A lamentation on this score was heard in England during the whole of the fifteenth, and the first half of the eighteenth centuries."*Capital*, I: 444.

45 "The more or less favourable circumstances in which the wage-working class supports and multiplies itself, in no way alters the fundamental character of capitalistic reproduction (...) This

quotes turn by turn the mercantilists Mandeville (the author of *Fable of the Bees*) and Eden who had understood after a gap of one century that "the surest wealth consists in a multitude of laborious poor" (Mandeville) and that "a portion at least of the society must be indefatigably employed" (Eden). Although the mercantilists had not theorised the exploitation of workers, they had understood its logic perfectly. Besides, Mandeville who lays stress on the need for the poor to work incessantly, especially if their wages are barely above subsistence level and they remain "ignorant", cynically viewed things from a typically mercantilist perspective: "for besides that they are the never-failing nursery of fleets and armies, without them there could be no enjoyment and no product of any country could be valuable." One hundred and fifty years later, we have moved from a demographic doctrine without a theoretical base, so characteristic of the mercantilists, to the theorisation by Marx of the constitution and the expansion of the proletariat. In order to convince his readers better, he explains a little later why the rise in wages does not change anything and cannot harm the capitalist system: if they continue to rise, the profits, as shown by Smith (quoted at length by Marx), will decrease, but the capital will always benefit by being invested because it will continue to earn interest and even if the interest is not very high, the process of accumulation will be strengthened. If, on the contrary, wages increase by slowing down accumulation, the relative surplus of work in relation to the capital will decrease and the rate of wages will fall. What really matters is not the change in the population of workers – whether there is an increase or decrease in absolute or relative terms – but the proportion of employed workers within the entire working class.[46] As the biological dimension of Malthus's thinking is eliminated, the population principle dependent on the sexual instinct ceases to be important. What continue to matter are the historicised individuals, i.e. workers selling their labour.

Marx's Primitive Accumulation Versus Malthus's Effective Demand

Even if it were admitted that once the accumulation process gets started it sustains itself, one question remains unanswered, viz. what is the starting point? Marx fully understands the difficulty: manufacturing cannot be divided and mechanisation can be introduced only in areas where large-scale production already exists and "a certain accumulation of capital (...) forms therefore the necessary prelim-

reproduction of labour-power forms, in fact, an essential of the reproduction of capital itself. Accumulation of capital is, therefore, an increase of the proletariat." Ibid.

46 "It is therefore in no way a relation between two magnitudes, independant of each other: on the one hand, the magnitude of the capital; on the other, the number of the labouring population; it is rather, at bottom, only the relation between the unpaid and the paid labour of the same labouring population." *Capital*, I: 447–448. Regarding this point, see Behar, 1974 and 1976.

inary of the specifically capitalistic mode of production."[47] On this subject, Marx repeats Smith almost word for word saying, "Work cannot expand to this extent without a preliminary accumulation of capital."[48] Once again his path crosses that of Malthus and his research on effectual demand. As a matter of fact, the latter had asked himself what gave rise to the initial investment and wondered about the origin of the real demand and the pre-existing purchasing power that set in motion the production of a particular good. To put it in present-day language, which potential market would offer sufficiently good prospects for the decision to invest? Let us recall Malthus's argument that Marx partly followed in his *Theories of Surplus Value*.

The Effective Demand

Malthus subscribes to the orthodox ideas of the classical economic theory, according to which supply is determined by the demand for labour.[49] And if Malthus rules out the idea that the growth of population (supply of labour) cannot govern production (demand for labour), it is so because there must be an existing demand in order to start a new line of production; in other words, there must be a pre-existent income and purchasing power independent of those that will be created when the production materialises.[50] On this point, Marx agrees with Malthus because the worker cannot buy from his capitalist employer the merchandise that he has been employed to produce, because the employer cannot realise any surplus value (in Marx's terms) and "his demand does not correspond to the supply."[51] Finally, when Malthus analyses the conditions of a strong and sustained demand, he examines the social groups and categories whose income is likely to create a strong and sustained demand for the product.[52] Marx, who follows the classical theory, (Malthus and Smith), according

---

[47] *Capital*, I: 452.

[48] I, footnote 14: 677.

[49] "...an increase of population, when an additional quantity of labour is not wanted, will soon be checked by want of employment, and the scanty support of those employed, and will not furnish the required stimulus to an increase of wealth proportioned to the power of production", *Principles of political economy*: 349–350.

[50] "There must be something in the previous state of the demand and supply of the commodity in question, or in its price, antecedent to and independent of the demand occasioned by the new labourers, in order to warrant the employment of an additional number of people in its production". *Principles of political economy*: 349.

[51] *Theories*...VI: 64–65.

[52] *Principles*...: 363–369. "If the conversion of revenue into capital pushed beyond a certain point must, by diminishing the effectual demand for produce, throw the labouring classes out of employment, it is obvious that the adpotion of parsimonious habits in too great a degree may be accompanied by the most distressing effects at first, and by a marked depression of wealth and population permanently (p. 369). Marx : "Class A [the capitalist class that produces the means of subsistence], has created a real surplus of food, an excess that is freely available, that can be accumulated or used like income for buying food or luxury goods." *Theories*...VI: 73. And: "If it

to which workers and capitalists cannot by themselves create a demand, concludes that Malthus was forced to find another category, viz. "unproductive consumers" (...) a class which "in society, will represent consumption for the sake of consumption, just as the capitalist class represents production for the sake of production".[53]

It is quite significant that Marx does not question this theoretical proposition. He says, "This is the only means of escape from overproduction, which exists alongside overpopulation relatively to production. Over-consumption by the class standing outside production is [recommended] as the best remedy for both overproduction and overpopulation"[54] However, he reproaches Malthus for his incoherence or rather the incompleteness of his demonstration and repeatedly asks from where this class obtains the means of payment. "Malthus does not explain. Anyway this is the basis of his plea for the greatest increase in the unproductive classes."[55] It is thus necessary to undertake a proper socio-economic inventory to find out which classes have purchasing power. Marx follows Malthus once more. First come the landowners and their employees and although Marx is not very explicit, he undoubtedly thinks that this social group is not large enough and that its consumption habits are such (which is what Malthus argued) that they cannot by themselves give rise to a sufficiently large demand. So it is necessary to resort to another source of purchasing power, as Malthus puts it, to sustain the effectual demand or, as Marx says, to stimulate the accumulation process.

But at this point, the tone changes drastically. Malthus suggests nothing less than "artificial methods", such as heavy taxes, State and Church sinecures, national debt and costly wars.[56] And Marx's scorn for these social groups irrupts in the following words, "We have the immense section of society which consists of parasites and self-indulgent drones, in part masters and in part servants, who appropriate gratuitously a considerable quantity of wealth – partly under the name of rent and partly under political titles – from the capitalist class, paying for the commodities produced by the latter above their value with the money they have taken from the capitalists themselves."[57] The reasons for Marx's violent reaction to Malthus's theoretical proposal regarding the unproductive classes are worth exploring. It is first and foremost an intellectual opposition. Marx does not fail to underline the contradiction between Malthus the economist and Malthus the demographer. "From

is accumulated further, there is a fall in demand from buyers who can afford to pay the price asked for and a contraction of the food market." *Theories*...VI: 75.

[53] *Theories*..., VI: 77–78: "The unproductive consumers not only constitute an enormous diversion for the products thrust on the market; further, they do not thrust products on the market; they do not thus compete with the capitalists; they simply constitute a demand without supply and thus compensate for the excess supply as compared to the demand from capitalists."

[54] *Theories*..., VI: 81.

[55] *Theories* ..., VI: 35.

[56] *Theories*..., VI: 78: Though they spend money for buying labour, it is essential that they do not employ productive workers, but just guests and domestic servants who will keep up the prices of food by buying without making the slightest contribution, the slightest increase."

[57] Ibid.: 80.

Malthus's theory of value there springs the whole doctrine of the necessity for an ever-increasing unproductive consumption, a doctrine which this theoretician of overpopulation (arising from lack of subsistence) has preached so emphatically."[58] It is also a quasi moral opposition as these parasitic classes are not subject to any work ethics and involves a dual stake – both theoretical and ideological – that is much more serious. These classes are essentially a relic of the old system of landownership and aristocracy, while Marx is more concerned with the present and the future of bourgeois society ruled by capitalistic production methods. It would appear that his mind refuses to admit the *logical* error that consists of proposing a solution applicable to an old system of production to solve a theoretical problem of capitalism in the 1860s, which amounts to mixing two different time frames. This interpretation is proved by the fact that the method he has chosen to solve the problem is radically different from the one used by Malthus. When analysing primitive accumulation, he proposes a *historicised* solution whose factual elements precede capitalistic accumulation. But there is more to come. As a matter of fact, what Marx cannot accept in Malthus's proposition is that it postpones the confrontation between the two classes – the only ones that matter economically – involved in the accumulation process. In other words, it delays the collapse of capitalism and the advent of the communist society.

These aspects are brought together in a very telling manner in the following passage that is rarely noticed: "Malthus's conclusion follows quite logically from his basic theory of value;[59] but this theory itself is curiously in accord with his aim – to act as an apologist for the state of affairs in contemporary England, with its landlordism, State and Church retired officials, tax collectors, tithes, national debt, stock exchange jobbers, law-court officials, parsons and hangers-on, against which the Ricardians fought as so many useless, outlived, detrimental and malignant phenomena of bourgeois production. Ricardo disinterestedly defends bourgeois production insofar as it stands for as unbridled a development as possible of the social forces of production. He is unconcerned with the fate of the agents of production, whether they be capitalists or workers (. . .). Malthus, too, wants as free a development as possible of capitalist production, insofar as only the poverty of its main agents, the working class, is a condition of this development; but according to him, this production should at the same time adapt itself to the 'needs of consumption' of the aristocracy and its representatives in State and Church, and serve as a material basis for the obsolete demands of those who represent interests inherited from feudalism and absolute monarchy."[60]

---

58 Ibid.: 63. Chapter 2 showed how to reconcile the two Malthuses.

59 We cannot deal with this point here. In Marx's eyes, Malthus commits a serious mistake: he believes that "the price and value of production are identical." Malthus therefore assumes the existence of profit, but does not wonder about its origin. *Theories. . .*, Vol. VI: 51 and footnote 1: 50.

60 Ibid. 79, 80.

Primitive Accumulation in the History of Capitalism

If the Malthusian solution of unproductive classes is rejected, the following question remains unanswered: how can the pump of capitalistic accumulation be set in motion? The solution proposed by Marx is radically different from the Malthusian analysis. He does not take into consideration the different economic actors and he totally rejects the economic theory in favour of economic and social history. The entire Section VIII of Book I, which concentrates on "The so-called primitive accumulation", and more particularly Chapter 31 ("Genesis of Industrial Capitalism"), are devoted to identifying the different stages of laying the foundations of capitalism since the sixteenth century. The problem is raised in the introductory chapter titled "The Secret of Primitive Accumulation". Capitalistic accumulation presupposes surplus value and surplus value presupposes capitalistic production", which in turn "presupposes the pre-existence of considerable masses of capital and of labour-power in the hands of producers of commodities." To come out of this vicious circle, it must be admitted with Adam Smith that "a primitive accumulation (previous accumulation according to Adam Smith) preceding capitalistic accumulation (...) [is] not the result of the capitalist mode of production, but its starting point."[61]

While Malthus presumed the existence of an *available* purchasing power at the time the decision to invest was taken, Marx preferred to demonstrate that the solution to the theoretical problem was necessarily of an *historical* nature. He believed that the means of production should have been violently snatched from the producers before the bourgeois world came into being. In a few pages of powerful writing, he shows that this is what actually happened when the feudal economic order made way for the capitalistic economic order.[62] It is well known that when the influx of gold and silver from the New World injected a considerable purchasing power into the European economy, England, Flanders and France developed their industry to raise their supply to meet the new level of demand. To satisfy the requirements of the wool industry, the area under pasture was expanded from the sixteenth century onwards through an expropriation drive (the famous *Bills for enclosures)* and the concentration of lands in the hands of aristocratic landowners. The *yeomen*, the small landowners who tilled their own land, being deprived of access to communal lands that provided them with the extra resources indispensable for the economic equilibrium of the family-based system, became proletarianised. By 1750, the *yeomen* had practically disappeared and were replaced by farmers. Marx starts with the enclosures movement, which was the first major social change, and illustrates the chapter with numerous examples of men being chased away from their lands by sheep. The second case of violence was the Poor Law going back to the sixteenth century which was denounced by Thomas More. Begging was severely repressed by Henry VIII, Edward VI, Elizabeth I and James I, while the Statute

---

[61] *Capital*,I: 527.

[62] *Capital*, I: 528.

of 1349, which came into effect during the reign of Edward III, worsened their situation. Wages were fixed, conspiracies banned and prison sentences imposed.[63] The proletarianisation of peasants and the confiscation of their lands did not however lead to a fall in agricultural production because these two movements were concomitant with an agricultural revolution of which England is a classic example, and to which Marx refers in one line focused on one of its major consequences: "the means of subsistence for a large part of the rural population were available while in the future they would be treated as an element of variable capital."[64] Let us briefly recall here that this was possible because of technical innovations: the disappearance of the practice of letting land lie fallow (following the introduction of a three-yearly crop rotation of cereals, turnips and clover), the introduction of artificial grasslands, irrigation and drainage, the replacement of the swing plough by the iron ploughshare and the use of multiple breaker ploughs. Jethro Tull invented the seeding machine, which made it possible to economise on seeds, while McCormick designed the first reaping machines in 1839. Bakewell (1725–1795) improved animal species through artificial selection thus increasing their weight in terms of meat. Advances in chemistry (Liebig) brought in nitrogenous fertilisers. Moving to the seventeenth and eighteenth centuries, he finally refers to the importance of trade, especially international trade, in a chapter on "The Genesis of Industrial Capitalism". Commercial capitalism served as a lever for the concentration of capital (the Bank of England was established in 1694), while the colonies opened up major sources of supply of raw materials and markets for products manufactured by the colonial power. By putting English capitalism of the 1860s in a historical perspective, Marx could give a factual demonstration of primitive accumulation and do without Malthus's argument on the effectual demand while retaining the essential points of his contribution. All these concepts and analyses must now be integrated in the theory of population.

Capitalism's Population Law: The Industrial Reserve Army

Marx's theory is supported by a wealth of data drawn from official censuses and surveys on employment and health available in his time and, on the theoretical side, by a profound knowledge of the writings of a large number of English, French and German authors. He then set about illustrating it with examples taken from life in England between 1846 and 1866. The theoretical part is somewhat complex as Marx takes into account several factors such as the decline, stability or growth of population, which are systematically related to changes in the organic composition of capital. Further, he constantly moves from the analysis of one particular branch to the entire capitalist system. It is quite evident that his aim was to demonstrate that capitalism was moving towards an aggravation of tensions that would end in an implosion. This analysis is accompanied by the identification of concrete changes in

---

63 I: 543–548.

64 *Capital*, I: 522.

the variable capital: he breaks up the industrial reserve army into several categories of population – floating, stagnant and latent – not forgetting to take into account the different methods of extending the working day, the rural exodus and the movement of the labour force from one sector to another and even from one country to another (e.g. Ireland) and the use of women and children in the place of male labourers. Finally, he condemns the physical deterioration, malnutrition and mortality of the labour force.[65]

Creation and Development of the Reserve Army

For the sake of convenience, we will confine ourselves to one particular branch before showing how capitalistic production methods embrace the entire economy. Let us recall the indispensable precondition, a direct legacy of Adam Smith and Ricardo, that Marx mentions specifically, namely that technical progress makes it possible to produce more with a given labour force and this can be done only through investments in capital. As observed in the case of the "puddlage" of iron before 1780, the organic composition of capital changes and its "constant" component (investment in machinery) increases at the cost of the "variable capital" (labour force) for the same amount of production.[66] But the fall in the share of variable capital (in the form of wages) is only relative and not necessarily absolute. The variable capital, or the demand for labour in the terminology of classical political economy, may even go up when the total capital (both constant and variable) *increases* at the rate x while the variable capital *decreases* at a rate lower than x. In such a case, the demand for labour (the disposable wage fund) and therefore the working population employed in that particular branch will increase in *absolute* value. Marx quotes the census figures of 1861 in support of his claim that this is exactly what happened in England between 1851 and 1861 in the cotton spinning and weaving industry (from 371,777 to 456,646) and in the iron industry (from 68,053 to 125,711) while, at the same time, other branches or sectors lost their labour force: agriculture (from 2,011,447 to 1,984,110), the silk industry (111,940 to 101,678) and long-stapled wool (from 102,714 to 79,249). The last three branches, where capital accumulation did nevertheless take place, illustrate the second variant in the change in the organic composition of capital translated by an absolute decrease in the wage fund.[67] As it

---

[65] Book III of *Capital* repeats in more simple terms the sometimes complicated arguments of Book I, but it limits itself to the economic mechanisms without considering the contribution of socio-historic data which constitute the real worth of Book I. In the case of Book III, see 215–216 (Chapter 13, Section III) and 244–251 (Chapter 15, Section III).

[66] Smith: "The growth of capital tends to increase the productive abilities of labour and makes it possible to use a smaller amount of labour to produce a larger quantity of work" (*Capital*, I: 449). Ricardo: footnote 115: 649; Andrew Ure: footnote 118: 650. On pudlage: *Capital*, I: 449–450

[67] "As long as the amount of capital does not change, any proportional decrease in its variable part amounts to its absolute decrease. For it to be otherwise, the proportional decrease should be counterbalanced by an increase in the total amount of the advance capital value." (*Capital*, I: 456).

is quite clear, everything depends on the idea, inspired by Barton, of changes in the organic composition of capital. Besides, Marx summarises in *Capital* what he had written about Barton's and Ricardo's theories of surplus value.[68]

However, the pace of technical progress is not the same in all branches with some witnessing a technical revolution before others. This was true of the textile industry where the revolution in spinning following the invention of the spinning jenny led to a bottleneck due to the lack of a similar advance in weaving. Marx logically inferred that it was a result of the interdependence of the two processes since "development in the productivity of labour" results in low-cost mass production. These products would stimulate other industries where there was no technical progress and the latter would respond to the stimulus by increasing the number of workers, especially in branches where manual labour continued to predominate. This is exactly what was observed in the census of 1861: "The increase of labourers is generally greatest since 1861 in such branches of industry in which machinery has not up to the present been employed with success." Regarding branches that had not yet been modernised, as it would be said today, "the centralisation of capital enabled them to set up enormous industrial armies."[69] Let us return to the branch (or branches) where technical progress resulted in the transformation of small factories into "large industries". Since this technical progress was made possible by the constant increase in capital, this meant that the relative diminution of the variable capital created a surplus population, which was surplus not due to demographic growth, but due to a fall in the number of jobs available.[70]

Let us now look at all the branches. Before they were mechanised, they attracted the major part of the industrial reserve army, but as the change in the organic composition of capital spreads to all the branches, a relative surplus population builds up in each of the branches. "But if a surplus labouring population is a necessary product of accumulation or of the development of wealth on a capitalist basis, this surplus population becomes, conversely, the lever of capitalistic accumulation, nay, a condition of existence of the capitalist mode of production. It forms a disposable industrial reserve army, that belongs to capital quite as absolutely as if the latter had bred it at its own cost. Independently of the limits of the actual increase of

68 *Capital*, I: 460–461. He also quotes two other economists, Jones and Ramsay.

69 *Capital*, I: 458. This is what Marx's contemporaries called "manufacturing industry".

70 "This accelerated relative diminution of the variable constituent, that goes along with the accelerated increase of the total capital, and moves more rapidly than this increase, takes the inverse form, at the other pole, of an apparently absolute increase in the labouring population, an increase always moving more rapidly than that of the variable capital or the means of employment. But in fact, it is capitalistic accumulation itself that constantly produces, and produces in the direct ratio of its own energy and extent, a relative redundant population of labourers, i.e. a population of greater extent than suffices for the average needs of self-expansion of capital, and therefore a surplus population (...) We call it relative because it is caused, not by a positive increase of the working class population which would cross the limits of wealth being accumulated but, on the contrary, of an accelerated growth of social capital that enables it to do without a more or less significant part of its labourers. Since this surplus population exists only in relation to the short-lived requirements of capitalistic exploitation, it can expand and contract all of a sudden." *Capital*, I: 459.

population, it creates, for the changing needs of the self-expansion of capital, a mass of human material always ready for exploitation."[71] In order to assess the importance of this theoretical construct, the above lines should be related to four operating conditions of the population law of capitalism as these conditions refer to certain basic elements of the Marxist theory.

Conditions for the Working of the Population Law of Capitalism

The first condition relates to labour as a commodity. Accumulation is possible only because labour, unlike other factors of production which are not renewable, is capable of reproducing itself indefinitely provided that care is taken to maintain it, a point dealt with at length in the second section of *Capital* (Chapters 6 and 7). When used in conjunction with labour as a factor of production, capital and land will create a surplus value which will rise, for instance in proportion to the duration of the working day. Thus in large industries, low-cost mass production makes it possible to obtain a surplus value thanks only "to the minimum wages paid, no more than requisite for a miserable vegetation, and to the extension of working time up to the maximum endurable by the human organism".[72] Capitalistic accumulation therefore presupposes the existence of an ever-increasing labour force.

The second condition relating to the availability of labour is actually a double condition: firstly, a worker does not sell his labour once and for all and, secondly, he has nothing else to sell. Marx repeats point by point Engels who, in 1844, had explained at length the difference between a worker and a slave. Engels' ideas were based on Adam Smith who said that work is a commodity like any other whose price and wage is regulated by supply and demand, the worker being in "in law and in fact the slave of the property-holding class". If the demand for workers decreases to such an extent that a number of them become "unsaleable if they are left in stock", they cannot survive and will die of starvation. "For, to speak in the words of the economists, the expense incurred in maintaining them would not be reproduced, would be money thrown away, and to this end no man advances capital; and, so far, Malthus was perfectly right in his theory of population". And continuing in line with Smith, he observes that this situation is no different from that of a slave, the only difference being that the worker is not sold once and for all, but piecemeal by the day, the week, the year. He therefore does not belong to a specific master, but to the property-holding class as a whole. It follows that this class is better placed than in a system based on slavery as it has no obligation towards the workers since it has not invested any capital; the worker therefore costs less than a slave.[73]

---

[71] *Capital*, I: 461. Regarding the relationship between the concepts of an industrial reserve army, relative surplus population and actual demographic growth, see Behar, 1974.

[72] *Capital*, I: 339. Marx refers here to wages corresponding to the minimum living wage.

[73] Engels: *Situation...*: 122–123. Marx: *Capital*, I: 131.

The third condition is that capitalism should have attained a certain level of maturity. Otherwise, it would not really be possible to increase constant capital at the cost of variable capital unless there is technical progress, as was the case before the development of modern capitalism. "This particular course of modern industry, which occurs in no earlier period of human history, was also impossible in the childhood of capitalist production. The composition of capital changed but very slowly. With its accumulation, therefore, there kept pace, on the whole, a corresponding growth in the demand for labour", whereas "The whole form of modern industry depends on the constant transformation of a part of the labouring population into unemployed or half-empoyed hands". [74]

The fourth condition refers to the pace of reproduction of the labour force. Marx agrees with Merrivale and Malthus on this point. Let us suppose that a new opportunity for industrial accumulation arises. It will trigger a demand for extra labour. But since the time needed for a new generation of workers to enter the labour market is 16–18 years, in the short run it is necessary to resort to a reserve stock of labour.[75] Marx does not fail to denounce the contradiction in which Malthus is caught and says, "Even Malthus recognises over-population as a necessity of modern industry, though, after his narrow fashion he explains it by the absolute over-growth of the labouring population."[76]

These four elements of the Marxist theory are therefore indispensable for establishing the validity of the concept of the industrial reserve army and, in the final analysis, the population law cannot be dissociated from accumulation. "The labouring population therefore produces, along with the accumulation of capital produced by it, the means by which itself is made relatively superfluous, is turned into a relative surplus population, and it does so to an always increasing extent. This is a law of population peculiar to the capitalist mode of production".[77] This gives rise to the famous statement that every historical mode of production has its own law. "An abstract law exists only for plants and animals, and only in so far as man does not interfere with them."[78]

---

[74] *Capital*, I: 461.

[75] Marx continues by quoting Malthus: "Prudential habits with regard to marriage, carried to a considerable extent among the labouring class of a country mainly depending upon manufactures and commerce, might injure it (...). From the nature of a population, an increase of labourers cannot be brought into market in consequence of a particular demand till after the lapse of 16 or 18 years, and the conversion of revenue into capital, by saving may take place much more rapidly; a country is always liable to an increase in the quantity of the funds for the maintenance of labour faster than the increase of population."*Capital*, I: 463.

[76] *Capital*, I: 463.

[77] *Capital*, I: 480.

[78] *Capital*, I: 460.

The Actual Working of the Population Law

Increasing the Industrial Reserve Army

The use of machinery has a direct impact on the labour force as it makes it possible to replace adult male workers by women and children.[79] But if the extra earnings represent for a working class family an amount of money higher than that provided earlier by the sole earnings of the head of the family, it means that the degree of exploitation has increased because now the entire family is employed by the large-scale industry. Marx thinks that this is so evident that he does not feel the need to analyse the family's microeconomics. He is satisfied with a note that raises the problem of the disappearance of the traditional function of production which foreshadows the situation of the family in industrialised countries in the twentieth century: "since certain functions like nursing and suckling children cannot be entirely suppressed, the mothers confiscated by capital must try substitutes of some sort. Domestic work such as sewing and mending must be replaced by the purchase of ready-made articles."[80] All through Book I of *Capital* (Chapters 10, 15 and 25 in particular), the labour of women and children is analysed at length and illustrated with precise examples. Members of the same family worked together making bricks, lace and woven straw products, but when large-scale industry gained predominance, the severe exploitation of children by their parents became the rule (Marx quotes at length the *Report from the Select Committee on Mines*). Further, the consequences of the exploitation of workers were documented in great detail, especially the figures regarding differential mortality and morbidity. For example, the rate of mortality of tailors in London was undoubtedly underestimated according to him. It was a labour force that had come from the countryside to learn or to improve its skills and was generally under thirty years of age. Numerous ageing workers or many others suffering from serious ailments came back to die. In the lace-making industry, there were numerous cases of consumption; in the match-making industry, poisoning caused by phosphorous was common among children (half the work force was under eighteen) and a specific disease that attacked the jaws; in the ceramic industry, the loss of weight and height and low life expectancy were common as attested by several doctors in the *First Report of the Children's Employment Commission.* Nutritional deficiencies gave rise in 1862 to a survey covering agricultural workers, silk weavers, dress-makers, glove-makers, cobblers and hosiers: the quantity of nitrogen and carbon in the food consumed by these children was measured and found to be lower than the required minimum. The manufacture of bread was also censured in

---

[79] *Capital*, I, 286–291, 340. For example, 463: "We have further seen that the capitalist buys with the same capital a greater mass of labour-power, as he progressively replaces skilled labourers by less skilled, mature labour-power by immature, male by female, that of adults by that of young persons or children, a Yankee by three Chinese."

[80] *Capital*, I, footnote 36: 641. Surprisingly, Marx does not make any mention of "the nursemaid industry" which was however known in his times.

1855. Lastly, London was considered to be the capital of the rag trade and a source of contagious diseases. In such conditions, alcoholism was rampant, promiscuity had reached such a high level that there was an abundance of illegitimate children and the consumption of opium derivatives was very common in some circles.[81]

How can the difference between the treatment of the two topics be explained? Why should the use of female and child labour be treated so briefly while giving numerous and detailed examples of working conditions and their effects on the working class? The first answer would be that Engels, like others, had described the process of substitution of labour and once the truth of his observations had been established, there was no need to proceed further. What is more surprising though is that Marx did not develop a microeconomic theory of fertility. In fact, this imbalance can once again be explained by the strategic importance of demonstrating the inevitable nature of accumulation. Since accumulation always leads to greater exploitation of the labour force, the demographic proofs provided by mortality and morbidity were evidently more obvious and convincing than the increase in fertility.

Besides greater exploitation, accumulation has another major demographic consequence. For the growth of the industrial reserve army, capitalism can have at its disposal an additional supply of labour when there is greater mobility of population. Marx quotes the figures of the census of 1861 pertaining to urban growth to which he alludes briefly. In the early nineteenth century, there was no other city apart from London having a population of 100,000 as against twenty-eight at the time he wrote *Capital*. Though he remarks on the deterioration of the environment and housing as a result of the rapid urbanisation, his essential contribution is the conceptualisation of the mobilisation of the labour force, which leads him to raise the question of relative surplus population.[82] This surplus population is present in many different forms. It may be floating, latent or stagnant, but it would be better to say that it can be divided into these three segments. In modern industry, surplus population is "floating" because it varies according to the economic situation, even if the population tends to grow on account of the progress made by this type of production as compared to manufacturing or domestic work, and even if variable capital decreases as compared to constant capital. When adult male labourers are replaced by women and children, he points out that "one consequence is that the female population grows more rapidly than the male", but he does not quote any figures in support of this statement.[83] The surplus population is "latent" in rural areas. There is an exodus from rural areas only if there are new employment opportunities in urban areas. One may add that for migration to take place, agriculture must suffer from veiled unemployment. But Marx does not say so clearly, he even contradicts himself when he analyses the technical revolution in agriculture: "If the use of machinery in agriculture is for the most part free from the injurious physical effect it has on

---

[81] Regarding these different points: Book I, Chapter 10: 187–188, 190–191; Chapter 15: 288, 333–335, 338, 356–359, footnote 182: 655; Chapter 25: 479–48, 498–500, 504.

[82] *Capital*, I: 468, 484–485.

[83] *Capital*, I: 468.

the factory operative, its action in superseding the labourers is more intense, and finds less resistance, as we shall see later in detail." So if it is a sustained structural movement ("without any after-effects"), it must be concluded that the push factors are more powerful than the pull factors and that the surplus population cannot be latent in rural areas.[84] The third component, viz. the "stagnant" surplus population, is a part of the *active* industrial army, and not the industrial "reserve" army. In other words, it is an employed work force but its activity is very irregular and the wages are at the lowest level. According to Marx this applies above all to the "domestic industry" whose demographic characteristics are specific and "call to mind the boundless reproduction of animals individually weak and constantly hunted down." It recruits itself constantly from the supernumerary forces of modern industries; it forms at the same time "a self-reproducing and self-perpetuating element of the working class, taking a proportionally greater part in the general increase of that class than the other elements. In fact, not only the number of births and deaths, but the absolute size of the families stand in inverse proportion to the height of wages, and therefore to the amount of means of subsistence of which the different categories of labourers dispose."[85]

This obscure passage calls for a brief clarification. In the case of a population earning the minimum living wage, it is understandable that its reproduction should be directly related to the price of the food it consumes. It grows when there is a *fall* in mortality or a *rise* in fertility or a combination of the two in an inverse ratio to food prices. Let us suppose there is a fall in food prices. This would cause a fall in mortality, but what is more surprising is the claim that there would be a rise in fertility. This is so in the case of agricultural workers, because their employers, the agricultural landowners, who are obliged to sell food at lower prices, will maintain their rate of profit by lowering wages. Agricultural workers will then increase their fertility to compensate for the fall in their purchasing power, thanks to the income resulting from child labour). But workers from other branches will on the contrary benefit from a higher purchasing power and have no reason to increase their fertility. But what workers is he referring to? Going by his classification, there is no doubt Marx is clearly thinking of the *active* industrial army. It must therefore be concluded that on this particular point Marx's reasoning is rather incoherent.

Apart from this classification, his perceptive analysis of the English agricultural proletariat, which takes up about twenty pages, is a mixture of historical analysis, accounts of observers (like Young, Wakefield and Hunter), statistical data regarding wages and malnutrition and information obtained from the social surveys of 1863, 1864 and 1865 on housing and health in rural areas. The lines referring to the types of surplus population in the counties of Worcestershire and Lincolnshire describe the contradictions arising from the seasonal nature of agriculture. Except for the peak season, labour was surplus in the rural areas and farmers gradually stopped hiring local labourers, who were too costly, preferring to hire gangs of ten

---

[84] Quotation: *Capital*, I: 362; see p. 508 regarding Worcestershire.

[85] *Capital* I: 470.

to fifty workers, mainly women and children, who were placed under the orders of a *gangmaster.* These gangs moved from farm to farm, a system that spread rapidly, and surveys covering the testimony of big farmers clearly indicate that they found it very profitable. There is no doubt that Marx greatly benefited by the remarkable social surveys conducted in the mid-1860s and published just as he was writing *Capital*, but he was very successful in synthesising these facts into the concept of relative surplus population: "The gang-system, which during the last years has steadily increased, clearly does not exist for the sake of the *gangmaster*. It exists for the enrichment of the large farmers, and indirectly of the landlords. For the farmer, there is no more ingenious method of keeping his labourers well below the normal level, and yet of always having an extra hand ready for extra work, of extracting the greatest possible amount of labour with the least possible amount of money, and of making adult male labour 'redundant'. From the exposition already made, it will be understood why, on the other hand, a greater or lesser lack of employment for the agricultural labour is admitted, while on the other, the gang-system is at the same time declared necessary on account of the want of adult male labour and its migration to the towns. The cleanly weeded land and the uncleanly human weeds of Lincolnshire are pole and counter-pole of capitalistic production."[86]

The International Dimension of Capitalism

We have already mentioned that Engels and Marx treated the crises of capitalism in a different manner. Marx, who looked at them from the perspective of the structural transformation of capital, shows that these crises are inherent in capitalism. But in the free-trading England of the 1860s, Marx ascribed the problem to the stagnation of international markets. Thus if a new market opens, "the technical conditions of the process of production themselves, machinery, means of transport, etc." now permit the fastest access to the new market. However, if this market is initially captured by selling goods at a lower price, sooner or later it will get saturated. Commercial crises and even financial speculation will add to the technical crises and there will be a "constant transformation of a part of the labouring population into unemployed or half-employed hands." Finally, resorting to credit to finance investment can only augment the commercial crisis.[87] Capitalism works on an international level and unemployment may be caused by crises in distant lands. Marx repeats this argument several times, often referring to the cotton famine of 1862 caused by the War of

[86] Farmers' accounts: footnotes 125, 126, 127: 685.

[87] *Capital*, I: 461–462. Also about credit: "with capitalist production an altogether new force comes into play – the credit system. Not only is this itself a new and mighty weapon in the battle of competition. By unseen threads it, moreover, draws the disposable money, scattered in larger or smaller masses over the surface of society, into the hands of individual or associated capitalists. It is the specific machine for the centralisation of capital." (*Capital*, I: 454).

Secession in the United States.[88] But the international outlook is not confined to just economic crises; it is also affected by structural changes like, for example, the destruction on the Indian cotton industry due to the import of English mill-made textiles from Manchester. He cites an unexpected source, the Governor General of India writing in his report in 1834–1835 that "the bones of the cotton-weavers are bleaching the plains of India."[89] Imperialism being the logical extension of capitalism, once the local industry is ruined, capitalism transforms the colony into a source of raw material. This is what happened in India which was forced to de produce cotton, wool, hemp and indigo. Between 1846 and 1865, cotton exports from India to England rose from 34.5 to 445.9 million pounds and wool exports from 4.5 to 20.6 million pounds.[90] The same was true of Australia. The capitalist system is therefore characterised by a new international division of labour since "industrial supremacy implies commercial supremacy."[91] Chapter 31 of Book I ("Genesis of the Industrial Capitalist") makes a brief mention of mercantilism, protectionism and the Dutch and English colonial regimes in the seventeenth and eighteenth centuries.[92] But the main point is that all these characteristics of the pre-capitalist period "increased gigantically during the infancy of Modern Industry."[93]

Challenging the Theory on the Basis of Demographic Facts

It is necessary to establish one last point. Since Marx proposes a population law and since he has quoted in its support all the demographic data that he could obtain, has he integrated this information correctly in his theory? And has the population law, which according to Marx explains population growth on the basis of capital accumulation and particularly the changes in its organic composition, been verified? The concept of relative surplus population, as we have seen, is closely linked with the observation of the rural exodus and urbanisation, which themselves are linked with the demand for labour in industry. The writings of English demographers and historians confirm Marx's statement that growth was more rapid in urban and industrial areas. On a long-term basis, for example between 1700 and 1750, the whole of England and Wales grew by 23%, much less than industrial areas like Lancashire (33%), Warwickshire (28%) and West Riding in Yorkshire (26%). On a smaller scale, between 1751 and 1831, the rural counties grew by 88% and urban counties

88 *Capital*, I, 326, 479–482. For example, the "cotton famine" of 1862 led to an attempt to develop its cultivation in some parts of India at the cost of local rice production. Due to the poor means of communication, local famines occurred as rice could not be transported to the regions suffering from a shortage.

89 *Capital*, I, 309.

90 *Capital*, I, 324, footnotes 156, 157.

91 *Capital*, I: 324, 559.

92 *Capital*, I, 556–564.

93 *Capital*, I, 562.

by 129%. And between 1764 and 1801, in the Vale of Trent studied by Chambers, the 62 farming villages grew by 38.7% while the 40 industrial villages grew by 96,5%.[94] On this point, Marx's contribution is not very original, in so far as he relies essentially on public sources, particularly the publications of the *Registrar General.* As for the gangs of agricultural workers who hired themselves out to landowners, he observes that the villages to which these gangs belonged were known for their sexual promiscuity and a very high rate of illegitimacy (up to half the children in villages like Bilford in Worcestershire were born out of wedlock), often among adolescents aged 13–14 years, and illegitimacy was undoubtedly accompanied by abortion and infanticide. And finally, there was widespread alcoholism aggravated by the consumption of opium derivatives fed by mothers to their infants.[95] Recent work by English historians (Hair, 1966, Sauer, 1978, Laslett and Oosterveen, 1973) confirms the magnitude of this problem of illegitimate births, the most "demographic" of the social consequences of the gang system, which was also seen in several other contexts, particularly in urban areas. But here again, the existence of this social blight was quite well known and Marx did not contribute anything new.

Much more interesting is the problem raised by a passage in Chapter 25 of *Capital,* in which Marx borrows a table from the *Registrar General*'s report containing the results of the census of 1861 (Table 5.1).

The slowdown of population growth in England between 1811 and 1861 does not give rise to any *specific* observations. Immediately after the table, Marx quotes just a series of figures to establish that the growth of capital and wealth was much faster during this period and contrasts it with the continuing poverty of the working class that he condemns vehemently.[96]

Table 5.1 Annual increase per cent of the population of England and Wales in decimal numbers

1811–1821	1.533
1821–1831	1.446
1831–1841	1.326
1841–1851	1.216
1851–1861	1.141

[94] For a more convenient summary, see Tranter, 1973.

[95] Housing and health: *Capital,* I: 492–511; illegitimacy: footnote 122: 685; opium: 288 and footnote 48: 642.

[96] The figures available today have been corrected by B.R. Mitchell and P. Deane (quoted by Tranter, 1973: 42, 53):

Year	Population	Years	Growth Rate
1821	12.0	1811–21	1.8
1831	13.9	1821–31	1.6
1841	15.9	1831–41	1.4
1851	17.9	1841–51	1.3
1861	20.1	1851–61	1.2

But he does not pursue these ideas further. Let us try to complete the demonstration by following the same line of reasoning as *Capital*. It is certainly very tempting to assume that Marx's comparison between the growth of wealth and poverty refers, in accordance with the analysis of the changes in the organic composition of capital, to the idea that constant capital grows faster than variable capital.[97] But if we begin by admitting the slowdown of the population growth rate to proceed further, it is at least necessary to separate the birth and death rates. Let us recall that each year the overall growth of a population results from the surplus of births over deaths (the so-called natural increase or decrease) and from the surplus of immigration over out-migration. By assuming that the figures involved in the natural increase are much larger than those pertaining to migration flows, the slowdown of the total growth may be due either to a constant fertility accompanied by an increasing mortality (reflecting a fall in the standard of living), or a fall in the mortality, compensated by a faster drop in fertility (which suggests an improvement in the standard of living).

Since Marx claims that poverty had increased, it implies that mortality had increased and that fertility *also* had increased or, at least, that it had remained constant. In fact, in macroeconomic Marxist terms, if the growth of variable capital (population) is slower than the accumulation of constant capital, proletarianisation spreads and at the microeconomic level workers should increase their fertility to compensate for the fall in wages. It is known today that the birth and death rates actually remained quite stable during this period (Table 5.2). So the first of the two hypotheses is confirmed and Marx's theory reflects reality.

Table 5.2 Birth rate and death rate (1841–1861)

Years	Birth Rate	Death Rate
1841–45	35.2	21.4
1846–50	34.8	23.3
1851–55	35.5	22.7
1856–60	35.5	21.8
1856–60	35.8	22.6

Table 5.3 Some data on migrations (1841–1861)[98]

Year of census	Total population (millions)	Period between censuses	Net migration (millions)	Rate of emigration
1841	15.9	1841–51	−0.483	−3.03
1851	17.9	1851–61	−1.368	−7.6

[97] *Capital*, I: 474–477, particularly 474 : "The increase of profits liable to income tax (farmers and some other categories not included) in Great Britain from 1853 to 1864 amounted to 50.47% or 4.58% as the annual average, that of the population during the same period to about 12%."

[98] Source: D. Glass, quoted by N. Tranter, 1973: 53.

But all this reasoning is vitiated by a hypothesis that we had adopted earlier and which does not hold because emigration far from being negligible, was actually massive (Table 5.3).

This has important implications. Firstly, it is obviously difficult to establish any theory in the absence of appropriate data. Marx evidently did not have these data at his disposal, but he wanted his population law to be demonstrated *only* by the overall rates of growth during the intercensal period. According to his own reasoning, the proof that he needed implied that he should at least have taken take into account the dynamic aspect of demography in its simplest form, the birth and death rates. Consequently, the slowdown cannot be explained by a change in the organic composition of capital that directly affected fertility and mortality, but by the growing emigration because the birth and death rates remained more or less constant. There is no doubt that the economic factors continued to rule demographic behaviour since poverty was the main reason for emigration as shown by the tragedy in Ireland where out of a total population of 8,175,000 in 1841, almost one million died due to famine in 1846 leading to the emigration of one and a half million Irish people during the famine, so that in 1851 Ireland's population had been reduced by 1,623,000 inhabitants as compared to 1841. But the major ideological implication is that emigration provides a safety valve during crises created by capitalism by reducing the industrial reserve army. Marx anticipated the objection and retorted that the fate of the "workers who had stayed back in Ireland and were freed from surplus population" did not improve in any case because "The revolution in agriculture has kept pace with emigration. The production of relative surplus population has more than kept pace with the absolute depopulation."[99]

But why did he not take into account the *other* international migratory flows, especially those from England to North America, Australia and New Zealand, when he analysed the crises of English capitalism in their international dimension? Since industrial capitalism was the most advanced in England, whereas Ireland, as he points out frequently, was still a rural and agricultural country, he should have taken migration into account in the case of England. We hold that Marx underestimated the importance of emigration in the case of England for the reason mentioned at the beginning of this paragraph, namely the *ideological* implications of such crises because the existence of large-scale out-migration weakened his prediction of the necessary collapse of capitalism. It is interesting to note the difference with Malthus who, on the contrary, *relied* on emigration, arguing that for England in particular it was the wrong solution for the problem of poverty because, in the long run, the population principle would ensure that the space vacated by emigrants was immediately occupied by others.

There is, however, one more point of criticism that has nothing to do with the problem of quantitative proof that Marx lacked. He could not ignore the fact that the proletariat was still in the process of being formed and that England had not yet reached the stage of the final confrontation between the proletariat and the capitalist. In Chapter 32 of Book I, he confines himself to *predicting* that such a confrontation

---

[99] *Capital*, I, p. 519. For a recent update, see Ross, 1998: 48–50.

would occur in due course. As we have seen, he nevertheless interprets the overall data regarding the population of England and Wales as if it *already* consisted only of workers and capitalists. Here is a serious conflict of timing as one cannot use figures pertaining to a current period to analyse a future context in which the economic and social structure will, Marx tells us, be different from the present structure. This error in reasoning is all the more surprising because in his *Critique of Political Economy*, Marx, who was so careful about timing and contextualisation, repeatedly insisted that figures should be anchored in social reality. For instance, he fully agreed with Malthus that the increase of fertility was too slow a response to satisfy the requirements of capital and that it was therefore necessary to depend on migration through the stock of rural labour. This opens up the ideological debate on the quality of Marx's forecast that capitalist society would be irresistibly drawn towards pauperisation. Demographic data show that after 1860, mortality and fertility followed an irreversible downward trend, a proof that the standard of living had gone up. We know that mortality fell due to an improvement in the food intake as a result of the agricultural revolution and a simultaneous drop in the severity of epidemics.[100] On the one hand, Marx, who lived in London where neo-Malthusian propaganda had begun to spread under the influence of Francis Place and George Drysdale, ignored the emerging reality of the drop in fertility among the middle classes.[101]

Demography and the Evolution of Capitalism

Almost everything separates Malthus from Marx: their intellectual approach, which is wavering in one and well structured in the other, their theoretical construction and, finally, their personal involvement in the political life of their time. But what they have in common is that each of them has formulated a law of population, which they have both put on a solid theoretical level, with Malthus believing in the universality of the principle of population in time and space and Marx claiming the existence of specific population laws for every mode of production and devoting himself exclusively to capitalism.

How should Marx's writings on population be interpreted? It is certainly necessary to verify the coherence of the theoretical construction from the economic angle because the law of population is also the law for a mode of production, paying special attention to central concepts like the demand for labour or the surplus value. At the same time, it is necessary to integrate the socio-demographic dimension of Marx's ideas, which were in actual fact inspired by Engels. The conclusion that the poverty of the working class is a reason for early marriage and high fertility, the

---

[100] For example: McKeown and Brown, 1955; McKeown and Record, 1972; McKeown, 1978.

[101] Petersen (1980: 192–193) notes that Marx, unlike the Socialists and later the Marxists, never referred to neo-Malthusianism, in spite of the stir created by the Bradlaugh-Besant case in 1877, six years before his death. But much before the establishment of the Neo-Malthusian League in 1877, there was considerable propaganda by Place and Drysdale.

recognition of various types of mobility especially the amplitude of the rural exodus, is a significant contribution while the analysis of morbidity, malnutrition and mortality among the working classes is equally important. So when Marx the economist proposed a population law for capitalism, he should have taken into account the socio-demographic behaviour of all classes: capitalists, workers as well as the other social classes, even if they were likely to disappear in the future. And although Marx is a remarkable sociologist of the working classes, he says very little about the demographic behaviour of the other social classes, which indirectly prevents the experimental verification of his theoretical propositions. Finally, having failed to make a distinction between what was specific to the working class and what concerned the entire population, Marx the sociologist either did not know or did not want to compare the theoretical implications of his very concrete observation of fertility, marriage, mortality and migration. While he brilliantly relates the analysis of the actual working of capitalism in England in the 1860s to the theory of capital accumulation, demonstrates that the concept of relative surplus population is useful for analysing the working of the labour market, makes good use of the demographic data relating to the condition of the working class, he fails to handle the overall demographic observations related to this same England of the 1860s, for the reason already mentioned. When he used the data relating to the entire population as if they were relevant to only one social class, the need to justify the prediction took the upper hand over sociological analysis.

Let us go back to our first question: why did Marx adopt such an ambivalent attitude towards Malthus? He acknowledged his worth as a theoretician while reproaching him for advocating a doctrinal approach perfectly consistent with his theoretical contribution. A careful reader of Malthus, he examined his arguments point by point and gave him credit for having perceived the risk of a general glut and for not trying to "conceal the contradictions of bourgeois production."[102] Unlike the optimism displayed by "vulgar" economists like Jean-Baptiste Say and his sacrosanct law of markets or Frédéric Bastiat and his theory of the harmony of interests, Malthus, by warning against the possibility of a lack of demand, effectively undermined once and for all the liberals' optimism about the evolution of capitalism. Keynes, who, by the way, shared this opinion, proclaimed that Malthus was the first of the Cambridge economists to have gone against Ricardo and foreseen the risk of a widespread crisis caused by an insufficient effectual demand.

But Marx firmly rejected Malthus's conclusion that crises can be avoided by multiplying the unproductive classes. The answer to the first question lies in the domain of ideological debate. From the point of view of social doctrine, Malthus pleads, in a very modern manner, in favour of a society largely composed of the middle classes which would make it possible to maximise demand. In the long run, industry as the principal source of the demand for labour can improve well-being

---

[102] In 1852, in a letter to Joseph Weydemeyer, journalist and member of the Communist League (*Lettres sur le Capital*, 5 March 1852: 59. The same opinion is expressed in a letter to Engels dated 14 June 1853 (641).

and resolve social problems due to the widespread practice of prudent restraint. It stimulates demographic growth without, however, any deterioration in the living conditions of the people. In the short run, regulation is possible due to fluctuations in the standard of living and the rate of marriage, both of which vary according to the demand for labour. Marx clearly sees the political stakes: "Malthus admits that bourgeois production, though it may not be revolutionary, is not a historical force either, but it creates a material base that is wider and more convenient for the old society."[103] As a matter of fact, if there is a solution for the crises arising from capitalism in the realm of consumption and if, in spite of the process of accumulation, stocks resulting from low-cost mass production can be sold in the market thanks to consumption by the middle classes, then the contradictions of capitalism will be solved. Marx could not but strongly oppose Malthus on this point. And he was not the only one to perceive the danger: the hostility of Clara Zetkin and Rosa Luxembourg to neo-Malthusianism follows the same logic.

In 1913, at the Berlin Congress, they opposed the arguments of the anarcho-syndicalists, who advocated a "strike of the womb" to stop production of canon fodder, opposed the arguments of the anarcho-syndicalists, who advocated a "strike of the womb" to stop the production of canon fodder, of bodies for labour and flesh for the pleasure of the bourgeoisie. The Communists, they held, were radically opposed to this strategy, because the larger the proletariat, the greater its revolutionary potential. But in the same year, Lenin published on 16 June 1913 a frequently quoted article in the *Pravda* whose line of reasoning is considerably different and which is particularly interesting for our study. Initially, he reaffirmed the Communists' "absolute" hostility to neo-Malthusianism. But, he added a clearly neo-Malthusian plea: "That does not prevent us from demanding a complete change in the laws banning abortion or the circulation of medical books dealing with contraception. These laws are nothing but hypocrisy on the part of the ruling classes." This stunning position was justified in the name of "the elementary democratic rights of citizens of both sexes." There is extreme doctrinal ambiguity in his utterances. If one follows the logic of the analyses in *Capital*, it is clear that the proletarian revolution must inevitably result in the economic contradictions peculiar to capitalism, while Lenin's "democratic" arguments are a plea clearly addressed to the middle classes. And while Clara Zetkin and Rosa Luxembourg addressed themselves to the workers and were naturally faithful to Marxian orthodoxy, Lenin's siding with the neo-Malthusians, if only for purely tactical reasons, was more dangerous because the spread of contraception posed the risk of social-democracy going adrift: with fewer workers offering their labour, they would be in a better position to negotiate their wages, improve their standard of living and ultimately become bourgeois. So Lenin was obliged to add that "the conscientious workers will always continue their ruthless struggle against the attempts to instil this reactionary and cowardly theory in the most advanced class of contemporary society, which is the strongest and the best

[103] *Theories...*, Vol. VI: 80; also see Vol. IV: 7.

prepared to face the great transformation."[104] In other words, taking into account the superstructure, which in this case is the legislation on contraception and abortion, it becomes necessary to move on to the level of the ideological combat to protect the future of the proletarian revolution.

Behind the laxity visible in Marx's analysis of the role of emigration in England and at the heart of the flagrant contradiction in Lenin's reasoning (e.g. contraception is good but neo-Malthusianism is reactionary), lies the problem of political strategy: how to persuade the working classes to accept the quasi Pascalian wager of the immediate absence of an improvement in their situation in the expectation of the golden age of a communist society? It is impossible to avoid politics. What Lenin proposed implicitly was reliance on the on the Bolshevik Party, the most advanced party and the most concerned about the well-being of the proletariat, which amounted indirectly to signing the death warrant of the purely economic prediction about the collapse of capitalism.

Annex: The Althusserian School and Population

Our analysis of Marx's thinking on population therefore favoured an epistemological approach based on economics, history and demography itself, taking into account the facts that Marx was aware of and which he had intentionally used to support his arguments. A major epistemological break occurred between 1845 and 1859, which inspired a purely philosophical interpretation of Marx's writings by the Althusserian School. It must now be seen if a philosophical reading can do justice to Marx's conceptualisation of population. In other words, what is the epistemological status of population?

In his book *Lire le Capital*, Althusser dismisses in a few lines all other forms of investigation, particularly historical investigation. Regarding the "relationship between economic theory and historical theory" that he believes is "imaginary", he claims that its success is a result of the "empiricist temptations of historians, who, on reading pages of 'concrete' history in *Capital* (the struggle for reducing the duration of the working day, the shift from small-scale manufacturing to large-scale industries, primitive accumulation, etc.) somehow felt 'at home' and raised the problem of economic theory in accordance with the existence of this 'concrete' history, without feeling the need to question its credentials. They followed a purely empirical method to interpret Marx's analyses which, far from being historical analyses in the real sense, i.e. supported by developing the concept of history, are really semi-finished historical data (cf. Balibar's text in Vol. II of this book), rather than a truly historical treatment of such data."[105]

It is known that Althusser and his disciples proposed a radically different analysis by reconsidering the very nature of *Capital* from a philosophical angle and

---

[104] *Classe ouvrière et le malthusianisme*. Quoted by Fréville, 1956: 290.

[105] *Lire le Capital*: 306–307.

showing that thanks to the epistemological break with Hegelian philosophy, Marx had rethought the concept of surplus value, which led him to question "the very purpose of economics."[106] After this, Marx created a radically new epistemological concept, namely *Darstellung*, which refers to structural causality: "structure is present in its effects" and "a structure's entire existence lies in its effects; briefly, this implies that structure which is only a specific combination of its own elements, should be nothing more than its effects."[107] This is the reason why he rejects the Cartesian tradition: "If economic phenomena are determined by their complexity (i.e. their structure), the concept of linear causality can no longer be applied as before and the new force of causality will be determined by the structure."[108] This interpretation led Althusser to challenge idealism and the historicist or humanistic interpretations of Marx's works and the "naïve anthropology" of the *homo œconomicus.*[109]

The Epistemological Status of Population

Considering this interpretation of *Capital*, do Marx's writings on population have only a secondary importance as "semi-finished historical data", or do they lead to a "truly historical treatment of this data"? From Althusser's viewpoint of historical materialism, defined as the science of history, what is the epistemological status of population? It should be noted that the term population does not appear at all in the 246 pages of Althusser's two books, nor in the contributions of Rancière, Machery and Establet. Balibar refers to it exactly four times.[110] Althusser does not even quote capitalism's population law though he celebrates "discoveries having far-reaching consequences: the general law of capitalistic accumulation, the tendential law of the fall in the rate of profit, the theory of rent, etc." thus mixing up Marx's and Ricardo's discoveries while claiming that classical economists had "ignored them" or "avoided them because they were incompatible with their premises."[111] However, if there is a law that Marx can claim to have discovered, it is indeed the population law of capitalism.

Let us concede that the epistemological status of population is so marginal and minor that none of the Althusserians found it worthwhile to dwell on it. This would explain why, although Althusser quotes twice the passage in which Marx denounces the abstract construction of the concept of population by economists, he clings to just one point, namely Marx's silence on the process of abstraction, but says nothing

[106] Ibid. 363.

[107] Ibid. 404–405.

[108] Ibid.: 399, 402.

[109] Ibid.: 310–344, 368–369. Also see Rancière's analyses: 99.

[110] He uses the expression "population of labour forces" (Ibid., 467), and mentions "relative surplus population" (Ibid.: 535–549).

[111] Ibid.: 256.

about the *object* of this silence, namely population.[112] We hold that attributing a *minor* epistemological status to population is not valid. On the contrary, we believe that even within the logic of the Althusserian interpretation of Marx's writings, population cannot be ignored either as a theoretical concept or in its empirical quantification, since they are obviously linked together; and in view of these conditions it must be concluded that this contradiction reveals the limitations of Althusser's theorisation of historical materialism. These limitations are obvious in the case of three key Althusserian theoretical points, which are far from marginal, namely the concept of productive forces, the paradigmatic value of the English example and, finally, the Althusserian concepts of reproduction and timing or "periodization" as proposed in *Lire le Capital*.

Three Key Theoretical Points

What does Balibar say? Since historical materialism was founded by Marx as a science of history and since it should be analysed according to the principles of structural logic, the result is that "in the realm of historical materialism as a scientific discipline", the analysis of productive forces, far from being a "technical or geographical precondition", is "on the contrary inherent in the definition of the social structure of a mode of production."[113] Since population is explicitly listed among the "fundamental concepts of historical materialism", along with "machinery, science, etc.", and Marx is quoted in support, population must at least be integrated in the structural analysis of *Capital*. Moreover, according to Balibar, "the most interesting aspect" is the rhythm or speed of development because rhythm is directly linked to the nature of the relationship between production and the structure of the mode of production.[114] Translated into demographic terms, "the speed of population" is actually its rate of growth, and it is one of the possible means of quantifying the population law of capitalism. Finally, Balibar points out that every specific combination "of the elements constituting the structure of the mode of production" defines the form of this structure, which takes us to one of Althusser's major contributions: the idea of a "matrix" of the mode of production.[115] Thus population, which certainly has the epistemological status of "a fundamental concept of historical materialism", has nonetheless been totally neglected in the philosophical interpretation he has proposed.

Secondly, the empirical data regarding England can hardly be described as "semi-raw material". Here again, there is a total contradiction with the letter and even the spirit of historical materialism. As is known, for Marx, the England of the 1860s

---

[112] Ibid.: 267–268. Marx's text is given above (128–129).

[113] Ibid.: 484.

[114] Ibid.: 466, 468.

[115] Ibid.: 447.

had a paradigmatic value, "In this work, I have to examine the capitalist mode of production and the conditions of production and exchange corresponding to that mode. Up to the present time, their classic ground is England. That is the reason why England is used as the chief illustration in the development of my theoretical ideas."[116] We have seen that Marx compared the rhythm of the growth of population and wealth to explain the increasing contradictions in English capitalism. What meaning would these data about population in England have for the Althusserians in their analysis of historical materialism? "We must consequently read all of Marx's analyses regarding the formation and dissolution of a mode production by looking for this second concept in it; it may exist explicitly or it may have to be prised out of it."[117] The proposed concept is that of "reproduction" and Balibar states later that reproduction assures "the continuity of production" and that it is "inscribed in the identity of the elements as they come out of one production process to enter into another."[118] This ambiguous wording needs to be clarified. Balibar proposes the concept of reproduction to explain "the passage from one mode of production to another."[119] That is exactly what the data collected by Marx helped to support or, to put it in Balibar's words, "the development of the structure according to a tendency, that is to say a law that does not include (mechanically) just the production of effects at a specific rhythm, therefore signifies that *the definition of the specific internal temporality* (emphasis Balibar's) of the structure belongs to the analysis of the structure itself."[120]

Finally, the Althusserians bypassed this aspect of population for two reasons. Firstly, because all their thinking revolved around the philosophical deconstruction of economics. Marx's historical analyses of primitive accumulation (Chapters 29–31 of Book I) have been played down because of their lack of logical coherence. This led to a "fragmented analysis" that does not have the fine structural causality that they found in the analysis of capitalism as a mode of production.[121] Marx, as Balibar rightly notes, is content to allow the elements explaining primitive accumulation to succeed one another. But he reproaches him for not producing a proper history in the theoretical sense "by taking into account the dependence of the elements on a structure."[122] The objection is valid only if the pre-eminence of philosophy is accepted and if the importance of the *Critique of Political Economy* for Marx is underestimated, though it is the sub-title of *Capital*... It is also necessary to mention a second reason. Population gives rise to a time analysis (referred to by Balibar as a

[116] Preface of the first edition of *Capital*. Surprisingly enough, Balibar quotes Marx on the importance of the English case, just after having disregarded the "semi-raw material" (Balibar: 496).

[117] *Lire le Capital*: 429.

[118] Ibid.: 500–501.

[119] Ibid.: 520.

[120] Ibid.: 541.

[121] Ibid.: 529.

[122] Ibid.

"periodization") which is *doubly specific*, and which Marx obviously accepts just as it is, though it differs considerably from the way it is conceptualised by Althusser and Balibar. All the lengthy articles devoted to "periodization" in *Lire le Capital* are actually intent on rejecting the distinction between synchrony and diachrony, denouncing the historians' empiricist conception of time and explaining the change from one mode of production to another.[123] The first peculiarity is that the five-yearly census data used by Marx are quite empirical. Should they be rejected as irrelevant for the structural understanding of *Capital* on the pretext that they constitute a fine example of reification by the bourgeois ideology that Marx condemned? Besides, they were put together by the ideological superstructure, namely the State machinery which, in this case, was the *Registrar General*. Quite the contrary, writes Althusser, "it is not possible to think of the relationship of production in their concept, while disregarding their specific conditions of existence as a superstructure." And still further, he says, "it is an absolutely theoretical condition that determines the definition of the economic situation itself."[124]

The contradiction with the text of 1859 that Althusser considered very important is quite obvious. It could either be that Marx was right to condemn the reification of population and he should not have used these data, or that the text of 1859 is not fundamental and, if it is so, Althusser's interpretation needs to be seriously questioned. The second peculiarity of demographic periodization is that labour as a commodity has the unique characteristic of being renewable and Marx fixes a period of 16–18 years for this renewal, following in this respect Merrivale and Malthus. Every new opportunity of industrial accumulation gives rise to a demand for extra labour, but since it is necessary to wait for at least one generation for the working class population to be able to satisfy the demand, in the short run, it is necessary to resort to stocks of labour. So in the short run, it is more advantageous to resort to immigration instead of depending on fertility. Generally speaking, Marx was more concerned, as we have seen, with identifying the historical mechanisms of primitive accumulation because Malthus's theory of value was incapable of resolving the problem of priming the accumulation pump. If our interpretation is correct, then structural interpretation completely bypasses the perfectly *coherent* theorisation seen in Marx's writings and an important contribution in the sphere of political economy.

Once again, the rejection of any other interpretation of *Capital* ends up in dealing with time only as an element of the structure instead of considering its place *within* the economic theory, as Marx explicitly meant it to be. There is no doubt that Marx believed that time is an exogenous variable.[125] But what is true of demographic time is *a fortiori* true of population as an "element" of production. This gives rise to a double paradox: firstly, in the very name of the method proposed, namely

[123] Ibid., Althusser: pp. 279, 285–290; Balibar: pp. 426–429.

[124] Ibid., pp. 389–390.

[125] Which explains the insistent tributes to Michel Foucault (Ibid.: 289, 490 for example).

the structural interpretation of *Capital*, the Althusserians leave out one important element that is considered to be inseparable from the structure's matrix; secondly, they do not take into account population, which, according to Marx, was important enough to warrant nothing less than a *law* that fits perfectly with historical materialism and which he deemed a major advance as compared to classical Malthusian economics. This is the price to be paid for rejecting interdisciplinarity.

Chapter 6
Beneath Demographic Issues

Even if we were to admit that political philosophy has always been the basis of thinking on population since Classical Greece, there is no doubt that its place was redefined in the eighteenth century when classical economics in England incorporated population into a totally different conceptual framework provided with new analytical tools. By defining an actor, namely *homo œconomicus*, in his dual role of producer and consumer, economics somehow removed population from the sphere of political philosophy, but without losing its footing in moral philosophy.[1] *Homo œconomicus* is a being endowed with reason and governed by the pursuit of his economic interests which enables him to reach a higher state of well-being. The utilitarian morality was all the more convincing because industrial development opened wonderful new avenues for the bourgeoisie to enrich itself, especially because the latter was prudent enough to control its reproductive instinct and develop economic activities based on the values of thrift and work. Besides, by conceptualising the three factors of production, namely land, capital and labour, and by defining markets where demand and supply balance each other in relation to a price, economics could theorise the dynamics of population. The latter increases along with the demand for labour and adjustment takes place through changes in marriage and fertility: employment opportunities encourage workers to marry earlier and have more children and since workers constitute the majority of the population, their behaviour leads to a growth of the population as a whole. Once this adjustment mechanism is defined, differences in demographic behaviour are automatically corrected: when fertility is too high, wages go down because there is more competition in the labour market.

The relation with moral philosophy underlies this intellectual construction: the individual is punished for not behaving rationally according to the principles of utilitarianism and for not maximising his interests and consequently his standard of living goes down and he may find himself faced with poverty and even death. The relationship with political philosophy also becomes evident in a short time. This strategy of rational behaviour, which is precisely what was advocated by

---

[1] Regarding the relationship between economic thinking and what Louis Dumont calls politics and morality, see: *Homo Æqualis*: 34–36, 47, 129 (on Adam Smith) and 199–202 (on Marx).

Y. Charbit, *Economic, Social and Demographic Thought in the XIXth Century*,
DOI 10.1007/978-1-4020-9960-1_6, © Springer Science+Business Media B.V. 2009

neo-Malthusianism, was recommended to *individuals* of other social classes, especially the working classes, in line with the bourgeois belief in the universality of its values. In more general terms, because moral philosophy proclaimed the convergence of interests, it was believed that society *as a whole* would find itself richer if all economic actors conducted themselves rationally. The idea of social progress based on economic prosperity, which is an invention of the nineteenth century, made it possible to express the ideas of justice and equality in new words. It joined hands with the doctrine of liberal democracy according to which it was enough for a Police State to guarantee the basic rights of its citizens since progress would automatically follow the free play of economic forces.

Thus the relationship between the ideas on population and economics is more evident and also more elaborate than the relationship with political philosophy because the conceptualisation of demographic variables occurred at the same time as the affirmation of the economic theory. Thinking on population thus finds itself at the confluence of political philosophy and economics. Population and its growth, as well as each of the main demographic variables gave rise to concepts and arguments borrowed from the two disciplines. Conversely, it could be imagined that while developing their own system, thinkers on population would have made significant theoretical progress *in the field of* political philosophy or economics. But there was no cross-fertilisation precisely because doctrinal or theoretical contributions logically followed a direction where population was progressively treated as an independent object within demography as a discipline.

Wealth and Power

For Malthus and his successors, the French economists, the central question was employment because wealth was assumed to increase if production and consumption went together. Marx with his concept of relative surplus population said the same thing while revealing the other side of the coin: capitalistic accumulation was the cause and consequence of the existence of a redundant population, not in absolute terms, but in terms of the possibility of finding employment.

This argument was not limited to national borders. Anything that contributed to power and wealth was good no matter where: views on colonisation, emigration and imperialism followed from this argument. The exploitation of the riches in the New World had greatly contributed to the emergence of the mercantilists' doctrine of the colonial pact and to their plea for putting the colonies under the king's authority.[2] That logic survived the mercantilists and it is quite legitimate to talk of "the imperialism of free trade", an expression that is only seemingly paradoxical. Marx, followed by Rosa Luxemburg and Lenin, had no doubts about its reality. As for the French economists, the drop in the birth rate gave rise to a triple problem in that it hampered industrialisation, weakened military power and slowed down the race for colonies.

[2] On colonisation in the French mercantilist system, see Charbit (2006).

In his quarrel with the English radicals, especially Godwin, Malthus brandished the formidable arm of the principle of population to refute the credo that bad governments were the cause of poverty, thus reducing the problem to its biological dimension, to which he added a pinch of utilitarianism.[3] When Proudhon and Marx entered the debate, they encountered this fearsome trap and Marx took great care to keep away from the interplay of demographic mechanisms by adopting an economical approach right away. This meant admitting that the demographic argument was almost unanswerable and it was better to leave the field open for Malthus. It was necessary to wait until the period between the two World Wars for the counterproof provided by the drop in the birth rate and the population slump to realise that his theory was obsolete. But Malthusianism was fortunate enough to rise from its ashes after the Second World War thanks to the so-called population explosion in the Third World.

Demographic Behaviour and Bourgeois Universalism

That several nineteenth writers could measure entire social groups against the yardstick of their demographic behaviour appears self-evident today. We can easily conceive that a century and a half ago liberal ideologues, when observing data on fertility simultaneously condemned the excessive fertility of the working class, which was the reason for its poverty, and the "catastrophic sterility" of the aristocracy responsible for its extinction, while praising the "prudence" and sagacity of the French peasants as well as the French and English bourgeoisie as the source of their well-being. Being used to thinking of society as such, we find it both normal and conceptually useful to attribute demographic, economic, cultural and other characteristics to various social groups, albeit after having carefully questioned their relevance.[4] A closer look shows that this interpretation of society is however quite recent, especially when political interests are involved. Plato provides a valuable reference: he thought only of the City's elite and was not in the least interested in the other social groups precisely because the politics of the City did not require counting all the social groups.[5] Similarly, the mercantilists were concerned only with the Prince and the plebeian masses, whose wretchedness did not actually matter as long as their labour was a source of revenue and their numbers were sufficient to man his armies. The true intellectual revolution explaining the emergence of demographic categories is the bourgeois proclamation of the *universality* of its own values: by claiming that it was, as a class, a reference model because the behaviour of its members was founded on reason and was the source both of their own individual happiness and of collective progress, the bourgeoisie imposed its

---

[3] Malthus's utilitarianism, see Halévy (1901) and Bonar (1885).

[4] Such qualifications are of course put on trial on the basis of available data and their relevance is evaluated on sociological theoretical grounds such as the autonomy of the actor.

[5] See Charbit, 2002.

criteria on other classes. From which it followed that all other groups were judged according to their demographic behaviour. Fertility and marriage played a crucial part in the arguments in support of the reform of the Poor Law in England in 1834, in France at the time of the "red spectre" in 1848 and again during the debates on the law on coalition in 1864. The "biological factor" became an integral part of the perception of others, as shown by Louis Chevalier's analysis of bourgeois opinion on the dangerous working classes of Paris in the first half of the nineteenth century.

Like fertility and mortality, space has a strong socio-political dimension whether it is analysed by itself as a static entity or in terms of its dynamic dimension, i.e. geographical mobility. In the eighteenth century, towns were described as "tombs of the race" and contrasted with the healthy life in the countryside; this Rousseau-like concept of nature's benevolence was first adopted by the bourgeoisie and later by the Romantics. Following industrialisation, new interests emerged in the nineteenth century and the terms of the debate changed radically: rural-urban migrations and urbanisation contributed to the enrichment of the bourgeoisie thanks to the availability of labour, which was, however, also a source of political danger. The classical English school and Malthus legitimised industrial production and its need for manpower against the defenders of a rural and agricultural economy, thereby reducing the physiocrats to a mere sect. It was just at this moment that new demo-economic concepts made an appearance: the distinction between the ideal types of consumer and producer was expressed more clearly and brought about the irreversible decline of the traditional rural family, a solidly built production and consumption unit, while Europe gradually turned away from the rural world into a considerably more unstable industrial society.

The State and the Family

The problem of the nature of the relationship between the state, the family and the individual are propped up by political interests. Notably in France, dissociating the reproductive function from the issue of authority caused a permanent tension from the second half of the nineteenth century: on one side, liberal ideology proclaimed the father's absolute freedom and his total power over his children guaranteed by the Napoleonic Code; on the other side, as a result of the drop in fertility, the State would get the citizens (at that time the heads of family) to accept its intervention – in the name of nationalism and the higher interests of the Nation – in the essentially private sphere of the family. The problem was expressed perfectly during a 1869 debate in the French Senate before the vote on a budgetary amendment to sanction additional expenditure for "clothing for aided children." The rapporteur of the budget, de Delmas, explained the contradiction very clearly: "We find ourselves between two extremes, one as formidable as the other: either we must undermine the paternal authority instituted by our laws and submit it in some cases to dominating action of public authority (...) which would mean controlling something, which by its very nature should remain absolutely free; or else we should not do anything and let the evil continue and grow further." In 1907, a comparable debate on the introduction of pre- and postnatal allowances no longer posed a problem: the awareness of declining fertility made it necessary, as also the higher interests of the nation.[6]

A total reversal occurred in the second half of the twentieth century with the appearance in France of a movement in favour of the liberalisation of contraception and of abortion and later with the "pro choice" movements in the United States. Albeit with some exceptions (notably the French communist party in the 1950s and 1960s), left wing democrats supported individualistic values while the conservative right, which had earlier held liberal views on the subject, favoured intervention. In brief, if thinking on population comes under political philosophy in so far as population is a constituent part of politics.

More specifically, following the revolution in 1789 and the affirmation of the right to private property independently of any religious legitimacy, the contribution of the theory of property to the conceptualisation of population blossomed in the nineteenth century when property was used to explain mortality, migration and of course fertility. There are numerous examples throughout the Second Empire: for example, property was supposed to raise the industrial worker to a middle-class status as it urged prudence in the matter of fertility. Finally, by condemning capitalistic exploitation Marx and Proudhon indirectly provided solid proof of the relation between property and population.

Theorising Versus Historicising

The belief that knowledge and science are the basis of power is certainly not peculiar to population thought, but the fact that the quantitative dimension is inherent in it has led to the pseudo-objectivisation of the discourse on population. Notwithstanding the differences in historical contexts, this characteristic is common to Malthus's double progression, the theory of the demand for labour in the writings of Adam Smith and David Ricardo and the free-trade theory of population advanced by economists. The temptation was so strong and its ideological advantage so evident that even those who did not subscribe to the established order had to resort to the argument of the scientific knowledge of population and its growth. Marx and Proudhon both advanced laws on population that they claimed were scientific: Marx framed a law suited to capitalism while Proudhon wished to relate his law to the solution of the economics contradictions. But the fundamental difference that separated them from those who justified power is that they historicised their theory of population. As a matter of fact, they had no choice: the conservatives justified the dominant order by stressing the concept of natural law which had been gradually built up since the sixteenth century while its other version, the analysis of society in

[6] On this point, see Charbit, *Les fondements idéologiques des politiques démographiques en France (1850–1900)*: 275–276.

biological terms, is an invention of the late eighteenth century. Marx's criticism of Malthus proves it: to refute the demo-economic theory which the latter formulated, Marx was obliged to totally ignore the role attributed by Malthus to moral restraint as the driving force behind growth on the pretext that it was just the product of a narrow ecclesiastic morality. That an analyst of his stature should have been mistaken is quite unlikely: if Marx retained from the Malthusian theory only the premonition that there was a fundamental flaw in the capitalist system and since he had studied the concrete mechanism of the crises of surplus production so deeply, it was a direct consequence of his obsessive desire to demonstrate *historically* that the collapse of capitalism was inevitable.

Refusing historicisation and calling for a higher unchanging order is typical of conservative thinking because it can give rise to a fierce polemic while claiming to be above partisan passions. Population lent itself perfectly to this ideological trick; the mechanism was simple as it sufficed to proceed by identifying oneself with larger social groups. The French economists are a typical example because it is possible to follow the development of their line of argument very precisely: from 1840, in order to reinforce their lobbying in favour of the establishment of free trade, they first identified the consumer with the general interest against the protectionists. Then when history accelerated between April and June 1848 during those few weeks of ideological upheaval, they tried to enter into an alliance with the short-lived socialist government, but this time it was the workers who were supposed to represent the general interest, not because they were workers, but because they were presented as constituting the largest consumer group, which was obviously not true considering the immense mass of peasants. In June 1848, they once again took up the defence of the common interest against the irresponsibility of the socialist government which claimed to guarantee the right to employment of the very same workers.

It was therefore absolutely necessary to solve the problem of the inevitable risk of a conflict between groups having vested interests. The assumption that there would be a convergence of individual interests leading towards the fulfilment of the general interest provided a theoretical solution. Jean-Claude Perrot takes note of this with reference to economics in the eighteenth century : "Let the nascent economy be modest enough to submit itself to the state's control and let it act as a complement of politics during the mercantilist phase, or let it become a competitor in the liberal analysis and claim to follow a society based on trade, which is formed spontaneously beyond the Prince's control and outside any social contract, and it will never stray away from philosophical individualism but will be bound to protect the artificial or natural combination of private interests."[7] This was even truer of ideas on population because their very object lent itself naturally to such behaviour: population is a disembodied aggregate that can therefore be immediately and spontaneously identified with the general interest. The physiocrats, who were great theoreticians, were able to perceive that good relations between the prince and his population

[7] *Histoire intellectuelle...*: 89.

depended on giving priority to the general interest. Le Mercier explicitly referred to the two stakes, wealth and power, which were in perfect accord with a third, namely populationism: "Would you like a society to reach the highest possible degree of wealth, population and power? Entrust its interests to liberty, make sure that this liberty is widespread (...) each person will always act for his greatest benefit and consequently contribute with all his might to the greatest possible growth of this type of private interest, whose convergence forms what could be called the common interest of the social organism, or the common interest of the chief and each of the members constituting this organism."[8]

One century later, the French economists solved the political problem through economics: thanks to the increasing well-being of the working class and the peasants and hence of the nation, social peace became possible. Proudhon however took the opposite view and denounced the socio-economic contradictions of the capitalist system. Marx went further and challenged as far back as in 1859 the reification of population into a statistical body, a prerequisite that enabled the bourgeois economy to hide the truth. When he affirmed that figures could not be considered independently of social classes and the links with production that give them a meaning, he was fighting a losing battle. Unfortunately, the *modern* concept of population was well and truly formed and the conditions were just right for the emergence of demography as an independent discipline, political arithmetic having refurbished its tools since the seventeenth century.

---

[8] *L'Ordre naturel*, I: 58. For a recent evaluation of the ideas on population of the physiocrats: Charbit, 2002.

Bibliography

Académie des Sciences Morales et Politiques, *Séances et travaux de l'Académie des Sciences Morales et Politiques* (Five series from 1842 to 1872).
Académie des Sciences Morales et Politiques, *Mémoires l'Académie des Sciences Morales et* Politiques (T. 1 to T. 13: 1837–1872).
Agulhon Maurice, "Vers le surpeuplement", in Duby Georges, Wallon Armand (dir.), *Histoire de la France rurale*, T. III, Paris, Seuil, 1976, 59–95.
Althusser Louis, *Avertissement*, in *Le Capital, Livre I*, Paris, Garnier Flammarion, 1969, 7–30.
Althusser Louis, *Pour Marx*, Paris, La Découverte/Poche, 1996. (Reprint of the first edition of 1965, with a foreword and a biographical note by Etienne Balibar).
Althusser Louis, Balibar Etienne, Establet Roger, Macherey Pierre, Ranciere Jacques, *Lire le capital*, Paris, PUF, 1996.
Anderson B.L., "Trends in Capital Accumulation in the Age of Malthus", in Turner Michael ed., *Malthus and his Time*, London, Macmillan, 1986, 201–221.
Annales de la Charité (1845–1853).
Annales de la Société d'économie politique (1848–1870. 8 volumes, published between 1889 and 1895).
Annuaire de l'économie politique et de la statistique (1844–1870).
Annales du Corps Législatif et du Sénat (1860–1870).
Ansart Pierre, *Sociologie de Proudhon*, Paris, PUF, 1967.
Ansart Pierre, *Naissance de l'anarchisme. Esquisse d'une explication sociologique du proudhonisme*, Paris, PUF, 1970.
Armengaud André, "Le rôle de la démographie", in Braudel Fernand, Labrousse Ernest, *Histoire économique et sociale de la France. III/1789–1880*, Paris, PUF, 1993 (First edition 1976), 161–237.
Aron Raymond, *Les étapes de la pensée sociologique*, Paris, Gallimard, 1967.
Assemblée Nationale, Compte rendu des séances de l'Assemblée nationale (1848–1849).
Audiganne Armand, *Les populations ouvrières et les industries de la France*, Paris, 1860.
Audiganne Armand, *Les chemins de fer aujourd'hui et dans cent ans*, Paris, 1862.
Augé-Laribé Michel, "Introduction" à *De la célébration du dimanche*, Paris, Marcel Rivière, 1926, 19–30.
Balibar Etienne, "Sur les concepts fondamentaux du matérialisme historique", in Althusser Louis et al., Balibar Etienne, Establet Roger, Macherey Pierre, Ranciere Jacques, *Lire le capital*, Paris, PUF, 1996, 419–568.
Bancal Jean, "Proudhon et le proudhonisme", *Encyclopædia Universalis*, 137–140.
Barber William J., *A History of Economic Thought*, Harmondsworth, Penguin Books, 1967.
Barral Pierre, *Le département de l'Isère sous la IIIème République 1870–1940*, Paris, Armand Colin, 1962.
Batbié Anselme, *Nouveau Cours d'économie politique*, Paris, 1866.
Baudrillart Henri, *Des rapports de la morale et de l'économie politique*, Paris, 1860.

Baudrillart Henri, *Manuel d'économie politique*, Paris, 1872.
Behar Cem, "Loi de population et science démographique", *La Pensée, Revue du Rationalisme moderne*, No. 186, avril 1976, 3–26.
Behar Cem, "Surpopulation relative et reproduction de la force de travail", *La Pensée, Revue du Rationalisme moderne*, No. 176, août 1974, 9–29.
Berelovitch Wladimir, "Les lectures de Malthus en Russie (avant la Révolution)", in Fauve-Chamoux Antoinette ed., *Malthus hier et aujourd'hui*, Paris, Editions du CNRS, 1984, 405–415.
Bertillon Jacques, *La statistique humaine de la France*, Paris, 1885.
Blanchard Marcel, *Le Second Empire*, Paris, Armand Colin, 1950.
Blanqui Jérôme-Adophe, *Tableau des populations rurales de la France en 1850*, Paris, 1850.
Blanqui Jérôme-Adophe, *Des classes ouvrières pendant l'année 1848*, Mémoires de l'Asmp, T. 7, 1850.
Blaug Mark, *La pensée économique. Origine et développement*, Paris, Economica, 1986 (4ème édition).
Block Maurice, *L'Europe politique et sociale*, Paris, 1869.
Block Maurice, *La Statistique comparée de la France avec les autres Etats de l'Europe*, Paris, 1861.
Boudin Jean Christian Marc François Joseph, *Eléments de statistique et de géographie générale*, Paris, 1860.
Boudin Jean Christian Marc François Joseph, *Statistiques de la population de la France et de ses colonies d'après les derniers recensements*, Paris, 1852.
Bonar James, *Malthus and his Work*, London, Allen and Unwin, 1927 (First edition 1885).
Bouglé Célestin, "Introduction", *Réformateurs sociaux. Collection de textes*. Paris, Félix Alcan, 1930, 1–11.
Boyer George R., "Malthus was Right after All: Poor Relief and Birth Rates in Southeastern England", *Journal of Political Economy*, Vol. 97, No. 11, 93–114.
Brackett James W., "The Evolution of Marxist Theories of Population: Marxism Recognizes the Population Problem", *Demography*, Vol. 5, No. 1, 158–172.
Breton Yves et Lutfalla Michel, dir., *L'économie politique en France au XIXè siècle*, Paris, Economica, 1991.
Broder André, "Le commerce extérieur: l'échec de la conquête d'une position internationale", in Braudel Fernand, Labrousse Ernest, *Histoire économique et sociale de la France. III/1789–1880*, Paris, PUF, 1993 (First edition 1976), 305–346.
Bruhat Jean, "L'affirmation du monde du travail", in Braudel Fernand, Labrousse Ernest,*Histoire économique et sociale de la France. III/1789–1880*, Paris, PUF, 1993 (First edition 1976), 769–827.
Buret Eugène, *De la misère des classes laborieuses en France et en Angleterre*, 1840.
Caire Guy, "Un ou deux Malthus?", in Fauve-Chamoux Antoinette ed., *Malthus hier et aujourd'hui*, Paris, Editions du CNRS, 1984, 276–283.
Cameron Maclachlan F., "The Ricardo-Malthus Debate on Underconsumption: A Case Study in Economic Conversation", *History of Political Economy*, Vol. 31, No. 3; 1999, 563–574.
Canguilhem Georges, *Etudes d'histoire et de philosophie des sciences sociales concernant les vivants et la vie*, Paris, Vrin, 2002 (First edition, 1968).
Cannadine David, "Conspicuous Consumption by the Landed Classes 1790–1830", in Turner Michael ed., *Malthus and his Time*, London, Macmillan, 1986, 96–111.
Cantillon Richard, *Essai sur la nature du commerce en général*. INED, Paris, 1952 (First edition 1755).
Castagno Azevedo Raimondo, "Marx et Proudhon contre Malthus", in *L'Europe en formation*, Nice-Paris, 1977, 159–179.
Charbit Yves, *Du malthusianisme au populationnisme, les Economistes français et la population, 1840–1870*, Paris, INED-PUF, 1981.

Charbit Yves, "Le destin de l'œuvre: histoire et idéologie", in Fauve-Chamoux Antoinette ed., *Malthus hier et aujourd'hui*, Paris, Editions du CNRS, 1984, 49–61.

Charbit Yves, "Les fondements idéologiques des politiques démographiques en France (1850–1900)", *Vème Colloque national de démographie. La fécondité dans les pays industrialisés, Lille, 24–26 Avril 1979*, Paris, Editions du CNRS, 1986, 263–278.

Charbit Yves, "Malthus populationniste? Une lecture transdisciplinaire", *Population*, No. 1–2, 1998, 113–138.

Charbit Yves, "La cité Platonicienne: histoire et utopie", *Population*, No. 2, 2002a, 231–260.

Charbit Yves, "L'échec politique d'une théorie économique: la physiocratie", *Population*, No. 6, 2002b, 849–878.

Charbit Yves, "Les colonies françaises au XVIIème siècle: mercantilisme et enjeux impérialistes européens", *Revue Européenne des Migrations Internationales*, Vol. 22, No. 1, 2006, 183–199.

Chatelain Abel, *Les migrations temporaires en France de 1800 à 1914*, Publications de l'Université de Lille-III, Lille, 1967.

Chatelain Abel, "La main-d'œuvre et la construction des chemins de fer au XIXe siècle", *Annales: E.S.C.*, 1953, Vol. 8, No. 4.

Chatelain Abel, "Les migrations temporaires au XIXe siècle. Problèmes. Méthodes. Documentation", *Annales de Démographie Historique*, 1967, 9–28.

Chevalier Louis, *Classes laborieuses et classes dangereuses à Paris pendant la première moitié du XIXème siècle*, Paris, Plon, 1958.

Chevalier Louis, *La formation de la population parisienne au XIXème siècle*, Paris, INED, 1950.

Chevalier Louis, *Le choléra, la première épidémie du 19ème siècle*, La Roche sur Yon, 1958.

Churchman Nancy, "Public Debt and Public Extravagance: The Ricardo-Malthus Debate", *History of Political Economy*, Vol. 31, No. 3, 1999, 563–574.

Clément Ambroise, *Recherche sur les causes de l'indigence*, Paris, 1846.

Clément Pierre, *Etudes financières et d'économie sociale*, Paris, 1859.

Coale Ansley, "The Demographic Transition Reconsidered", *Congrès de l'IUSSP*, Vol. I, 53–72, Liège, IUSSP, 1973.

Coats A.W., "Malthus et la science économique britannique: interprétation classique, néo-classique et keynesienne", in Fauve-Chamoux Antoinette ed., *Malthus hier et aujourd'hui*, Paris, Editions du CNRS, 1984, 307–315.

Cocks Edmond, "Malthus in a War-Based Economy", in Turner Michael ed., *Malthus and his Time*, London, Macmillan, 1986, 222–235.

Cole W.A., Deane Phyllis, "The Growth of National Incomes", in Habakkuk H.J. et Postan M., *The Industrial Revolutions and After: I. Incomes, population and technological change* (The Cambridge Economic History of Europe, Vol. VI), Cambridge, Cambridge University Press, 1966, 1–55.

Coontz Sidney H., *Population Theories and the Economic Interpretation*, London, Routledge and Keagan Paul, 1961.

Corbin Alain, *Archaïsme et modernité en Limousin au XIXème siècle*, Paris, Marcel Rivière, 1975.

Cottrell Allin F., Darity William A., Jr., "Marx, Malthus, and Wages", *History of Political Economy*, 1988, Vol. 22, No. 2, 173–90.

Courcelle-Seneuil Gustave, *Traité théorique et pratique d'économie politique*, Paris, 1858.

Crouzet François, "Essai de construction d'un indice de la production industrielle française au XIXème siècle", *Annales: E.S.C*, 1970, Vol. 25, No. 1, 56–91.

Crouzet François, "The Growth of British Exports 1783–1820", in Turner Michael ed., *Malthus and his Time*, London, Macmillan, 1986, 189–200.

Cuvillier Armand, "Introduction", *De la création de l'ordre dans l'humanité*, 5–31.

De Parieu Félix, "Succession", *Dictionnaire de l'économie politique*, 1853.

Daly Herman E., "A Marxian-Malthusian View of Poverty and Development", *Population Studies*, 1971, Vol. 25, No. 1, 25–37.

Dameth Henri, *Le mouvement socialiste et l'économie politique*, Paris, 1869.

Dameth Henri, *Introduction à l'étude de l'économie politique*, Paris, 1872.

Daumard Adeline, "Progrès et prise de conscience des classes moyennes", in Braudel Fernand, Labrousse Ernest, *Histoire économique et sociale de la France. III/1789–1880*, Paris PUF, 1993 (First edition 1976), 897–929.

Désert Gabriel, "Prospérité de l'agriculture", in Duby Georg, Wallon Armand dir., *Histoire de la France rurale*, T. III, Paris, Seuil, 1976, 221–253.

Dome Takuo, "Malthus on Taxation and National Debt", *History of Political Economy*, Vol. 29, No. 2, 1997, 275–293.

Dow Louis A., "Malthus on Sticky Wages, the Upper Turning Point", *History of Political Economy*, Vol. 9, No. 3, 1977, 302–321.

Dumont Louis, *Homo Æqualis, I. Genèse et épanouissement de l'idéologie économique*, Paris, Gallimard, 1985 (First edition 1977).

Dunham Arthur, *The Anglo-French Treaty of Commerce of 1860 and the Progress of the Industrial Revolution in France*, Ann Arbor, University of Michigan Press, 1930.

Duroselle Jean-Baptiste, *Les débuts du catholicisme social en France (1822–1870)*, Paris, PUF, 1951.

Duval Jules, *Histoire de l'émigration européenne asiatique et africaine au XIXème siècle*, Paris, 1862.

Duveau Georges, *La vie ouvrière sous le Second Empire*, Paris, Gallimard, 1946.

Eccleston Bernard, "Malthus, Wages and Labour Market in England 1790–1830", in Turner Michael ed., *Malthus and his Time*, London, Macmillan, 1986, 143–156.

Engels Friedrich, *Esquisse d'une critique de l'économie politique*, Paris, Editions Allia, 1998.

Engels Friedrich, *La situation de la classe laborieuse en Angleterre en 1844*, Paris, Éditions Sociales, 1961.

Eversley David E.C., *Social Theories of Fertility and the Malthusian Debate*, Oxford, Oxford University Press, 1959.

Fayet Pierre, *Mémoire sur l'accroissement de la population de la France*, Paris, 1858.

Fohlen Claude, *L'industrie textile au temps du Second Empire*, Paris, Plon, 1956.

Fohlen Claude, *Une affaire de famille au XIXème siècle: Méquillet-Noblot*, Paris, Armand Colin, 1955.

Foley Duncan K., "Comment" in *Mini symposium: Locating Marx after the Fall, History of Political Economy*, 1995, Vol. 27, No. 1 pp. 159–165.

Foucault Michel, *L'archéologie du savoir*, Paris, Gallimard, 1969.

Fréville Jacques, *La misère et le nombre I. L'épouvantail malthusien*, Paris, Editions sociales, 1956.

Gani Léon, "Jules Guesde, Paul Laffargue et les problèmes de population", *Population*, 1979, No. 6, 1023–1044.

Garbouleau Paul, *De la dépopulation des campagnes*, Montpellier, 1869.

Garnier Joseph, "Machines", *Dictionnaire de l'économie politique*, 1853.

Garnier Joseph, *Du principe de population*, Paris, 1857.

Garnier Joseph ed., *Le droit au travail à l'Assemblée nationale*, Paris, 1848.

Gide Charles, Rist Charles, *Histoire des doctrines économiques depuis les physiocrates jusqu'à nos jours*, Paris, Sirey, 1929 (First edition 1926).

Gilbert G., "Economic Growth and the Poor in Malthus's Essay on Population", *History of Political Economy*, 1980, Vol. 12, No. 3, 83–96.

Gille Bertrand, *La sidérurgie française au XIXème siècle*, Genève, Droz, 1968.

Gimenez Martha E., "Fetishized Nature–Dead–End Politics: Reflections on the Malthusian Heritage", *Organization and Environment*, 1998, Vol. 11, No. 4, 461–465.

Gonnard René, *Histoire des doctrines de population*, Paris, Nouvelle librairie nationale, 1923.

Grampp William D., "Malthus and His Contemporaries", *History of Political Economy*, 1974, Vol. 6, No. 3, 278–304.

Green Francis, "Marx, Malthus, and Wages: A Comment", *History of Political Economy*, 1991, Vol. 23, No. 1, 95–99.

Gurvitch Georges, *Proudhon*, Paris, PUF, 1965.

Hair P.E.H., "Bridal Pregnancy in Rural England in Earlier Centuries", *Population Studies*, 1966, Vol. 20, No. 2, 233–243.

Hajnal John, "European Marriage Patterns in Perspective", in Glass David, Eversley D.E.C. eds., *Population in History*, London, Arnold, 1965, 101–143.

Harrisson John, "Introductory Essay", in *The Malthus Librairy Catalogue, The personal collection of Thomas Robert Malthus at Jesus College*, Cambridge, Pergamon Press, New-York, 1983, 15–25.

Halévy Elie, *La formation du radicalisme philosophique. I. La jeunesse de Bentham*, Paris, 1901.

Halévy Elie, *La formation du radicalisme philosophique. II. L'évolution de la doctrine utilitaire de 1789 à 1815*, Paris, 1901.

Halévy Elie, *La formation du radicalisme philosophique. III. Le radicalisme philosophique*, Paris, 1904.

Harvey-Phillipps M.B., "Malthus Theodicy: The Intellectual Background of His Contribution to Political Economy", *History of Political Economy*, 1984, Vol. 16, 591–608.

Heilbroner Robert L., *Les grands économistes*, Paris, Seuil, 2001.

Hobsbawm Eric J., *Avant-Propos* to Fengels F., *La situation de la classe laborieuse en Angleterre en 1844*, Paris, Éditions Sociales, 1961, 7–23.

Hollander Samuel, "More on the Post-Napoleonic Depression", *History of Political Economy*, 1969, Vol. 1, No. 1, 306–325.

Hollander Samuel, *Classical Economists*, Basil Blackwell, Oxford, 1987.

Hollander Samuel, "Malthus and Agricultural Protection", *History of Political Economy*, 1995, Vol. 27, No. 3, 531–537.

Hutchinson, E.P., *The population Debate: the development of conflicting theories up to 1900*, Boston, Houghton Mifflin Company, 1967.

Huzel J.P., "The Demographic Impact of the Old Poor Laws: More Reflections on Malthus", in Turner Michael ed., *Malthus and his Time*, London, Macmillan, 1986, 40–59.

INSEE, *Annuaire statistique de 1946*.

Journal de la Societe de Statistique de Paris (1860–1873).

Keyfitz Nathan, "The Evolution of Malthus's Thought", in Dupâquier J., Fauve-Chamoux A., Grebenik E., eds., *Malthus Past and Present*, Academic Press, London, 1983, 3–15.

Keynes John M., *Essays in Biography. Collected writings*. Vol. X, Macmillan, London, 1972, pp. 71–108.

L'Economiste Français (1860–1869).

La Revue des Deux Mondes (1840–1870).

Labrousse Ernest ed., *Aspects de la crise et de la dépression de l'économie française au milieu du XIXème siècle*, La Roche-sur-Yon, 1956.

Labrousse Ernest, "A livre ouvert sur la élans et les vicissitudes de la croissance", in Braudel Fernand, Labrousse Ernest, *Histoire économique et sociale de la France. III/1789–1880*, Paris, PUF, 1993 (First edition 1976), 961–1024.

Lambert Paul, "Lauderdale, Malthus et Keynes", *Revue d'économie politique*, 1966, Vol. 76, No. 1, 3–56.

Lambert Paul, "Malthus et Keynes. Nouvel examen de la parenté profonde des deux œuvres", *Revue d'économie politique*, 1962, Vol. 72, No. 6, 783–829.

La Revue des Deux Mondes (1840–1870).

Laslett Peter, Oosterveen Karla, "Long-Term Trends in Bastardy in England", *Population Studies*, 1973, Vol. 27, No. 2, 255–286.

Laurent Robert, "L'utilisation du sol: la rénovation des méthodes de culture", in Braudel Fernand, Labrousse Ernest, *Histoire économique et sociale de la France. III/1789–1880*, Paris, PUF, 1993 (First edition 1976), 663–684.

Laurent Robert, "L'utilisation du sol: une agriculture de spéculation", in Braudel Fernand, Labrousse Ernest,*Histoire économique et sociale de la France III/1789–1880*, Paris, PUF, 1993 (First edition 1976), 685–712.

Laurent Robert, "Les mutations de la société rurale", in Braudel Fernand, Labrousse Ernest,*Histoire économique et sociale de la France. III/1789–1880*, Paris, PUF, 1993 (First edition 1976), 739–767.

Le Bras Hervé, Garden Maurice, "La dynamique de la population française", in Dupâquier Jacques dir., *Histoire de la population française. T. 3: de 1789 à 1914*, Paris, PUF, 1988, 117–166.

Legoyt Alfred, *Du progrès des agglomérations urbaines et de l'exode rural*, Paris, 1867.
Le Journal de la Société de Statistique de Paris (1860– 1870).
Le Journal des Débats (1848–1867).
Le Journal des Economistes (1842–1872).
Le Libre-Echange (February-June 1848).
Le Play Frédéric, *Les ouvriers des deux mondes*, Paris, 1879.
Legoyt Alfred, *Du progrès des agglomérations urbaines et de l'exode rural*, 1867.
Lemahieu L.D., "Malthus and the Theology of Scarcity", *Journal of the History of Ideas*, 1979, Vol. 40, No. 3, 467–474.
Léon Pierre, *La naissance de la grande industrie en Dauphiné, fin du XVIIème siècle-1869*, Paris, PUF, 1954.
Léon Pierre, "Morcellement et émergence du monde ouvrier", in Braudel Fernand, Labrousse Ernest, *Histoire économique et sociale de la France. II/1660–1789*, Paris, PUF (First edition 1970) pp. 651–689.
Léon Pierre, "L'élan industriel et commercial", in Braudel Fernand, Labrousse Ernest, *Histoire économique et sociale de la France. II/1660–1789*, Paris, PUF, 1993 (First edition 1970), 499–528.
Léon Pierre, "Les nouvelles élites", in Braudel Fernand, Labrousse Ernest, *Histoire économique et sociale de la France. II/1660–1789*, Paris, PUF, 1993 (First edition 1970), 601–649.
Léon Pierre, "L'épanouissement d'un marché national", in Braudel Fernand, Labrousse Ernest, *Histoire économique et sociale de la France. III/ 1789–1880*, Paris, PUF, 1993 (First edition 1976), 275–304.
Léon Pierre, "L'affermissement du phénomène d'industrialisation", in Braudel Fernand, Labrousse Ernest, *Histoire économique et sociale de la France. III/ 1789–1880*, Paris, PUF, 1993 (First edition 1976), 475–616.
Leroy Maxime, *Histoire des idées sociales en France. II De Babeuf à Tocqueville*, Paris, PUF, 1950.
Leroy Maxime, *Histoire des idées sociales en France. III D'Auguste Comte à Proudhon*, Paris, PUF, 1954.
Leroy-Beaulieu Paul, *De l'état moral et intellectuel des populations ouvrières*, Paris, 1868.
Leuillot Paul, *L'Alsace au début du XIXe siècle*, Paris, 1959.
Levasseur Emile, *Histoire des classes ouvrières en France depuis la conquête de Jules César jusqu'à la révolution. Tome II*. Paris, 1859.
Levin M. Samuel, "Malthus and the Idea of Progress", *Journal of the History of Ideas*, 1996, Vol. 27, No. 1, 92–108.
Lubac Henri de, *Proudhon et le Christianisme*, Paris, 1945.
Lux André, " Le Malthus des *Principes*, arbitre des deux Malthus de l'*Essai* ", in Fauve-Chamoux Antoinette ed., *Malthus hier et aujourd'hui*, Paris, Editions du CNRS, 1984, 63–74.
Mac Cleary G.F., *The Malthusian Population Theory*. London, Faber and Faber, 1953.
Magnusson Lars, "Malthus in Scandinavia 1799", in Turner Michael ed., *Malthus and his Time*, London, Macmillan, 1986, 60–70.
Mingay G. E., "The Course of Rents in the Age of Malthus", in Turner Michael ed., *Malthus and his Time*, London, Macmillan, 1986, 85–95.
Malthus Thomas Robert, *An Essay on the Principle of Population, as it affects the future improvement of society, with remarks on the speculations of MR. Godwin, M. Condorcet and other writers*, Harmondsworth, Penguin Books, 1970. (First edition 1798).
Malthus Thomas Robert, *Observations on the Effects of the Corn Laws and of a Rise or Fall in the Price of Corn on the Agriculture and General Wealth of the Country* (1814).
Malthus Thomas Robert, *Grounds of an Opinion on the Policy of Restricting the Importation of Foreign Corn* (1815).
Malthus Thomas Robert, *Essay on the Principle of Population*, London, Dent, Everyman's Library, 1965 (7th edition of 1827).
Malthus Thomas Robert, "A Summary View on the Principle of Population", in Malthus, *An Essay on the Principle of Population*, Harmondsworth, Penguin Books, 1970, 220–272. (First edition 1830).

Malthus Thomas Robert, *Principles of Political Economy*, Pullen John ed., Cambridge, Cambridge University Press, 1989 (Fac simile of the 1820 edition).
Ministère de l'agriculture, du commerce et des travaux publics, *Enquête agricole 1866*, Paris, 1869.
Markovitch Tibor J., " La crise de 1847–1848 dans les industries parisiennes", *Revue d'histoire économique et sociale*, 1965, No. 2.
Marx Karl, *Contribution à la critique de l'économie politique*, Paris, Éditions Sociales, 1968.
Marx Karl, "Gloses critiques en marge de l'article 'Le Roi de Prusse et la réforme sociale'", *Vorwärts*, 7 et 10 août 1844, in *Œuvre. III. Philosophie*, Bibliothèque de La Pléiade, Paris, Gallimard, 1982, pp. 398–418.
Marx Karl, "Gloses critiques en marge de l'article 'Le Roi de Prusse et la réforme sociale'", *Vorwärts*, 7 et 10 août 1844, in *Œuvre. III. Philosophie*, Bibliothèque de La Pléiade, Paris, Gallimard, 1982, pp. 398–418.
Marx Karl, *Histoire des doctrines économiques (Theories of surplus value)*. Traduit par J. Molitor. Paris, Costes, 1947. *T. IV: Ricardo. T. V: Ricardo, suite et fin. T. VI: De Ricardo aux économistes vulgaires*.
Marx Karl, *Le Capital, Livre I*, Paris, Garnier Flammarion, 1969.
Marx Karl, *Le Capital, Livre II*, Paris, Editions sociales, 1976.
Marx Karl, *Le Capital, Livre III*, Paris, Editions sociales, 1976.
Marx Karl, *Les luttes de classes en France (1848–1850)*, Paris, Edition sociales, 1967.
Marx Karl, *Le Manifeste du Parti Communiste*, Paris, UGE, 1962 (Collection 10–18).
Marx Karl, *Le 18 Brumaire de Louis Bonaparte*, Paris, Edition sociales, 1968.
Marx Karl, *Misère de la philosophie*, in Proudhon, Marx *Misère de la philosophie. Philosophie de la misère*, Paris, UGE, 1964 (Collection 10–18), 398–500.
Marx Karl, Engels Friedrich, *Correspondance. Lettres sur Le Capital.* Presentation and notes by Gilbert Badia. Translation from German by Gilbert Badia and Jean Chabert. Translated from English by Paul Meier. Paris, Editions Sociales, 1964.
Marx Karl, Engels Friedrich, *La Nouvelle Gazette Rhénane*, Introduction and notes by Lucienne Netter. Paris, Éditions Sociales, 1er juin-5 septembre 1848: T.I, 1964. 14 février 1849–19 mai 1849, T.II, 1971.
McKeown Thomas, Brown R.G., "Medical Evidence Related to English Population Changes in the Eighteen Century", *Population Studies*, 1955, Vol. 9, 119–141.
McKeown Thomas, Record R.G., "Reasons for the Decline of Mortality in England and Wales During the Nineteenth Century", *Population Studies*, 1972, Vol. 26, No. 1, 94–121.
McKeown Thomas, "Fertility, Mortality and Causes of Death. An Examination of Issues Related to Modern Rise of Population", *Population Studies*, 1978, Vol. 32, 535–541.
McQuillan Kevin, "On the Development of Marxist Theories of Population", *Canadian Studies in Population*, 1982, Vol. 9, 109–116.
Meek Ronald L., *Marx and Engels on the Population Bomb*, Berkeley, The Rampart Press, 1971. (First published as *Marx and Engels on Malthus* London, Lawrence & Wishart, 1953).
Mertens Clément, "Le marxisme et les problèmes de population", *La Vie économique et sociale*, mai 1962, No. 3, 201–217.
Meublat Guy, "Au sujet de la théorie marxiste de la population. Un débat entre Rosa Luxemburg et Otto Bauer", *Population*, 1975, No. spécial, 197–219.
Mingay G.E., "The Course of Rents in the Age of Malthus", in Turner Michael ed., *Malthus and his Time*, London, Macmillan, 1986, 85–95.
Molinari Gustave de, "Emigration", *Dictionnaire de l'économie politique.*
Molinari Gustave de, *Malthus*, Paris, s.d.
Molinari Gustave de, *Principes d'économie politique*, Paris, 1846.
Moreau de Jonnes Alexandre, *Annuaire de l'économie politique pour 1849*, Paris, 1850.
Moreau de Jonnes Alexandre, *Eléments de statistique*, Paris, 1856.
Morley Neville, "Political Economy and Classical Antiquity", *Journal of the History of Ideas*, 1998, vol. 59, No 1, 95–114.
Notestein Frank, "Economic Problems of Population Change", *Proceedings of the Eight Conference of Agricultural Economists*, London, Oxford University Press, 1953, 13–31.

Oualid William, "Proudhon Banquier", in *Proudhon et notre temps*, Paris, Chiron, 1920, 131–155.
Paglin Morton, *Malthus and Lauderdale. The anti-Ricardian tradition.* New-York, 1961.
Passy Frédéric, *Conférence sur la paix et la guerre donnée à l'Ecole de Médecine de*, Paris, 1867.
Passy Frédéric, *L'industrie humaine*, Paris, 1868.
Passy Frédéric, *Les machines et leur influence sur le développement de l'humanité*, Paris, 1866.
Passy Frédéric, *Les maux de la guerre et les bienfaits de la paix*, Paris, 1869.
Passy Frédéric, *Mélanges économiques*, Paris, 1855.
Passy Hippolyte, *Des systèmes de culture et de leur influence sur l'économie sociale*, Paris, 1853.
Perelmann Michael, "Marx, Malthus and the Organic Composition of Capital", *History of Political Economy*, 1985, Vol. 17, No. 3, 461–490.
Perrot Michelle, "Malthusianism and Socialism", in Dupâquier J., Fauve-Chamoux A., Grebenik E., eds., *Malthus Past and Present*, Academic Press, London, 1983, 257–274.
Petersen William, "The Malthus-Godwin Debate, then and Now", *Demography*, 1971, Vol. 8, No. 1, 13–26.
Petersen William, "Marxism and the Population Question: Theory and Practice", in Teitelbaum Michael, Winter Jay M. eds., *Population and Intellectual Resources in Western Intellectual Traditions*, Supplement to *Population and Development Review*, Vol. 14, 1988, 77–101.
Petersen William, *Malthus. Le premier anti-malthusien*, Paris, Dunod, 1980.
Picard Roger, Introduction à *Système des contradictions économiques*, Paris, Marcel Rivière, 1923, 5–32.
Pierrard Pierre, *La vie ouvrière à Lille sous le Second Empire*, Paris, Bloud et Gay, 1965.
Pinkney David, *Napoleon III and the Rebuilding of Paris*, Princeton, Princeton University Press, 1958.
Pirou Gaëtan, "Proudhonisme et marxisme", 175–202 in *Proudhon et notre temps*, Paris, Chiron, 1920.
Poussou Jean-Pierre, Lepetit Bernard, Courgeau Daniel, Dupâquier Jacques, "Migrations et peuplement", in Dupâquier Jacques, dir., *Histoire de la population française. T. 3: de 1789 à 1914*, Paris, PUF, 1988, 167–227.
Pouthas Charles, *La population française pendant la première moitié du XIXème siècle*, Paris, INED-PUF, 1956.
Prévost-Paradol Pierre, *La France nouvelle*, Paris, 1868.
Proudhon Pierre Joseph, Unpublished *Carnets*: Fonds Proudhon, Bibliothèque municipale de Besançon; Nouvelles acquisitions de la Bibliothèque nationale.
Proudhon Pierre Joseph, *Avertissement aux propriétaires*, Paris, Marcel Rivière, 1938, pp. 167–248 (1842).
Proudhon Pierre Joseph, *Carnets de P.J. Proudhon*, Vol. I: Carnets I, II, III, IV (19 July 1843–24 December 1846). Paris, Marcel Rivière, 1960.
Proudhon Pierre Joseph, *Carnets de P.J. Proudhon*, Vol. II: Carnets IV, V, VI, (3 January 1847–24 February 1848). Paris, Marcel Rivière, 1961.
Proudhon Pierre Joseph, *Carnets de P.J. Proudhon*, Vol. III: Carnets VI, VII, VIII (25 February 1848–9 August 1850) Paris, Marcel Rivière, 1968.
Proudhon Pierre Joseph, *De la capacité politique des classes ouvrières*, Paris, Marcel Rivière, 1924 (1865).
Proudhon Pierre Joseph, *De la célébration du dimanche* (Mémoire couronné en 1839 par l'Académie de Besançon). Paris, Marcel Rivière, 1926, 35–96.
Proudhon Pierre Joseph, *De la création de l'ordre dans l'humanité, ou principes d'économie politique*, Paris, Marcel Rivière, 1927, 33–464 (1843).
Proudhon Pierre Joseph, *La guerre et la paix*, Paris, Marcel Rivière.
Proudhon Pierre Joseph, *Le droit au travail et le droit de propriété*, Paris, Marcel Rivière, 1938, 415–462 (5 October 1848).
Proudhon Pierre Joseph, *Philosophie du progrès*, Paris, Marcel Rivière, 1946, 29–131.
Proudhon Pierre Joseph, *Philosophie de la misère. Système des contradictions économiques*, Paris, Marcel Rivière, 1923 (1846).

Proudhon Pierre Joseph, *Programme révolutionnaire aux électeurs de la Seine*, Paris, Marcel Rivière, 1938, 301–333. (Published in *Représentant du Peuple* 31st May, 1st and 5 June 1848).
Proudhon Pierre Joseph, *Qu'est-ce que la propriété?*, Paris, Marcel Rivière, 1926, 19–353. (This refers to the first Mémoire, published in June 1840. The second Mémoire was published on 24 April 1841).
Proudhon Pierre Joseph, *Philosophie de la misère. Système des contradictions économiques*, Paris, Marcel Rivière, 1923 (1846).
Puech Jules L., Ruyssen Théodore, "Introduction" à *Philosophie du progrès*, Paris, Marcel Rivière, 1946, 5–28.
Pullen J.M., "Malthus' Theological Ideas and Their Influence on his Principle of Population", *History of Political Economy*, 1981, Vol. 13, No. 1, 39–54.
Pullen J.M., "Correspondence Between Malthus and his Parents", *History of Political Economy*, 1986, Vol. 18, No. 1, 133–154.
Pullen J.M., "Some New Information on the Rev. T.R. Malthus", *History of Political Economy*, 1987, Vol. 19, 127–140.
Pullen J.M., "Introduction" to Malthus Thomas Robert, in Pullen John ed., *Principles of Political Economy*, Cambridge, Cambridge University Press, 1989, Vol. I, xv–lxix.
Pullen J.M., "Malthus on Agricultural Production, an alternative View", *History of Political Economy*, 1995, Vol. 27, No. 3, 517–529.
Ranciére Jacques, "Le concept de critique et la critique de l'économie politique des 'Manuscrits de 1844' au 'Capital' ", in Althusser Louis et al., Balibar Etienne, Establet Roger, Macherey Pierre, Ranciére Jacques, *Lire le capital*, Paris, PUF, 1996, 81–199.
Rashid Salim, "Malthus' Model of General Gluts", *History of Political Economy*, 1977, Vol. 9, No. 3, 366–383.
Rashid Salim, "Malthus' *Principles* and British Economic Thought", *History of Political Economy*, 1981, Vol. 13, No. 1, 55–79.
Rashid Salim, "Richard Wathely and Christian Political Economy at Oxford and Dublin", *Journal of the History of Ideas*, 1997, Vol. 38, No. 1, 147–155.
Reybaud Louis, *Jérôme Paturot à la recherche d'une position sociale*, 1843.
Reybaud Louis, *La laine, nouvelles études sur le régime des manufactures*, Paris, 1867.
Ricardo David, *The Principles of Political Economy and Taxation*, Everyman's Library, Dent, London, 1965. (First edition 1817).
Rosen Frederick, "The Principle of Population as Political Theory: Godwin's *Of Population* and the Malthusian Controversy", *Journal of the History of Ideas*, 1970, Vol. 31, No. 1, 33–48.
Ross Eric B., *The Malthus Factor, Poverty, Politics and Population in Capitalist Development*, London, ZED Books, 264 p.
Rossi Pelegrino, *Cours d'économie politique*, Paris, 1865.
Sainte-Beuve Charles-Augustin, *P.-J. Proudhon, sa vie et sa correspondance*, Paris, 1872.
Santurri N. Edmund, "Theodicy and Social Policy in Malthus' Thought", *Journal of the History of Ideas*, 1982, Vol. 43, No. 2, 315–330.
Sauer R., "Infanticide and Abortion in Nineteenth-Century Britain", *Population Studies*, 1978, Vol. 32, No. 1, 81–93.
Sauvy Alfred, "Les marxistes et le malthusianisme", *Cahiers internationaux de sociologie*, 1966, Vol XLI, 1–14.
Sauvy Alfred, De Malthus à Mao Tse-Toung, Paris, Denoël, 1958.
Sauvy Alfred, "A propos d'un calcul de Proudhon", *Population*, avril-juin 1959, 356–358.
Sauvy Alfred, *Malthus et les deux Marx*, Paris, Gonthier, 1966.
Sauvy Alfred, *Théorie générale de la Population*, Paris, 1966.
Say Jean-Baptiste, *Cours d'économie politique*, Paris, 1832.
Say Jean-Baptiste, *Traité d'économie politique*, Paris, 1841.
Schumpeter Joseph, *History of Economic Analysis*, London, Routledge, 1994. (First edition 1954).
Simon Jules, *L'ouvrière*, Paris, 1863.
Simons B. Richard, "T. R. Malthus on British Society", *Journal of the History of Ideas*, 1955, Vol. 16, No. 1, 60–75.

Singer-Kerel Jeanne, *Le coût de la vie à Paris de 1840 à 1954*, Paris, Armand Colin, 1961.
Skinner Quentin, "Meaning and Understanding in the History of Ideas", *History and Theory*, 1969, Vol. 8, 3–33.
Smith Adam, *The Wealth of Nations*, Penguin Books, Harmondsworth, 1970. (First edition 1776).
Sorlin Pierre, *La société française: 1840–1914*, Paris, Arthaud, 1969.
Specklin Robert, "Les progrès techniques", in Duby Georges, Wallon Armand (dir.), *Histoire de la France rurale, T. III*, Paris, Seuil, 1976, 194–219.
Spengler Joseph J., "French Population Theory since 1800", *Journal of Political Economy*, October 1936, 577–611, December 1936, 743–766.
Spengler Joseph J., *Economie et population. Les doctrines françaises avant 1800. De Budé à Condorcet*, Paris, INED/PUF, 1954. (*French Predecessors of Malthus, A study of Eighteenth Century Wage and Population Theory*, Durham, Duke University Press, 1942).
Spengler Joseph J., *France Faces Depopulation*, Durham, Duke University Press 1938 (First edition 1936).
Spengler Joseph J., "Malthus on Godwin's *Of Population*", *Demography*, 1971, Vol. 8, No. 1, 1–12.
Spengler Joseph J., "Malthus' total population theory, a restatment and reappraisal", *Canadian Journal of Economics and Political Sciences*, February 1945, 83–110; May 1945 234–264.
Spiegel Henry William, "Theories of Economic Development: History and Classification", *Journal of the History of Ideas*, 1955, Vol. 16, No. 4, 518–539.
Stapleton Bernard, "Malthus: The Origins of the Principle of Population", in Turner Michael ed., *Malthus and his Time*, London, Macmillan, 1986, 19–39.
Statistique de la France, Résultats généraux du dénombrement de 1856, Paris, 1859.
Statistique de la France, Résultats généraux du dénombrement de 1861, Paris, 1862.
Statistique de la France, Résultats généraux du dénombrement de 1872, Paris, 1873.
Szreter Simon, 1993, "The Idea of Demographic Transition and the Study of Fertility. A Critical Intellectual History", *Population and Development Review*, 1993, Vol. 19, 659–701.
Thompson E.M., *Louis Napoleon and the Second Empire*, Oxford, Oxford University Press, 1954.
Thompson Warren, "Population", *American Journal of Sociology*, 1929, Vol. 34, 959–975.
Thuillier Guy, *Aspects de l'économie nivernaise au XIXème siècle*, Paris, Armand Colin, 1966.
Thuillier Guy, *Georges Dufaud et les débuts du grand capitalisme en Nivernais au XIXème siècle*, Paris, SEVPEN, 1959.
Toutain Jean-Claude, *Le produit de l'agriculture française de 1700 à 1958. II: la croissance,* Cahier de l'I.S.E.A., série AF, No. 2, Paris 1961.
Toutain Jean-Claude, *La population de la France de 1700 à 1959*, Cahiers de l'ISEA, série AF, No. 3, Paris, 1963.
Tranter Neil, *Population since the Industrial Revolution. The case of England and Wales*, London, Croom Helm, 1973.
Turner Michael, "Corn Crises in Britain in the Age of Malthus", in Turner Michael ed., *Malthus and his Time*, London, Macmillan, 1986, 112–128.
Vamplew Wray, "Malthus and the Corn Laws", in Turner Michael ed., *Malthus and his Time*, London, Macmillan, 1986, 129–139.
Van de Walle Etienne, "Pour une histoire démographique de l'avortement", *Population*, 1998, janvier-avril, 273–289.
Vial Jean, *L'industrialisation de la sidérurgie française 1814–1864*, Mouton, Paris, 1967.
Vidalenc Jean, *Le peuple des campagnes*, Paris, Marcel Rivière, 1970.
Vigier Philippe, *Essai sur la répartition de la propriété foncière dans la région alpine*, Paris, SEVPEN, 1963.
Villermé Louis, *Sur les cités ouvrières*, Paris, 1850.
Villiaumé Nicolas, *Nouveau traité d'économie politique*, Paris, 1867.
Von Tunzelmann G.N., "Malthus's Total Population System", in Coleman David, Scholield Roger eds., *The State of Population Theory. Forward from Malthus*, London, Blackwell, 1986, 65–95.
Waterman A.M.C., "Malthus as a Theologian: The First Essay and the Relation Between Political Economy and Christian Theology", in Dupâquier Jacques, Fauve-Chamoux A., Grebenik E. eds., *Malthus past and present*, London, Academic Press, 1983, 195–209.

Waterman A.M.C., "Malthus on the Long Swing", *The Canadian Journal of Economics*, 1988, Vol. 21, No. 1, 206–207.

Waterman A.M.C., *Revolution Economics and Religion. Christian Political Economy 1798–1833*, Cambridge, Cambridge University Press, 1991.

Waterman A.M.C., "Reappraisal of Malthus the Economist, 1933–97", *History of Political Economy*, 1998, Vol. 30, No. 2, 293–334.

Webb Sidney et Beatrice, *English poor law History. Part I: The Old Poor Law*, London, Frank Cass, 1963 (First edition 1927).

Webb Sidney and Beatrice, *English poor law History. Part II: The Last Hundred Years*, London, Frank Cass, 1963 (First edition 1929).

Weeks, John R., *Population. An Intoduction to Concepts and Issues*, Wadsworth, Belmont, 1992.

Wiltgen Richard J., "Marx's and Engels's Conception of Malthus: The Heritage of a Critique", *Organization and Environment*, 1998, Vol. 11, No. 4, 451–460.

Winch Donald, *Riches and Poverty. An Intellectual History of Political Economy in Britain (1750–1834)*, Cambridge, Cambridge University Press, 1996.

Wollf Jacques, "The Economic Thought of T.R. Malthus", in Dupâquier J., Fauve-Chamoux A., Grebenik E., eds., *Malthus Past and Present*, London, Academic Press, 1983, 61–81.

Wrigley Anthony E., Schofield Roger S., *The Population History of England. 1541–1871*, London, Edward Arnold, 1981.

Wrigley Anthony E., "Malthus's Model of a Pre-industrial Economy", in Dupâquier J., Fauve-Chamoux A., Grebenik E., eds., *Malthus Past and Present*, London, Academic Press, 1983, 111–124.

Wrigley Anthony E., "Elegance and Experience: Malthus at the Bar of History", in Coleman David et Schofield Roger eds., *The State of Population Theory. Forward from Malthus*, London, Blackwell, 1986, 46–64.

Index

P

R